DELIVERING ON THE PROMISE

of the 95% Reading and Math Goals

DELIVERING ON THE PROMISE

of the 95% Reading and Math Goals

Lynn Fielding
Nancy Kerr
Paul Rosier

The New Foundation Press, Inc.
Kennewick, WA
2004

To obtain additional copies of *Delivering on the Promise,* please use the order form on page 292, Appendix A.

For permission to reproduce parts of this material, please contact the publisher at:

The New Foundation Press
114 Vista Way
Kennewick, WA 99336
Phone (509) 783-2139
Fax (509) 783-5237

Second Printing 2006

Library of Congress Catalogue Card Number: 2004111263
ISBN: 0-9666875-1-5
Typset by A Melody
Printed in the United States of America

About the Authors

Lynn Fielding has served 18 years as a director of Kennewick Schools, 8 years as a director of the Washington State School Directors Association, and is in his second year as a director of the Northwest Evaluation Association. He has presented at eight National School Board Association conferences, and at Nebraska, Iowa, Washington, and Idaho School Board conferences. Co-founder of the National Children's Reading Foundation and initial author of its READY! for Kindergarten curriculum, he is available both for presenting and consulting with school districts interested in leveraged educational reform from birth through grade 12. With a LL.M. in taxation from Georgetown University, he is a practicing tax and business lawyer.

Nancy Kerr has served as the president of the National Children's Reading Foundation since 1998. In this role she has received national and state awards. She is a former classroom teacher, school board director, and assessment developer/trainer for the National Board for Professional Teaching Standards, (Princeton). She has chaired local and state school funding elections for over 20 years. She has a B.S. from Brigham Young University and M.Ed. from Washington State University.

Paul Rosier, Ed.D., is the superintendent of Kennewick (Washington) School District (15,000 students) and president of the Washington Association of School Administrators (WASA, 2004-05). Other administrative positions in his thirty-four-year career include superintendent of Mesa County Valley School District in Grand Junction, Colorado (18,000 students), and Page (Arizona) Unified School District (3,000 students). Rosier's doctoral dissertation in 1977 focused on initial reading strategies which moved Navajo children at Rock Point, Arizona, from the 25-30th percentile to the 50th percentile, an increase equivalent to two grades.

Contact Information

Lynn Fielding: lynnfielding@hotmail.com
Nancy Kerr: nankerr@clearwire.net
Dr. Paul Rosier: rosipa@ksd.org
Kennewick School District: www.ksd.org
The National Children's Reading Foundation:
www.readingfoundation.org or (509) 735-9405

What others are saying about *Delivering on the Promise* and its predecessor, *The 90% Reading Goal.*

"This is a must-read for all Boards of Education, superintendents, principals and teachers who truly want every child to succeed. It is written by those who have, and who continue to dramatically increase the achievement level for all students. The maxims included in the final chapter serve as excellent filters for examining every district's current instructional practices."

— *Jim Huge, President, Jim Huge and Associates*

"The Kennewick experiment is proving that amazing progress is possible, even in poorer communities."

— *The Tampa Tribune, Florida, 1999*

"These individuals [Lynn Fielding, Nancy Kerr, Paul Rosier] are strong and capable leaders, and their organization is lean, cost-effective, and easy to replicate. . . . I will continue to offer my support for their dedicated efforts in helping children become strong readers and achieve academic success."

— *Gary Locke, Governor, State of Washington (2002)*

"These books describe a plan that can be implemented in any town, school, or district that refuses to allow one child to be permanently disabled because he or she cannot read. American Fidelity will work to provide leadership and coordination of efforts with any educators who want to network to bring encouragement and success to deliver on the promise of achieving the 90% reading goal!"

— *John Rex, President,*
American Fidelity Assurance Company, Oklahoma

" No goal is more important in a school than teaching children to read–on time and well. These inspiring and data-driven accounts tell how one school district with a vision and with a Reading Foundation mobilized a whole community to do just that. For anyone concerned about our littlest learners at K-3, these books are indispensable."

— *Chieko Okazaki, Colorado, Utah, and Hawaii*
Educator and Community Leader

"A 'hands on,' 'no excuses,' 'here's how to get the job done' road map of teaching all students to read. A **must read** for all K-12 education leaders.

— *Anne Loring, School Board Director*
Reno (Washoe County), Nevada

"Creating catch-up growth is tough to do. *Delivering on the Promise* suggests down-to-earth, powerful, and common-sense ways to achieve it. This book should be required reading for board members and administrators."

— *Chuck Namit, Board President, North Thurston, WA*
Assistant Executive Director, Washington State School Director's Association

"From the ground up, Kennewick has provided a comprehensive plan to address the needs of its individual students on a grand scale. *Delivering on the Promise* could very well be the key to raising literacy rates nationwide."

—*Pete Hall, Principal, Anderson Elementary School*
(50% minority, 90% free or reduced lunch count school)
Reno, (Washoe County), Nevada

"During my year as national president I saw many outstanding programs as I criss-crossed the country. The Reading Foundation and its third grade 90% reading goal was one of the two best that I saw."

— *Sarah Ann Long, President,*
American Library Association, 1998

"The Tennessee PTA adopted the '90% reading goal' in November, 2001. It has been so well received and we sincerely appreciate your books and what extremely valuable tools they have been to us in our efforts."

— *Evelyn M. Pelletier, Tennessee PTA,*
President-elect, 2004

"The establishment of the South Sound Reading Foundation has been the most meaningful achievement of my career."

— *Shirlee Lehnis, Director of Instruction,*
North Thurston School District, WA

"The most powerful way to improve education is to collect the right data and to keep it in front of the right people."

— Lynn Fielding

"Without focused leadership and without using proven strategies, what is the chance that 95% of the students in your school or district will read and do math at or above your state standards by 2014?"

— Paul Rosier

"It's a pity more school districts don't assess incoming kindergarten students. It's the first thing boards and superintendents in low performing school districts need to have—data on the new wave of students who enter school each September, many of whom are already two to three years behind."

— Nancy Kerr

Contents

Tables and Figures

Executive Summary:
Kennewick's Approach To No Child Left Behind

This is a "how to" book — how to get 95% of your students to your state's reading and math goals.

America is in the midst of a long educational reform. The aim of the reform is to assure that our top 60% of students continue to make annual growth while the remaining 40% of students, who do not achieve minimum standards, make annual growth plus significant catch-up growth. Teaching all children to read and do math proficiently has always been the promise of public education.

No Child Left Behind (2001) is current legislation that urges delivery on that long overdue promise for our 40% lowest-achieving students.

The No Child Left Behind (NCLB) legislation, in effect, sets 95% reading and math goals. Ninety-five percent of students must be tested. One hundred percent of tested students must achieve minimum standards in reading and math by 2014. Achieving these 95% goals is a puzzle with many pieces. Over the last decade, Kennewick has learned much about those pieces as a result of our 90% third-grade reading goal adopted in 1996.

What we have learned appears in four parts.

Part One deals with the most urgent piece of the puzzle—proven techniques that provide immediate accelerated growth for lagging students. We describe Kennewick's model for assuring that 90% or more of our students read at grade level, as well as our experience with what worked and what did not over the last eight years.

Early reading is a big piece of the "adequate yearly progress" puzzle both at a student and a district level. Students who fail to read early rarely develop into great students in middle and high school.

Smaller pieces of the reading and math puzzles that must fit together include increased use of data, increased direct instructional time, and instruction that is more skilled and more flexible. For this to occur, superintendents, boards, principals, and professional teacher associations must work together in new ways. Part One deals with the students currently in our K-12 system.

Part Two deals with the larger national perspective of why we have the new 95% goals, why we measure their growth with "adequate yearly progress," and why the push for reform is not going away. It explores the economic, social, and legislative forces that resulted in new legislation in all 50 states and on the federal level. Additionally, Part Two explains why state standards have been set at different levels and what your district should know about the differences. It describes another global educational change: for the last 50 years, public schools focused on achievement or end point measurements—for example, what students score on the SAT, the number of high school graduates, or GPA's at the end of a semester. Now, public schools must focus on the data of both *annual growth* and *annual achievement* for each student. How does a principal make sure that every student makes a year of math growth each year in elementary school? Where do board members find data on catch-up growth for students who are behind? Which district testing systems generate this kind of essential data?

Part Three is the second major common-sense strategy to catch up children who are behind. Research data suggest that about 20% of students enter kindergarten with language and math skills typical of three-year olds. Another 20% enter with skills typical of four-year olds.

That is, in their first five years of life, 40% of children have made only two, three, or four years of normal language and pre-math growth. They enter kindergarten already years behind their classmates, *and the problem persists*. While they make annual growth each year in reading and math, the other students grow as well. These lagging students manage only to keep the same place at the end of the line.

Currently, elementary schools are locked into catching up the 40% of each new batch of students who come to kindergarten already behind. This catch-up focus will continue. By the year 2014, 95% of all these students must read at grade levl by third or fourth grade to comply with the mandated requirement of "adequate yearly progress."

How can we assure that age-appropriate literacy and math growth occurs during the first five years of their life? Part Three outlines the targets, tools, and training Kennewick is using to assure that more children enter kindergarten with language and math skills typical of five year olds. Part Three is a look outside the K-12 box.

Part Four describes four of the many faces that are changing the structure of education. It ends with 99 maxims that summarize the book. The maxims are a quick way to overview the principal points of the book before you start as well as a quick way to review them after you are finished. We recommend that you turn to them now.

This book is an invitation. If you are seeking to jump-start reform in your district or searching for significant insights on how to create sustainable annual and catch-up student growth in core subjects, we offer our experience.

At an average adult reading speed of about 300 words a minute, and skipping nothing from the title page to the back cover, you can read this entire book in 6 hours and 18 minutes. Reading Part One, including sidebars, kickers, and footnotes, and spending 5 minutes on each figure and table, will take 2 hours and 38 minutes.

PART ONE

THE KENNEWICK STORY: THE TAG LOOP

About Kennewick

Kennewick is located in southeastern Washington where the Columbia, Snake, and Yakima rivers meet. With neighboring cities Pasco and Richland, it forms the Tri-Cities, the largest metropolitan area between Portland and Spokane. Each city has its own government and school system. With the adjacent smaller communities of Benton City, Burbank, Connell, Finley, and Prosser, the urban area has a population of 185,000 and a student population of over 40,000. Kennewick serves 15,000 students with thirteen elementary schools, four middle schools, and three high schools. Twenty-five percent of Kennewick's students are ethnic minorities, and 48 percent of elementary school students are eligible for federal lunch programs. The school district operating budget is $112 million.

CHAPTER ONE

The Kennewick Model: Targeted Accelerated Growth

"We thought the board was crazy."

— David Montague, Principal
Washington Elementary, Winter 1996

In the spring of 1995, the Kennewick School Board conceived and adopted the goal that 90% of our third graders would read at or above grade level by the end of third grade by 1999.[1]

Our goal had most of the elements of the current No Child Left Behind (2001) federal legislation. It set a clear target. It focused on our poorest readers. It assumed incremental growth from an initial baseline by each elementary school and by the district to our target over a given time period.

There are other similarities. Most of our educators viewed the goal as impossible. No school district of significant size had ever achieved it. Our teachers were stunned and skeptical. No one thought it was possible. School administrators were concerned that it would make us look bad.

---

[1] Lynn Fielding, Nancy Kerr, and Paul Rosier, *The 90% Reading Goal* (Kennewick, WA: New Foundation Press, 1998), provides an account of the early years of this goal.

Table 1.1
Percentage of Kennewick School District Third Graders Reading at or above Standard, Spring 1996-2004

	(1)	(2)	(3)	(4)	(5)	(6)	(7)	(8)	(9)	(10)	(11)	(12)	(13)
School	2003 % Free or Reduced Lunch	2003 % Minority Enroll-ment	2003 % English Language Learners	% Enrolled only in 2nd or 3rd Grades	1996	1997	1998	1999	2000	2001	2002	2003	2004
Washington	54	25.7		33.3	72	72	68	78	94	96	99	94	98
Cascade	35	14.4		35.6	78	79	72	83	88	91	99	96	93
Vista	50	24.4		30.6	83	73	90	79	80	93	91	95	94
Southgate	20	12.2		29.6	92	80	81	86	88	82	90	93	91
Ridge View	23	21.9	13.9	24.7	80	69	78	88	79	84	94	90	92
Hawthorne	60	33	20.8	30.3	69	62	62	78	73	87	90	92	80
Canyon View	38	28.7		34.2	71	66	78	65	83	76	90	90	90
Sunset View	9	11		18.2	82	86	92	85	84	87	89	95	93
Lincoln	41	21.8		22.9	79	75	73	85	87	86	78	99	92
Westgate	80	37.3	30.9	36.1	58	55	47	51	57	49	55	76	82
Eastgate	82	68.2	60.8	19.1	53	55	52	40	53	54	67	68	80
Amistad	76	67.7	47.2	39.7	66	65	55	52	44	47	51	65	80
Edison	73	58.6	43.4	45.3	66	68	71	54	53	55	53	46	74
District	48	21	14.7	30.3	74	70	71	72	77	78	82	86	88

Table 1.1 shows the percentage of students at or above Kennewick's reading standard from 1996 through 2004 by each of our 13 elementary schools. Column 1 shows the percentage of students on free and reduced lunch in 2003. Columns 2 and 3 show the percentage of minority enrollment and English Language Learners (ELLs) by school. (ELLs are students who are learning English as a second language). Column 4 shows mobility—the percentage of third grade students who first entered the Kennewick school district as second or third graders and who were not here during kindergarten and first grade. Columns 5-13 list the percentage of students at or above the reading standard by elementary school in the spring of each year from 1996 through 2004. The bottom line is the district average. *In calculating the averages, we have used all students in the denominator.* Shaded cells highlight the years each elementary school achieved or exceeded the 90 % goal. Schools have been ranked in order of their long-term effectiveness in teaching students to read at or above grade level.

The reactions of parents and community members produced yet another problem. They thought we already knew how to teach all our students to read at grade level.

The current reactions to the federal 95% reading and math goals mirror those Kennewick experienced in 1995-1997 — internal shock, belief that achieving these goals is impossible, concern about looking bad, and communities perplexed about why their public schools were not already teaching most students to read and do math at minimum levels.

What might you learn from Kennewick's experience? District-wide, 90% of our students are not reading at or above the standard. We began at 57% in the spring of 1995. **We reached 77% in spring of 2000, 82% in 2001, 86% in 2003, and 88% in 2004.**

In the last three years, seven to nine of our 13 elementary schools reached the 90% reading goal with one school at 98% in the spring of 2004. More importantly, our lowest school in 2004 scored higher than our district average in 1997, 1998, and 1999.

Individual schools are now meeting the goal with consistency. Three elementary schools have reached the goal two years in a row. Three have reached it three years in a row. Washington Elementary has reached it five years in a row.

On the way to the 90% reading goal, we learned a lot about what works and what does not. These principles and some pitfalls, layered together, are explained throughout this book. We have learned that the same principles can be applied to middle and high school as well.

Excellent leadership, excellent initial instruction, and excellent data systems have always been essential pieces of high performance schools. These themes will surface repeatedly in Part One. The four-step Targeted Accelerated Growth (TAG) loop principles are new. Diagnostic testing, proportional increases in instructional time, focused teaching to the deficient sub-skill, and retesting to assure that learning has actually occurred are common-sense strategies and central to how we catch up students who are behind.

May we suggest an analogy with the aircraft industry? The Wright Brothers proved that powered flight was possible in 1903. However, it wasn't until 1935 that flight became commercially feasible. In the intervening years, a myriad of experiments with commercial flight failed. More than 30 years passed until a series of interdependent component technologies came together to form something that could not only get off the ground but also soar. This is when Douglass Aircraft (later to merge into McDonnell Douglass) brought together five critical component technologies necessary to make the plane both aeronautically sound and capable of carrying a commercially feasible payload. Those five elements were:

> the variable-pitch propeller, retractable landing gear, a type of light-weight molded body construction called "monocque," radial air-cooled engines, and wing flaps. To succeed, the DC-3 needed all five; four were not enough. One year earlier, the Boeing 247 was introduced with all of them except wing flaps. Lacking wing flaps, Boeing engineers found that the plane was unstable on take-off and landing and had to downsize the engine.[1]

Creating annual growth for all students and catch-up growth for those who are behind requires multiple technologies. Creating annual growth for more students usually means better execution in the traditional areas of excellent leadership, excellent initial instruction, and excellent data systems. Creating catch-up growth means adding the new layers of targeted accelerated growth. Layers of processes, some of which may not even currently exist in your district, must be carefully added and must work together. In addition, the governance structure must interact in different ways to create and sustain these changes.

We offer our "lessons learned" to show how we fit the pieces together. We believe that most of our lessons about the 90% reading goal will be relevant to America's 15,000 school districts as they work to achieve the new 95% educational requirements in No Child Left Behind.

Answers to questions about implementing accountability by superintendents, board members, and principals can be found at www.readingfoundation.org.

[1] Peter M. Senge, *The Fifth Discipline: The Art and Practice of the Learning Organization* (New York: Doubleday Currency, 1990), 6.

CHAPTER TWO

Washington Elementary: "No Exceptions, No Excuses"

"The Targeted Accelerated Growth (TAG loop): (1) diagnostic testing to identify the deficient sub-skills for lagging students, (2) proportional increases in direct instructional time, (3) teaching to the sub-skill, and (4) retesting to be sure students are actually catching up."

— Kennewick School District Strategic Plan

Dave Montague has been principal at Washington Elementary for twenty-one years. He started back when a principal's job was to manage the building, discipline the kids, and do whatever was necessary to keep problems from going downtown. A visitor at the door of his office might expect to see him relaxed in a scuffed leather chair with worn armrests, sagging comfortably from two decades of continuous use. Instead, Dave Montague's chair is a roller-mounted, spiffy, blue-cloth-covered design from Office Max. The desk is glass-covered, clear, and gleaming.

A photograph of Washington's Governor Gary Locke and the school staff hangs next to a plaque honoring the school as the recipient of the National Title I Directors Award in 2002, the State Reading School of the Month in January 2003, and the State Title I Distinguished School Award in 2003-04. Pithy education adages punctuate the walls.

Most importantly, Dave Montague's chair is empty. He is nowhere in his office. It's 8:45 a.m., and that means he is in one of Washington's 25 classrooms with his famous list of "look-fors."

"I understand unavoidables—nose bleeds, parents coming in unexpectedly, an accident at home," explains Dave. "But barring something fairly major, our two-hour reading block starts at 8:45 and runs to 10:45. Start 20 minutes late or stop 20 minutes early and do that every day during first, second, and third grade, and your students lose the equivalent of an hour daily of direct reading instruction during their first three years. Losing an hour of direct instruction in this school means losing about three-fourths of a year of reading growth."

Instructional Supervision Look-Fors
Dave Montague, 2002-03

- If it's reading, are you teaching Open Court?
- In reading, are you starting on time?
- Are you using direct instruction both hours?
- Are all students engaged in what you are teaching all the time?
- Are you instructing students? Or are students working individually?
- If kids are working individually, what are you doing?
- If kids are using felt pens, crayons, scissors, etc., are they spending more time on the artwork than on the reading?
- Are the para-eds working with kids the whole time?

Instructional time is treated as a critical commodity at Washington. The 120 minutes of the reading block are inviolate. There are no assemblies, no announcements, and no interruptions during this time. Every student gets 120 minutes. One hundred and twenty minutes creates annual growth for all students. Kids who are behind get more.

"We focus on direct, eyeball-to-eyeball instruction during the morning period, when students are fresh." Montague continues, "Everyone teaches, including the aides, the librarians, and the music and P.E. specialists. I look for students getting instruction from the teacher, not working alone."

Students who are behind have been placed in small groups of four or five. Those furthest behind are working with the most skilled instructors. Students at grade level work in larger groups. After the first 60 minutes, the class reconvenes to continue through a series of tightly organized, highly integrated, and prescriptive activities. Washington Elementary gets these smaller teaching units by mobilizing virtually every adult in the school to teach during the block. These precious 120 minutes are focused exclusively on reading. Every minute gets used. (Read Chapter 4 to see how it works.)

"When students are behind in reading, they need more instructional time depending on how far behind they are. Some need 30 minutes, some need an hour, and some need more. We give them whatever they need to reach the goal," Montague explains. "Time is proportional to their deficiency. The greater the deficiency, the more time they get."

How much do they need? Superb diagnostic testing pinpoints and predicts the need. Excellent leadership sets the priority of proportional increases in direct instructional time. Chapter 3 demonstrates a simple way to calculate how many more instructional minutes it typically takes a student in the 14th percentile to catch up to grade level in two years. The rational delivery structure only emphasizes the elegance of the instruction.

"Direct instruction is becoming an art form in our school," Montague reflects. "Minute for minute we use it perhaps twice as effectively as we did five to eight years ago. Direct instructional time is too valuable to waste practicing. Students can practice later in the school day, or after school. "

Direct instruction is the dance between the instructor and his or her students to the music of the curriculum. The dance is always a combination of the quantity of actual minutes spent in instruction and the quality of superb instruction during those minutes. It is eyeball-to-eyeball, highly energetic, and highly interactive.

Chapter 4 models and Chapter 5 explores the concepts of rigor, engagement, and purpose as elements of direct instruction. Most of the learning goes on during direct instruction using guided exercises, not during individual practice. "Practice" includes the use of work sheets, silent sustained reading, and in-class seatwork.

Montague continues, "We focus this 'catch-up time' on what they lack. Is it phonemic awareness? Is it phonics? Is it accuracy or fluency? Is it comprehension? The afternoon catch-up time is targeted to these specific skills. To clearly see the weak sub-skills, you have to look at the data. You have to embrace data. The increased time needs to actually target the deficient sub-skill. The student who is deficient in hearing the sounds of the letters will get little benefit from increased time if the instructor merely reteaches the morning's lesson. We test way more than the district or the state requires us to, even though many educators think that this much assessment is absurd—just like the quotation in my office."

Which one? Dave's walls are peppered with quotations:

> "Never confuse motion with action."
>
> "If we don't model what we teach,
> we are teaching something else."
>
> "All kids can learn.
> We can teach them.
> No exceptions.
> No excuses."

However, the one he's probably referring to is taped to his file cabinet: "The fact that an opinion has been widely held is no evidence whatsoever that it is not utterly absurd." While there may be principals who spent the last decade complaining about district, state, and national testing requirements, principals in Kennewick's elementary schools have become skilled at looking at the data from their mandated tests. In addition, most of them even added a layer of diagnostic testing to better identify deficient sub-skills. Excellent schools test far more than most districts or states require. (Chapter 6 discusses diagnostic assessment and teaching to the deficient sub-skill.)

Dave is emphatic. "After you have diagnostically tested to identify the deficient sub-skills, proportionally increased the instructional time, and used the extra time to teach to the sub-skill, you have to retest to assure the student has actually made the needed growth. When we started using our afternoons for remediation with the students who needed it—this was in 1999-2000—we went from 78% at or above the reading standard to 94% in one year."

The 120-minute block assures that students achieve a year of reading growth during the school year. Catch-up growth happens beyond the 120- minute block when retesting pinpoints weak skill areas and when teachers focus additional instruction on those areas. This process is intelligent, intensive, and challenging, because when retesting shows that interventions aren't working, it presses the educators to adjust instruction. Principals and teachers have to understand on deeper levels what is not working and adjust the strategy. It works because retesting assures that instructional change at the building level is driven by what students are learning.

Dave, lightly graying at 54 and eligible to retire two years ago, is an obviously intelligent, energetic, and resourceful leader. He has stayed in one school in a mid-size town in a rural section of the state for one reason.

"It's become more fun," he says. "Instructional leadership is a lot more rewarding than building management. More stressful, but more rewarding. Twenty-one years ago, I was hired to manage the building. During the next ten years, I got pretty good at it. Instructional leadership wasn't even on the radar screen. There was a lot of talk about instruction, but no one ever asked to see my data. During the first decade I was principal, no one said, even once, 'Dave, show me data that proves what you're doing is actually making a difference.'"

Students who fail to learn to read in the primary grades rarely develop into great readers in middle and high school. They generally enter kindergarten behind, read two to three years behind grade level in elementary school, and are still two to three years behind their average classmates in middle and high school. Districts that lack the organization and the will to teach their children to read at or above grade level by second or third grade, when it is relatively easy and inexpensive to do so, rarely do so thereafter when it is much harder and more expensive.

The culture of Washington Elementary, like every other elementary school, bears the fingerprints of its principal on its reading goal. Not every principal in Kennewick has approached the goal in the same way. Each one, with his or her teachers, brings a different focus and different skills. Different student populations call for custom-tailored responses. (Chapter 7 explores some ways principals approach the needs of their distinctive student populations.)

"In January 1995, there was a meeting downtown with the board and Dr. Rosier. Any elementary teacher who was interested in reading was invited," explains Montague. "By the time the meeting ended, someone proposed as a goal that 90% of kids should read on grade level by third grade within the next three years.[1] When the board appointed a district committee to discuss it, I knew the goal was dead for sure. But in the summer, the goal was included in the district strategic plan as an indicator. Then, just before Christmas of 1995, the board allocated $500,000 for it from the levy. That's when I knew this was not another flavor-of-the-month. It began to look like they were serious—like this goal was here to stay."

A year after the goal was first articulated, the board and superintendent released the first draft of the Reading White Paper (Appendix B). The White Paper gave elementary principals the freedom to change their reading programs while holding them responsible for the results.

The current reaction to the No Child Left Behind legislation is an eerily exact replay of the shock, incredulity, and complaints voiced by Kennewick principals and teachers about the 90% reading goal in 1996. There had never been specific and measurable academic goals in our district or state. Not in the last 30 to 50 years. Perhaps never. Weren't schools being set up for failure? No one had ever taught 90% of third graders to read at grade level. Hadn't educators been working hard enough? Were jobs now on the line? There was also the shock from our suburban community that large numbers of students were not *already* reading at grade level. All of this grief over some political goal!

---

[1] The actual proposal was 90% at second grade but it was modified to third grade within three months prior to its adoption into the district's Strategic Plan.

The 1995 Kennewick Reading White Paper:
A Seven-Point Summary

1. **A BUILDING APPROACH:** Primary planning and program change will be on an elementary school-by-school basis.
2. **PLANNED, INCREMENTAL, AND CONTINUOUS GROWTH:** The district expects planned, incremental, and continuous improvement at kindergarten through third grade from each school's baseline to the goal over the next three years.
3. **PRIMARY ACCOUNTABILITY:** Primary accountability is with building principals.
4. **INCREASED RESOURCES:** Each elementary school should identify and alter decade-old paradigms that limit the amount of existing resources that are spent on reading.
5. **K-3 CHANGES:** Our primary approach is intervention in grades K-3, not remediation commencing in the fourth grade.
6. **RESULTS ORIENTED**: Programs will be evaluated on the basis of progress shown.
7. **EXPECTATIONS**: We expect all children, including those from low socioeconomic backgrounds, to reach the reading goal.

"We thought the board and the superintendent were crazy," confessed Dave. "I saw in the White Paper that elementary principals were responsible and said, 'Why don't they come down to our building and see the kids that come to our school?' I mean, our kindergarten kids seem to enter school every year with lower skills. We had 54.2% free-or-reduced lunch counts in 1994-95, a 13.8% ethnic minority, a high turnover rate—and every year the numbers all grew. One of my colleagues wrote a biting six-page response to the district's reading White Paper, and I was one of the 13 elementary school principals who jointly sent it downtown as our collective response. We all but mutinied: 'Why are we elementary principals primarily responsible? Why not the superintendent? Why not the board?'"

It was a situation that could have instantly channeled everybody's available energy into recriminations and counterattacks. The board and superintendent, whatever their personal feelings, accepted the letter with stoicism and kept forging ahead with their discussions, workshops, and commitment to the goal.

"After that, the whining died down. The goal started to grow legs," Dave recalls. "Principals are messengers. When you're in the message business, it doesn't help to criticize the message. It drives a wedge. It empowers those who don't want to change. Since we're responsible for implementation, it makes no sense to send a mixed message. Principals cannot play 'loyal opposition' harping against accountability and at the same time provide effective leadership for growth."

Once elementary principals began looking at the situation instead of their frustration, they saw the logic. Who better to assure that their students could read? It was not the legislators at either the state or federal levels who could look at student and classroom data, determine use of time, choose curriculum, assign teachers, and make building level adjustments. The discussion slowly swung away from the adult concerns and began focusing on what the students needed. Reading is the language of learning. The first thing parents want schools to do is to assure their children's physical safety. And the second thing they wanted schools to do is to teach their children to read. If the elementary schools do not teach their students to read early and well, it matters little what else we teach them.

> *"We did notice one particularly provocative form of economic insight that every good-to-great company attained, the notion of a single 'economic denominator.' If you could pick one and only one ratio—to systematically increase over time, what x would have the greatest and most sustainable impact on your [elementary school's] engine?"*
>
> —Jim Collins in *Good to Great* [2]

The superintendent and board began to hold a public workshop every two weeks at one of the 13 elementary schools. Meeting minutes circulated throughout the district after each workshop, highlighting the positive aspects of the school's strategies and identifying the pivotal role each principal was playing.

[2]Jim Collins, *Good to Great* (New York: Harper Business, 2001), 104.

Historically, elementary schools in Kennewick had not received much board attention. Now they were in the spotlight, and none of our principals was going to publicly announce that his or her elementary school could not teach its students to read. Chapter 8 provides a deeper look at what this process looked like from the superintendent and board levels.

"We began to have serious staff meetings," Dave remembered. "We began going through the district White Paper and looking at the Northwest Evaluation Association test data to see how far behind some of our kids were. It was the first time Washington had ever had such precise data. In the fall of 1995, 23% of our third-grade students were reading at second-grade level and 41% of our third-graders were reading at a kindergarten or first-grade level. It was professionally unacceptable to have that many of our students so far behind." [3]

Washington Elementary wasn't alone. According to the fall 1995 scores, only 57% of Kennewick's third graders were on track to achieve the district reading standard. Yet by the spring of 1996, 75% of third graders across the district reached the standard. Schools were jubilant. The extra money had hardly kicked in yet. No school had even held school-wide staff training. At that point, decisions about how staff-training dollars were spent were still made by individual teachers. Getting to the 90% goal was going to be easier than anyone thought.

"We celebrated in the spring of 1996," Dave recalls. "At Washington, we had moved 72% of our students to the standard. Our hard work and focus had paid off. The following year we worked more intentionally. During the summer, we selected the Consortium of Reading Excellence (CORE) [4] as our school-wide training model for

---

[3]Northwest Evaluation Association (NWEA) is a not-for-profit organization that provides beginning, middle, and end of year on-line assessments of student achievement and growth. The data can be used by classroom teachers for diagnostics and classroom instruction as well as by administrators for program measurement and accountability. NWEA is located at 5885 SW Meadows Rd. Suite 200, Lake Oswego, OR 97035; www.NWEA.org; phone: (503) 624-1951; fax: (503) 639-7873.
[4]CORE stands for Consortium on Reading Excellence. Address: 5855 Christie Ave. Suite A, Emeryville, CA 94608. Phone: (888) 249-6155. Fax: (888) 460-4520. Website: corelearn.com. CORE has provided training in over 750 schools and 70 school districts.

kindergarten through fifth grade and spent 30 hours in training.[5] Our teachers focused on reading, and we studied our data from NWEA more carefully. We were shocked when we only got to 72% again in spring of 1997 and stunned when we fell to 68% in spring of 1998."

Table 2.1 shows the district's discouragingly flat-growth period—four long years from 1996 to 2000. We realized later that our first year pop in test scores was from the three to five months of extra gain that came from additional focus and curriculum alignment in third-grade classrooms. Three to five months of growth lifted the students nearest the standard over it, boosting the percentage of students above the standard the first year. But the second year, the same amount of effort moved the new wave of students only up the same three to five months. Replicating the first-year growth with the new third graders during the second year means no system growth during the second year. Gains during the first year come from harder work and curriculum alignment. Gains in the subsequent years have to come from other strategies.

"By the third year, we had exhausted our work-harder-at-third-grade strategy," Dave recalls. "More of the catch-up gain had to be made at second and first grade. Our first- and second-grade teachers realized that they had to become more accountable for their students' learning. Even our kindergarten teachers, who had spent most of their class time on social activities, began the transition to teaching phonemic awareness along with letter and sound recognition."

At the beginning of the fourth year (1998-99), the district extended the NWEA reading tests to second grade. Other assessments were implemented at kindergarten, first, and second grades. The new tests showed what was happening in the early years. After the tests were instituted at second grade, second-grade scores jumped six points. The following year, the higher scoring second graders became third graders and made growth typical of what we had done the previous three years. The five-point district-wide jump in 2000 (see column 7 of Figure 2.1) was primarily a result of more gain during second grade of the prior year.

---

[5]Three full days were spent in training in August, October, and June with two all-day site visits from CORE instructors in 1996-97 and two training and two site visit days again in 1997-98.

"By the fifth year, I was convinced high performance reading was about more time and better use of that time," says Montague, rubbing his jaw thoughtfully. "Students who were behind needed more direct instruction. Some of them started getting 60 to 90 minutes extra each day for a total of 180 to 210 minutes a day. We spent that additional time on the sub-skills they hadn't mastered."

Table 2.1
Percentage of Washington Third Graders Reading at or above Standard, Spring 1996-2003

	(1)	(2)	(3)	(4)	(5)	(6)	(7)	(8)	(9)	(10)
School	1996 Free or Reduced Lunch	2003 Free or Reduced Lunch	1996	1997	1998	1999	2000	2001	2002	2003
Washington Elementary	43	54	72	72	68	78	**94**	**96**	**99**	**94**
District	39	48	**74**	**70**	**71**	**72**	**77**	**78**	**82**	**86**

It was during the fifth and sixth years that Washington really broke away from the pack. Sunset and Southgate, two schools with a high socio-economic population, hit the 90% reading goal early on but without consistency. Washington was the first to repeat.

Curriculum became not a personal option but a carefully honed tool. "Before year 7, we used MacMillan for curriculum and CORE for training," recalls Montague. "After year 7, we changed to Open Court for both curriculum and training. Open Court starts with phonemic awareness, moves to phonetics, and then quickly to comprehension. Open Court has more extensive daily classroom materials and activities. However, Open Court is very prescriptive and works best when every teacher teaches every lesson."

Each elementary school in Kennewick is free to choose its own reading curriculum, staff-training programs, and allocation of direct instructional time. The board is hard on results, liberal on methods. Before the 90% goal, each teacher was an individual provider—adding, improvising, creating the curriculum as he or she saw fit. This attitude has shifted over the years. Now teachers rarely see themselves as composers working in isolation. In the metaphor coined by Dr. Edward J. Kame'enui (pronounced come-ME-new) Department of Special Education, University of Oregon at Eugene, the publishing companies are the composers, the principal is the conductor, and teachers are the performers. The shift has been slow but is bringing significant results. Elementary teams, using carefully developed curriculum, are consistently getting better results than collections of individual providers using an eclectic collection of curriculum, no matter how gifted they are individually. These results have encouraged principals like Dave Montague and his teachers to bring demanding rigor to their curriculum. If it doesn't work deep enough, fast enough, and hard enough, it isn't good enough. (See Chapter 5 on instructional leadership.)

"Washington has a great team," affirms Dave. "This is not an easy school. Teachers think twice about coming, but once here, almost no one transfers."

From early days, schools with high levels of collaboration and teamwork made greater gains than schools where teachers worked in isolation using traditional concepts. At Washington Elementary, teachers collaborate at and between grade levels, discussing techniques that work with certain kinds of kids and reorganizing the mix between classes, especially during the reading block. Grades 4-5 generally gave up resources so that K-3 could front-load what it needed—sometimes with more hope than faith in the results. However, such cooperation with the school's priorities has paid off. Washington Elementary has reached the 90% reading goal every year since 2000.

Targeted Accelerated Growth (TAG) Loop

- Diagnostic testing to determine the deficient sub-skills of those behind
- Proportional increases in direct instructional time
- Teaching to the deficient sub-skill
- Retesting to assure that adequate catch-up growth actually occurred

Dave celebrates but with humility. "There are schools in our district with more difficult populations. The difficult populations are not those with high free and reduced lunch counts. The research is fairly clear that poverty correlates with low performance only when it's aggregated on school levels, not by individual student.[6] No, the difficult populations are those with mobility and second language learners. Our hat is off when we see the gains that schools like Amistad, Eastgate, and Westgate are making."

Washington Elementary's enviable record is no fluke, no flash of charisma. Instead, it stems from an insistence on getting good data, student by student, then following where it leads. Dave Montague could have written the book on Targeted Accelerated Growth. In fact, in some ways, TAG simply gave his program a name. A student who can't tell the difference between "d" and "b" is not going to learn it drilling on "-tion" and "-ation" suffixes.

Washington Elementary's Targeted Accelerated Growth loop (TAG) may be the most intensive individualized instruction these students will ever receive, and it seems to be working.

[6] Catherine E. Snow, M. Susan Burns, and Peg Griffin, eds., *Preventing Reading Difficulties in Young Children* (Washington, DC: National Research Council/National Academy Press, 1998), 126-27. "When the average SES [socio-economic status] of a school (or district) and the average achievement level of the students attending that school are obtained for a large sample of schools, a correlation between SES and achievement can be calculated using the school as the unit of measurement. In a meta-analytic review of the findings for 93 such samples, White (1982) found that the average size of the correlation was .68 which is substantial. . . . When achievement scores and SES [socio-economic status] are measured *individually* for all children in a large sample, however, the strength of the association between SES and achievement is *far lower*. In White's (1982) meta-analysis, for instance the average correlation between reading achievement and SES across 174 such samples was .23. Similarly, the correlation was .22 in a sample of 1,459 9-year old students whose scores were obtained through the National Assessment of Educational Progress (NAEP) evaluations (Walberg and Tsai, 1985). . . . In other words, within a given school or district, or across many districts within a country, SES differences among children are relatively weak predictors of achievement. Thus, all else being equal, coming from a family of low SES (defined according to income, education, and occupation of the parents) does not by itself greatly increase a child's risk for having difficulty in learning to read after school income level has been accounted for."

CHAPTER THREE

Proportional Increases in Direct Instructional Time

"An academic day has 375 minutes (6 ¼ hours). How many of those minutes are spent in direct instructional time? What about reading? What if the schedule shows a 60-minute reading block, but the teacher rotates from the high-skill, to medium, to low-skill groups? If so, each student is getting only 20 minutes of direct reading instruction."

— Marlis Lindbloom, Assistant Superintendent, Curriculum and Instruction, Kennewick

For most of Kennewick's high-performance elementary schools, increasing the amount of time spent on direct reading instruction was an intuitive decision. They tried more time. It worked, and they kept on doing it. It was merely an extension of what remediation was about. Principals and many teachers at these schools saw the direct connection between increasing instructional time and increasing reading growth. Students who were a little behind needed a little more instructional time. Students who were a lot behind needed a lot more time.

Increased instructional time is perfectly consistent with the landmark research of the Carnegie Institute done in the 1950s. Time on task has a high correlation with increased learning.

Students of substantially equal intelligence need similar amounts of time to learn the same concepts. When students don't "get" a concept, they may need a different teaching technique or need to have the concept recast in a form more compatible with their learning style. But they always—ALWAYS—need to spend more time on it as well.

Some Kennewick educators (and perhaps some in your district as well) initially saw no innately proportional relationship between increases in instructional time and increases in student growth. Others did not differentiate between instructional time and practice time. Any increase in time except for Title I students[1] also ran counter to decades of school culture. It violated the assumptions of traditional master schedules in which every student received the same minutes of instruction in virtually every subject. Increasing direct instructional time in these schools did not occur until the Kennewick central office introduced Time and Focus Reports (described later in this chapter) at the elementary schools and began requiring Principal Scheduling Reports (Chapter 17) at middle and high schools.

Proportional increases in direct instructional time for lagging students is the second element in the TAG loop—right after diagnostic testing to determine the sub-skill deficiency. Here's how it works. Suppose your state has set its fourth grade reading standard at the 50th percentile. Suppose a student named Tony finishes second grade scoring in the 12th percentile. What will it take to get him to the standard?

Tony will be making "good" growth from the excellent teaching he receives in his 120-minute block described in the next chapter. Because seriously struggling students are at risk of falling further behind, we call their achievement of normal annual growth "good" growth. However, "good" or annual growth merely perpetuates Tony's reading deficiency. Tony must grow at an accelerated rate to erase his three-year deficiency.

---

[1] Federal legislation is divided into "titles." Title I of the relevant legislation provides extra funding to districts based on the percentage of students in a county who qualify under the "Aid for Dependent Children" program. Districts, in turn, are required to allocate the money within the districts under formulas targeting need. In Kennewick, the funding is proportionally allocated to the six elementary schools with the highest free or reduced lunch counts. Teachers hired with these funds are called Title I teachers. Students that qualify to be served by the programs are often called Title I students. No funding is available for qualifying students at non-qualifying schools.

Stated more precisely, how many minutes of direct instructional time should Tony's principal schedule for Tony in third and fourth grade to reasonably assure that he makes annual growth plus enough catch-up growth to move from the 12th to the 50th percentile by the end of fourth grade?

Let's fill in what we know. Typically, most elementary schools teach reading in a 60-to-80-minute block, delivered by 20 minutes of direct instruction to one of three reading groups while students in the other two groups practice at their seats. If Tony gets 27 minutes of direct instruction and 53 minutes of practice each day, he will most likely make one year's growth. That's the good news. However, all the other students are also getting 60-80 minutes, and they will also make a year's growth from wherever they started. The bad news for Tony is that, with the normal 60-80 minutes of instructional time, he will still be in the 12th percentile at the end of fourth grade.

Now, let's work on the part that we don't know. How many years of normal growth are there between the 12th and the 50th percentile in reading at the elementary schools? A rough rule of thumb is that each unit of 13 percentile points from the 50th percentile equals a year of growth.[2] Let's apply this to Tony.

State standard in percentiles is..................	50th percentile
Tony's second grade status in percentiles is...	-12th percentile
The difference is..................................	38 points
Percentile point difference divided by 13 is....	2.9 years

Tony is behind about three years—in other words, he is entering the third grade with the literacy skills of the typical five-year-old entering kindergarten. (See Chapter 21 for skills typical of five-year-olds.)

Now that we have figured out how many normal years of growth Tony is behind using percentile data, how do we convert that into daily

[2] A year of growth at third grade = 13 percentile points = 8 NWEA RIT points. We use RIT points, defined and described in the explanation for Figure 3.1, because they provide a finer scale and because our testing system by Northwest Evaluation Association uses it. The relationship of a year of growth = 13 percentile points = 8 RIT points can be seen by measuring the distance between the midpoint of the quartile marked by the lines in Figure14.1 derived from Northwest Evaluation Association's RIT Scale Norms for Use with Achievement Level Tests and Measures of Academic Progress, August 2002, Appendix A 6-7.

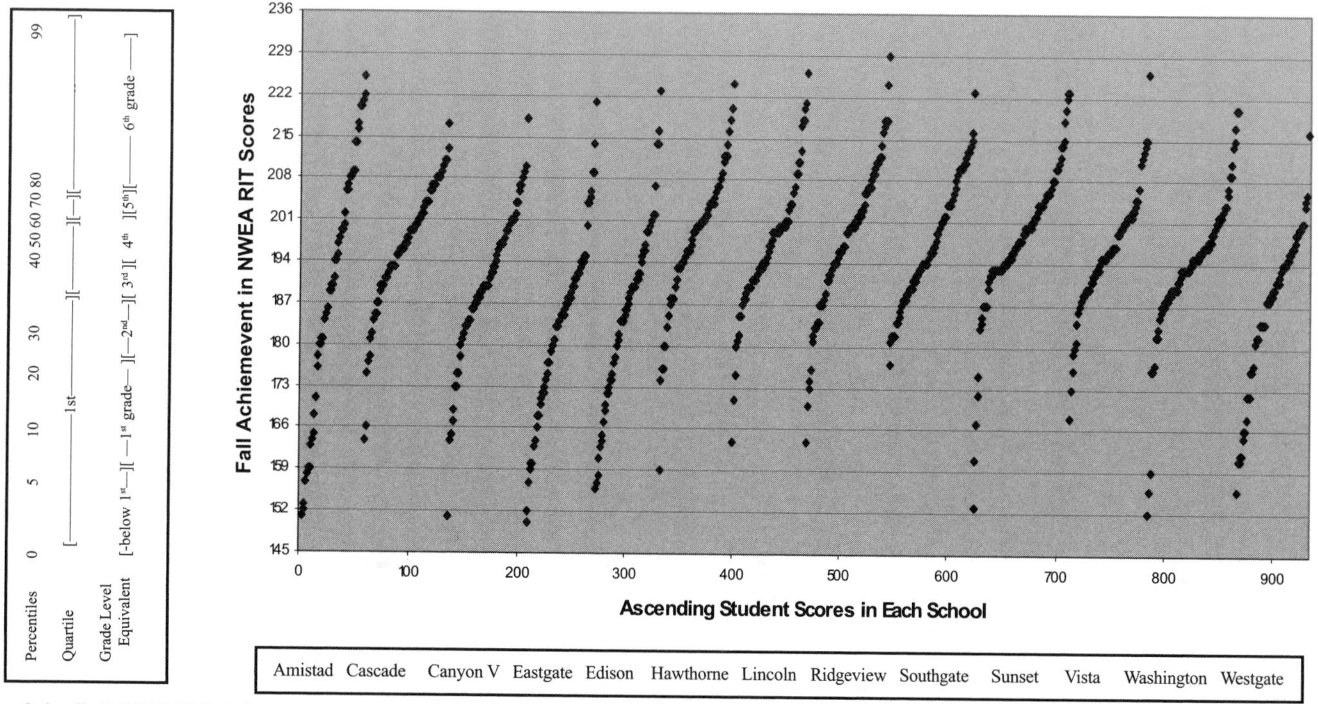

Figure 3.1. Fall 2002 Third Grade Reading RIT Scores for Kennewick's 13 Elementary Schools. Our "caterpillar" chart is probably the single clearest view of the six-year reading span. Each "caterpillar" represents a school. Each dot in the 13 "caterpillars" represents an individual third grader. Our students scored as low as 149 (NWEA RIT scale, on the left) and as high as 229 at the beginning of third grade. The "tail" of each caterpillar starts with the score of its lowest student and moves upward with the next highest student score toward the "head." Paralleling the RIT scores are the traditional ways of showing student proficiency: percentile, quartile, and grade equivalent. For example, Amistad Elementary's lowest-scoring student is the 149 dot. This left-hand box further explains that this student is a fourth percentile reader, is in the first quartile, and is below first-grade level. The top-scoring third-grader at Amistad scored 225, is in the 90th percentile, is in the fourth quartile, and is reading at a sixth-grade level. Kennewick's reading target in RIT points is 194. The students above a RIT score of 187 in the fall can reach the target of 194 with annual growth. Students who score above 187 in the fall are on track to reach the 90% reading goal without intervention. Students below 187 in the fall are behind. They will need proportional increases in direct instruction time to assure annual growth plus necessary catch up to reach the 90% reading goal.

instructional minutes? From this point, there are several ways to do the math. Here's a simple method:

Daily minutes required for annual third grade growth		80
Daily minutes required for annual fourth grade growth		80
Additional daily minutes to make three additional years of growth	+	240
Total third and fourth grade daily minutes.............		**400**

Dividing the instructional time equally between third and fourth grade shows that Tony needs 200 minutes of direct reading instruction in both third and fourth grades to reach the 50th percentile by the end of fourth grade.

Or we can do the math like this. Knowing that Tony must make normal growth each year plus another 1.5 years *each year,* Tony's direct instructional time must be 1 x 80 minutes (for annual growth) plus 1.50 x 80 minutes (for catch-up growth) or a total of 200 minutes a day during third and fourth grade. Of course, Tony may learn more quickly as he gains skills and confidence, or with a more skillful teacher or small instructional group of two to six students or with one-on-one tutoring. A good assessment system like Kennewick's will identify the actual growth achieved, allowing rapid adjustments in instructional time. Either way, this is what Dave Montague means when he talks about proportional increases in direct instruction time.

Figure 3.1 graphs the six-year range of reading abilities of Kennewick's 933 third graders, distributed among its thirteen elementary schools, tested in the fall of 2002. Each dot represents an actual student score. The scale on the left is measured in RIT (from **R**asch un**it** scale) points, an equal interval unit of measurement developed and used by Northwest Evaluation Association, which is Kennewick's testing system. It is a numeric assignment that can show relationships with quartiles, percentiles, and grade equivalents without translation or adaptation. Let's reflect on this for a minute.

Typically, people who look at our chart, or one from their own school that shows the same kinds of data, have some questions:

1. How do I know where my state has set the reading standard in percentile equivalents? Are all state standards set at the same place?

Thanks to the federal No Child Left Behind legislation, 2003 was the first time in the history of public schools that minimum academic standards were set earlier than high school graduation nationwide. Because states can set their own standards, there's a lot of variation. California has set its reading standard at the 14th percentile for its 10th graders—which is very low. Wyoming has set its standard at the 67th percentile for the same group of students—which is very high. Larger districts and the Office of Public Instruction in most states have typically compared the scores of their students on state tests to those on nationally normed tests and can closely approximate the percentile where the standard is set. Chapter 15 deals at greater length with where states have set standards in reading and math.

2. Can a second-grade student actually be three years behind in reading? That's as long as he's been in school.

When children enter kindergarten with the math and literacy skills of a two or three year old, they start two to three years behind. If they make annual growth in kindergarten, first, and second grade, they will still be three years behind. As in the Tony example, they will be 12th percentile second graders with the literacy skills of the average five-year-olds entering kindergarten. Typically, a five-year-old enters kindergarten knowing how to spell his name, identifying the shapes and sounds of a few letters and numbers, and recognizing a few words. Isn't this about the skill level of very low second graders?

Let's think about this another way. If Tony makes annual growth for the next three years, he will still be in the 12th percentile and will still be three years behind. This means that Tony as a fifth grader will have reading skills of an average (50th percentile) second grader. He will struggle to sound out (decode) words of two and three syllables. He will not read fluently—about 70 to 90 words a minute instead of 130 to 140 words a minute. His reading recognition vocabulary will be about a third of what is average for his age or his classmates. Again, isn't this about typical for a very low fifth grader?

3. Doesn't the pullout time funded by Title I catch these students up?

In schools that qualify for the funding, Title I provides students with about 30 extra minutes a day. Assuming the validity of our math and our rule of thumb, 30 extra minutes a day will move Tony each year about 5 percentile points—from the 12th percentile to the 17th percentile during third grade and to the 22nd percentile by the end of fourth grade.[3] The gain may be a little higher, because pullout classes are smaller and the instruction will probably be tailored more closely to Tony's needs. Even though this is good progress, it still falls considerably short of the state standard in our example of the 50th percentile. When you reflect on your own local data, isn't this kind of gain typically optimistic of the Title I pullout time? Could this be why, after 30 years of Title I, large numbers of students are still reading below grade level?

4. Where do I find data about the number of minutes of direct reading instruction students are getting in my elementary schools?

In Kennewick, we created the Time and Focus Report that appears in Table 3.1. The Kennewick district office prepares spreadsheets for each school to complete with information for each student below the 50th percentile. Separate forms are necessary for reading and math, and the forms differ slightly for elementary, middle, and high school. Column 2 lists the individual student's fall Reading RIT score, and Column 3 indicates the national percentile of that score. Column 4 displays the number of minutes each child receives daily in his or her classroom's standard reading block of direct instruction. Columns 5, 6, and 7 show the intervention, the skills 1-5 covered, and the daily minutes spent. The district reading or other reading specialists generally provide the intervention time in our elementary schools. Columns 8-13 provide space to document other interventions. RR is Reading Recovery. Study Buddies is an after-school, twice a week, hour-long program of direct reading instruction unique to Washington Elementary. Column 14 shows the total of columns 4, 7, 10 and 13 — the total number of daily minutes for each child spent in direct reading instruction.

[3] Thirty minutes a day in a normal 80-minute instructional period is 30/80 or 3/8 of a year of catch-up time. Three-eighths of a year of catch-up instruction multiplied by 13 percentile points is about 5 percentile points, well short of the 38 percentile points needed to move a student to the 50th percentile.

Table 3.1
Washington Elementary's Time and Focus Report

	(1)	(2)	(3)	(4)	(5)	(6)	(7)	(8)	(9)	(10)	(11)	(12)	(13)	(14)
Name	Student ID (altered)	Reading RIT Score	Pct	Reading Block Daily Minutes	Name of Intervention and Skill Focus		Minutes Per Day	Name of Intervention and Skill Focus		Minutes Per Day	Name of Intervention and Skill Focus		Minutes Per Day	Total Daily Minutes
(removed)	601393	176	26	120	District	1-5	48				St. Buddy	1-5	24	192
(removed)	604226	187	47	120	District	1-5	48				St. Buddy	1-5	24	192
(removed)	604249	177	27	120	District	1-5	48				St. Buddy	1-5	24	192
(removed)	604809	162	11	120	District	1-5	45				St. Buddy	1-5	24	189
(removed)	600762	156	7	120	RR	1-5	24				St. Buddy	1-5	24	168
(removed)	600754	177	27	120	District	1-5	48				St. Buddy	1-5	24	192
(removed)	600739	185	43	120							St. Buddy	1-5	24	144
(removed)	600703	182	36	120	District	1-5	48				St. Buddy	1-5	24	192
(removed)	794792	159	9	120	District	1-5	30	RR	1-5	30	St. Buddy	1-5	24	180
(removed)	600786	188	50	120	District	1-5	45				St. Buddy	1-5	24	189
(removed)	604396	183	38	120	District	1-5	48				St. Buddy	1-5	24	192
(removed)	600702	188	50	120	District	1-5	45				St. Buddy	1-5	24	189
(removed)	770609	182	36	120	District	1-5	45				St. Buddy	1-5	24	189
(removed)	604467	186	45	120	District	1-5	45				St. Buddy	1-5	24	189
(removed)	600697	187	47	120	District	1-5	48				St. Buddy	1-5	24	192
(removed)	600740	176	26	120	District	1-5	48				St. Buddy	1-5	24	192
(removed)	600787	189	52	120							St. Buddy	1-5	24	144
(removed)	604366	197	72	120	District	1-2	15				St. Buddy	1-5		135
(removed)	720774	189	52	120							St. Buddy	1-5	24	144
(removed)	720642	191	57	120	District	1-5	45				St. Buddy	1-5	24	189
(removed)	720760	191	57	120	District	1-5	48				St. Buddy	1-5	24	192
(removed)	604255	194	65	120	District	1-5	48				St. Buddy	1-5	24	192
(removed)	604235	196	54	120							St. Buddy	1-5	24	144
(removed)	604846	NEW		120							St. Buddy	1-5	24	144
(removed)	632406	152	1	120	RR	1-5	24				St. Buddy	1-5		144
(removed)	770698	194	65	120	District	1-5	48				St. Buddy	1-5	24	192

Skill focus is as follows: 1= Phonemic awareness, 2 = Decoding, 3= Fluency, 4 = Vocabulary, 5 = Comprehension

"The power of Kennewick's program is that we are responsible for getting 90% of our students to the goal, not that we have a specified number of minutes to teach reading. A quick way to gut this program would be to get obsessed with inputs rather than results."

—Ted Mansfield, Principal, Ridge View Elementary

Instructional minutes of each of the elementary school's standard reading block are summarized in Table 3.2. It includes only direct instructional time. It excludes time spent on "reading in the content area," silent sustained reading, and writing time. Although many intuitively feel that reading blocks are generally uniform, they actually vary widely between schools in the same district as Table 3.2, reporting the situation in Kennewick's elementary schools, demonstrates. Prior to the report, length of reading blocks also varied widely among classes in the same grade level within the same school.

Table 3.2
Standard Reading Block Minutes in Kennewick's Elementary Schools by School by Grade, 2002-2003

School	1st Grade	2nd Grade	3rd Grade	Total minues
Canyon View	195	135	150	480
Westgate	160	120	120	400
Lincoln	150	130	120	400
Southgate	120	120	150	390
Hawthorne	150	150	90	390
Washington	150	120	120	390
Amistad	120	140	130	390
Eastgate	120	120	120	360
Vista	120	120	120	360
Ridge View	135	120	90	345
Cascade	120	90	75	285
Edison	90	90	80	260
Sunset View	90	90	75	255
District	**132**	**119**	**111**	**362**

Kennewick has imprecise data on instructional time prior to 2000. However, Greg Fancher, director of Elementary Education, after consulting with our elementary principals, believes that reading time averaged about 70-90 minutes but that it varied as much as 50-70% between classes in the same grade in the same school. He estimates that only 20-30 minutes consisted of the kind of explicit, direct instruction now counted in the Time and Focus Report summarized above; students spent the remaining time in independent seatwork.

Table 3.3
Standard Reading Block Plus Intervention Block Minutes
Kennewick Elementary Schools
by School by Grade for 2002-03

School	Free or Reduced 2003	% at or above the 90% Goal	1st Grade	1st Grade Intervention	2nd Grade	2nd Grade Intervention	3rd Grade	3rd Grade Intervention	3 Year Cumulative Total of Standard and Remedial Direct Instructional Minute
Sunset View	9	95	90	5	90	30	75	52	342
Edison	73	46	90	26	90	52	80	29	367
Westgate	80	76	160	36	120	41	120	46	523
Cascade	35	96	120	60	90	30	75	40	415
Ridge View	23	90	135	30	120	30	90	30	435
Vista	50	95	120	10	120	25	120	40	435
Lincoln	41	99	150	5	130	45	120	21	471
Washington	54	94	150	10	120	24	120	55	479
Canyon View	38	90	195	54	135	42	120	30	576
Eastgate	82	68	120	30	120	80	120	55	525
Hawthorne	60	92	150	30	150	30	90	78	528
Amistad	76	65	120	80	140	81	130	66	617
Southgate	20	93	120	60	120	56	150	75	581
District	39	86	132	23	119	44	99	47	465

5. Is it possible to give a student 200 minutes of reading instruction in one day?

An elementary school day is generally 6 1/4 hours long, or 375 minutes. Typically 40 minutes goes to recess, 30 minutes for lunch, and 30 minutes for such "specials" as assemblies, P.E., library, computer lab, etc. That leaves 275 minutes. If a principal is willing to cut almost everything else but math, it is possible to give a student 200-220 minutes of direct reading instruction.

Table 3.3 reports on the standard reading instruction offered at each Kennewick grade school by grade for 2002-03, interspersed (shaded columns) with the additional catch-up minutes of direct reading instruction given to students who are below the 90% reading goal. The schools are arranged from fewest to most total minutes. Sunset has the least time with 342 minutes. Southgate has the most with 581 minutes.

In Tony's case, the growth he needed to catch up by fourth grade could have been less concentrated if the school had started in kindergarten instead of the beginning of third grade. Then there would have been almost five years instead of just two to make up the three years Tony was behind.

What was surprising, of course, before we started to treat direct instructional time as a valuable resource, was the huge range in instructional time between schools and between classrooms at the same grade level in the same school.

If Tony's additional instructional time begins in early November instead of the second week of school in September, he will lose 2/9ths or 22% of his intervention time. If Tony needs 200 minutes and his extra 120 minutes begin in November, he loses an average of 26 minutes a day over the course of the year.

6. Don't schools run their standard reading blocks and interventions in similar ways?

There are more similarities between college football offenses than between elementary school reading interventions. Not only does the amount of direct instructional time vary wildly, but the *use* of the time varies significantly as well. The most cost-effective way to provide extended reading instruction to virtually all students is to lengthen the standard reading block and make direct reading instruction time proportional to *need* instead of available time slots. The flexibility and nimbleness of each elementary school are critical factors in this process. Obviously, as the quality of initial instruction improves, its quantity can be decreased.

7. Is growth really dependent on time? Don't 30-40 minute programs in most districts catch kids up?

The caterpillar charts in Figure 3.1 emphasize how far some students have to progress before they are caught up. Growth is directly proportionate to the quality and quantity of instructional time. When we looked at our data student by student, we saw a painful fact with painful clarity: Most students who start behind stay behind. Time-starved reading programs that rely on sudden growth bursts from extraordinary instruction rarely move students from the 5th-30th percentiles up to grade level.

8. Isn't it wrong to cut art or social studies and especially science to make room for more reading instruction?

> *"In all the other First World countries, grades 1-3 are primarily about teaching reading and math."*
>
> —Tony Wagner, Co-director,
> Harvard Graduate School of Education
> Change Leadership Group

In the United States, public schools deliver 85%[4] or more of their curriculum by reading textbooks, whiteboards, worksheets, and computer screens. Students must read to do well. It matters little what else they learn in elementary school if they do not learn to read at grade level. Even math depends on reading. There are far more words than numbers in math books. As math concepts become

[4] "In the United States, an estimated 85% of classroom time spent on instruction involves using textbooks." João Oliveria, "Textbooks in Developing Countries," in *Promoting Reading in Developing Countries*, edited by Vincent Greaney (Washington, DC: World Bank, 1996), 78, citing L. Anderson, "The Environment of Instruction: The Function of Seatwork in a Commercially Developed Curriculum," in *Comprehension Instruction: Perspective and Suggestions*, edited by G. G. Duffy, L. R. Roehler, and J. Mason (White Plains, NY: Longman, 1984), 93-103; and State of Florida, *Instructional Materials Committee on Training Materials* (Tallahassee: State of Florida Department of Education, 1993), 93-103.

more complicated, the verbal descriptions become more involved as well. As Kennewick has focused on reading, our math scores have improved at a rate similar to our reading scores. The reading problem becomes more obvious in middle school where students who cannot read well struggle to absorb content in all other subjects. In high school, it is these same students who begin to drop out. The body count underscores the message: Art, social studies, science, and math cannot compensate for the loss of learning to read fluently.

9. Are there other short-term alternatives?

Kennewick's experience is that there are not. First-quartile students do not learn faster than fourth-quartile students. If anything, students require more instructional time when they are behind. Look carefully at the three flat years of growth at the district level in Kennewick from the fall of 1996 to the spring of 1999 shown in Table 1.1.

During these painful years, Kennewick's educators spent a lot of time exploring many alternatives besides increased instructional time. These alternatives uniformly provided little gain.

With the exception of the WSU volunteer program at Cascade and about 130 volunteers organized through a program called Team Read Tutoring, used primarily at Amistad, Westgate, Eastgate, and Edison, we opted against trying to raise our reading scores by one-on-one tutoring by professionals because of the cost.

Reducing the size of the reading group is an effective strategy, but it's very expensive. The cost of 30 daily minutes of additional instruction per year in a one-on-one pullout is about $5,200 per child. The cost of the same 30 minutes daily of additional instruction in groups of four is $1,300 per child.[5]

This left us with two primary strategies: to improve curriculum and improve instruction. Improved curriculum and instruction

[5] If a reading instructor's salary is $40,000 per year with an additional $12,000 in benefits and if he or she teaches 10 30-minute daily sessions over a school year, each session will cost $5,200. (Salary of $40,000 plus benefits of $12,000 equals $52,000. $52,000 divided by 10 daily sessions for 180 days equals $5,200 per 180-day session.) If the session is for one child, the cost per child is $5,200. If the session is used for four, the cost is $1,300 for each student each year.

are necessary but not sufficient. Quality alone was not getting the job done. What turned the corner for us in the 4% growth per year in 1999-2003 was increased instructional time—raw quantity. Increased time in the standard block created space for more direct instruction. Increased time in the intervention block created more space for diagnostic intervention.

"Sometimes the truth is so obvious it eludes us for years," Dan Yankelovich observed.[6] Students who are behind do not learn more in the same amount of time as students who are ahead. Catch-up growth is driven primarily by proportional increases in direct instructional time. Catch-up growth is so difficult to achieve that it can be the product only of quality instruction in great quantity.

> *"Students who are behind do not learn faster than those who are ahead."*
>
> —Lynn Fielding

One of our four schools that began the 2002-03 school year with a backlog of lagging students resisted increasing the amount of instructional time. It retained its traditional 80-minute reading block and 30-minute average intervention block at third grade and continued to experience a significant decline in the numbers of its students who were meeting the reading goal. In contrast, each of the other three schools lagging in 2002 that increased their instructional time made significant improvement in the numbers of their students at or above grade level. While these three schools have substantially increased reading time at each grade level starting in 2002-03, and test scores showed an immediate jump by 3 to 13 points, it will still take two or three more years for the cumulative impact of increasing instructional time at kindergarten to show up at third grade.

10. So what is the relationship between quantity and quality?

Quantity of instructional time can be doubled or tripled in a semester. *Quality* of instructional time cannot. Filling an enlarged instructional window with quality instruction does not happen without

[6] Dan Yankelovich, "How Public Opinion Really Works," *Fortune Magazine*, October 1992. Yankelovich is cofounder, with former Secretary of State Cyrus Vance, of Public Agenda, the nonprofit research foundation that published the seminal educational research *First Things First* in 1994.

excellent curriculum, rigorous training and diagnostic assessments. Improving quality occurs over extended periods of time, at different rates among teachers in the same school, and as a constant process of arduous, intelligent labor. This is why the primary and immediate strategy for catch-up growth is proportional increases in direct instruction time.

This insight is critical—not only at elementary school but in middle and high school as well. Catch-up growth rarely occurs unless principals and teachers have good data, know each student's learning needs, and schedule proportional increases in direct instructional time. Proportionally increased time, however, is enhanced when instructors become more skilled and when the curriculum better aligns to the student's *current* need.

11. So the other long-term alternative is getting better instruction?

That's right. While seven points of NWEA RIT growth is the average for 60-80 minutes of instruction, not all teachers get the same amount of growth in the same amount of time. Our data show that one teacher's students might average three RIT point increases in student scores with 60 extra minutes while another teacher's students will average 12 points.

The next two chapters explore what makes the difference. This chapter has made Kennewick's best case for quantity time — increasing direct instructional time proportional to the individual student's needs. The next two chapters deal with the excellent instruction that creates quality time and enhances "growth per teacher per hour."

CHAPTER FOUR

SUPERB DIRECT INSTRUCTION: STEPHANIE'S CLASSROOM

"Differences in teacher effectiveness are the dominant factors affecting student academic growth in all subjects."

— Dr. William Sanders[1]

The bell rings at 8:35 a.m. and a new school day begins in Stephanie Walton's first grade classroom at Washington Elementary. After the flag salute and lunch count, her 22 students swiftly break into six small groups for the first hour of the morning reading block. Three students go to the district reading specialist, three to the Title I teacher, while four head next door to learn with other students of their ability level. The teacher in the neighboring classroom sends over three of her students, and they take their seats at a table with three of Stephanie's students. In the back of the room, seven students gather for direct instruction with a para-educator who follows Stephanie's lesson plan and is within her listening range. In the hall, two students join a small reading group with the P.E. teacher. At Washington everyone teaches reading the first two hours of the day.[2]

---

[1] William Sanders, Ph.D., is currently a Senior Research Fellow with the University of North Carolina and employed by SAS Institute in Cary, North Carolina. See Chapter 27.

[2] In February 2002 Washington Elementary was chosen as the Washington State Reading School of the Month. This honor includes a visit from the Governor and Superintendent of Public Instruction. The problem was that the Governor's office wanted to schedule the ceremony during the morning reading block. This time is so protected and inviolate that the staff seriously discussed whether to allow this interruption.

Students with the lowest skills are assigned to the most qualified instructors. Everyone uses the SRA Open Court Reading Program.[3]

At 8:45 A.M. Stephanie writes *igh* on the large white board by her desk. She directs the six children to a sound card on the wall to review the "i" and "i-e" spellings they already know. She points to the *igh* explaining that this is another way to say the long *i* sound.

i g h[4]

She clearly says the sound, "I."
"I," the students in her group echo.
Quickly Stephanie writes a *t* on the board.

t

"What sound?" she asks.
"Ttt," her group repeats.
"The sounds together?" she prompts.

t i g h

"Tie," they respond in unison.
She beams while adding a *t* at the end, "Word?"

t i g h t

"T-igh-t" the students chant.

Stephanie writes an *e* on the board and covers *tight* with her hand. "Sound?"

---

[3] All available staff except the receptionist and the principal teach reading during this block. Today Stephanie is teaching from SRA Open Court Reading, Level 1-C, Unit 5 Lesson 9, Teacher's Edition, (Columbus, Ohio: McGraw-Hill, 2000).

[4] What appears in large type is what Stephanie writes on the board. What appears in "..." is a phonemic approximation of what is being said.

"Excellent reading instruction is systematic. It starts with phonemic awareness and the alphabetic principle (phonics), then moves to comprehension and fluency."

— Claudia Glover, District Reading Specialist,
Washington Elementary

e

She adds an "n" next to the e while still covering *tight*.
"Sound?"
"N," the group answers.

n

"Together?" she says removing her hand.

e n

"En!" the group swiftly responds.
Stephanie removes her hand from the other letters,
"Now blend them." [5]

t i g h t e n

Again covering *tight*, she erases the *en* and adds *l*. "Sound?"
"Lll," the children say.
In a split second she writes a *y*. "Sound?"
"Eee."
"Together?" the teacher prompts.

l y

"Leee!"
"That's right! Blend."

[5] Teachers at Westgate Elementary School used money from the Bill and Melinda Gates Foundation to purchase Smart Boards. The letters automatically sail on to the board, allowing for smoother blending.

t i g h t l y

"Tightly," the students respond.

All this has transpired in five minutes. As Stephanie Walton teaches, she verifies what her students are learning, teaches more, verifies, corrects, and continues teaching. Now she extends the *ight* sound to another pattern.

b r i g h t

b r i g h t e n   b r i g h t l y   b r i g h t n e s s

Twenty minutes fly by, with students blending words and sentences using the *igh* spelling pattern. Stephanie reminds the students that *igh* words usually rhyme with each other. On the board she writes:

The light at night is very bright.

"Max, can you read the words with the long *i* sound?"

"Amy, can you come to the board and circle the *igh* spelling in these words?"

The sight of it gave me a fright.

The students are having fun. The lesson moves quickly and holds their full attention. They know the routine and teacher expectations. This is a safe classroom to take risks and learning is exciting. Stephanie is warm and inviting, smiling and calm. She is also working hard. This is direct, eyeball-to-eyeball instruction.

At the other end of the classroom, the para-educator goes through the same patterns with a slightly larger, slightly more advanced group. She is also highly skilled, continuously involving the students, incrementally increasing the difficulty, verifying understanding, reviewing, reteaching, advancing, and rechecking.

Ten years ago we would have seen three reading groups with seven students each. Stephanie would have been the only adult, except on the days when she was able to get a mom to volunteer to help with the art project that accompanied the reading unit. Stephanie would have spent 20 minutes providing direct instruction to each group, while the other two groups did seat work or read silently. The 60-minute reading block would have predominantly focused on comprehension utilizing whole language techniques. Often the worksheets would be from yesterday's social studies, math, or health lesson, attempting to integrate reading instruction with other subjects.

At 9:05 Stephanie gives the students today's decodable reading book, *The Opossum at Night*. They look at the High-Frequency Word Wall to review words they will see in this book: *does, the, too* and *to*.

"Carlos, will you read the title of this book, please?"
"Has anyone ever seen an opossum?"

A lively discussion begins about the pronunciation of *opossum* (uhpossum) and animals the children have seen on television, in their neighborhood, and on trips. Now that the children are fully engaged in the topic, Stephanie calls on a different child to read each page of the story aloud. She helps them blend difficult words. The group rereads the story. To assess comprehension she asks lighthearted questions:

"Shalom, why doesn't the opossum like the light?"
"It is too bright."
"Yes. Greg, what does the opossum feed her babies?"
"Bugs!"
"Yuck! Would you like to eat bugs?"
"My brother read about people who eat bugs. They live in Australia."
"That's true. People in many countries cook and eat bugs."
"Sonnet, what does the opossum tell her babies?"
"She tells them to go to sleep."
"Good. What else does she tell her babies, Carlos?"
"They can play again tonight."
"Are you ready to read to each other? Read the book two times with the person sitting next to you. Girls read even-numbered pages and boys read odd-numbered pages. Go."

As they read, Stephanie monitors attentively. When they finish, she promptly collects the small booklets and distributes their Reading and Writing Workbooks while praising their efforts:

"You guys are becoming amazing readers! Stop and remember what you could read in September, think of what you can read now, and imagine what you will be able to read by the end of the year!"

"Oh yeah," "Cool," "Wow!" the six children reflect. They are happy about their accomplishments.

At 9:30 Stephanie guides her small group to a page in their workbooks that reinforces the long *i* spelled *igh.* They also practice writing and blending compound words such as *lightbulb, nightshirt,* and *tightrope.* When Max and Amy struggle with the assignment, she intervenes by writing the first word on the board, having the children blend it, adding the second word, having the children blend it, then having them blend the whole word. She decides that tonight she will send home another worksheet for additional practice.

It's 9:43. Glancing up, Stephanie smiles at the students who are returning from other classes. "Your options are cards or workbook." They know exactly what to do, and get right to work. She continues teaching until the rest of the students come back into the room as silently as the first three, go to their seats, and take out cards or workbooks.

At 9:47 Stephanie asks the entire class to come to the carpet area at the front of the room. In less than two minutes they are settled in the story area gazing at the cover of *Things That Go*. The 24-inch picture book features photographs and text about pony carts, oxen, rickshaws, fire engines, and monorails. The children expand their vocabulary while Stephanie points at a world map where they could find oxen and rickshaws (India), trains (Denmark), trolley (Germany), and monorails (Seattle, Washington).

"Where in the world do you suppose we would find rickshaws, Nina?" Stephanie pauses almost six seconds, refusing to take answers from other waving hands while Nina thinks. "Yes, India, that's right. They have rickshaws in India. Now Peter, would you like to be pulling the rickshaw or riding in the rickshaw?"

> *Few adults have ever been in a classroom where direct eyeball-to-eyeball, student-engaged teaching goes on for 55-58 minutes out of every hour. Videotapes of this kind of instruction may be purchased from the Kennewick School District at (509) 222-5000.*

Most of the boys want to pull. Most of the girls want to ride. They are making connections with the words: oxen, rickshaws, trains, and monorails. Five minutes later they are comparing (trains and monorails both carry lots of people) and contrasting (trains use two tracks and monorails use only one). The next five minutes are spent on position words: "on," "beside," "behind," "in," and "over." Some children stand to demonstrate the relationships asother children are called on to describe them. In twenty-five minutes, they use the same thematic material to do five different exercises.

Stephanie ends the session by saying, "Please go back to your seats and turn to page 18 in your workbooks. Hands and pencils should be down."

By 10:19 they are back in their seats, a transition that takes less than 90 seconds. They spend the next ten minutes on two workbook exercises that reinforce the five position words they have just learned, holding their answers up as they go. Stephanie is actively moving up and down the three rows of desks, checking her students' work and providing individual attention. By 10:30, the students are writing on their 8" x 12" white boards, spelling extensions of words they did earlier, showing their teacher, as they review ten to twelve words.

Stephanie's direct instruction is highly structured, highly sequenced, and highly integrated, and occurs 90-95% of the time. By 10:45, the students have tucked the white boards, erasers, and markers back in their desks. Stephanie distributes their corrected writing papers, and the children cheer. This is the final phase before they are photographed with their polished story and it is displayed in the hallway.

"Where are we going to put these stories?" she asks.
"In the hall for everyone to read!" the student's chorus.
"Do we want to do our best work?" Stephanie asks.
"We always want to do our best!"

It's 10:47, and continuous direct instruction goes on. If you missed the transition, the two-hour standard reading block is over. Washington Elementary's first graders have moved on to writing. Reading remediation occurs in the afternoon for students who need more time.

Occasionally a gifted teacher, the right curriculum, and a magical class can produce such results spontaneously. But consistent achievement emerges from the intelligent and rigorous application of a curriculum that has been carefully selected to produce sequential learning from simple to complex skills. In the spring of 2003, 20 of Stephanie's 22 first-graders scored 12 or higher on the Diagnostic Reading Assessment (DRA) scale, which indicates that 91% of them are on track to meet the 90% Reading Goal. Of the two who didn't, one had just moved into the school district.

Professionals like Stephanie are committed to continual professional growth through staff development, teaming with colleagues, and studying educational research and journals. They use precise data about students to guide instructional decisions and adjust lesson plans to target the learning levels of each child. Excellent instruction is essential for annual growth.

Spring third grade reading scores are a result of all that comes before. The work of third grade teachers builds on the expert instruction of second grade teachers. Their efforts, in turn, build on the outcome of the labor of teachers like Stephanie. Stephanie's work builds on the results of kindergarten teachers.

We estimate that in the spring of 1996, less than ten percent of Kennewick kindergarten students could read. Those who were able to read often learned at home. Kindergarten, in many classrooms, was considered a time for social transition and not academic skill development.

In the spring of 2004, 71% of Kennewick kindergarten students were reading. They were not reading Shakespeare or even Garfield. However, they were reading words in sentences and could explain what they were reading. More precisely, they got 36 of 42 words correct on the Developmental Reading Assessment which contains simple, repetitive text like, *I see a blue pond* and *I can see a yellow sun.*

The complex field of teacher development and in-service training is beyond the scope of this book. However, Stephanie has just modeled classroom instruction of high rigor where each student was appropriately challenged, high student engagement where each student actively participated in the learning, and a clear lesson purpose where the materials were intentionally designed to achieve the targeted learning. The results were mastery of reading sub-skills.

In the spring of 2004, 71% of Kennewick kindergarten students were reading.

Chapter 5 shows how administrators can use this powerful instructional framework in their role as instructional leaders.

CHAPTER FIVE

INSTRUCTIONAL LEADERSHIP: OUR CRAFT

"Instructional leadership is our craft."

— Paul Rosier

Initial Achievement + Growth = Ending Achievement

While the statement seems fairly self-evident, it wasn't until the fall of 1995 that Kennewick had accurate initial achievement data for students for reading and math. It was several years after that when Kennewick began awkwardly but successfully predicting student academic outcomes. When we realized we could predict and actually control the outcomes, we started to take responsibility for them.

Initial achievement always has the highest correlation to ending achievement. The correlation of reading level (achievement) between the beginning and end of third grade in Kennewick is .83. This is a very high correlation, yet it is a simple restatement of "start ahead, stay ahead; start behind, stay behind." The initial academic starting point will always be the largest predictor of individual ending outcomes. This is especially true when students' initial starting points cover a six-year range. Even when the lowest 40% of students make one to three years of growth and even when we extend the interval to measure between the beginning of third grade to the end of fifth grade or end of seventh grade, the initial academic starting point will always emerge as the highest predictor. That is what we learned about initial achievement.

Growth is the second major factor in the equation. Growth, we learned, is a function of *the amount of time* multiplied by the *rate of growth*. Chapter 3 focused on the *amount of time* component of instruction.

What controls the *rate of growth*? We expect students' overall growth to substantially increase, perhaps double when direct instructional time is doubled. Yet even when students receive the same amount of instructional time, all students do not grow the same. What accounts for the variation? Is it primarily student motivation? Is it socio-economic background?

Factors Accounting for .43 of the Differences in Growth[1]

Minutes of instructional time	.18
Instructor	.13
Socio-economic status and years in the district	.13

Research initially done by Dr. William Sanders, director of the University of Tennessee's Value-Added Research and Assessment Center for 34 years, and paralleled, in part, in Kennewick, indicates that one of the highest factors correlating with different rates of growth among students is the instructor. After the amount of direct instructional time, the individual instructor predicts the amount of growth students make. Some instructors create minimal growth, other instructors create average annual growth, and still others create high amounts of growth in equivalent amounts of time. In analysis of growth factors we can control, the instructor is the big dog.[1]

Differences among instructors should come as no surprise. Some lawyers specialize in trial work and excel at it. Give them complex construction contract work and expect a different result. Michael Jordan was a phenomenal NBA outside player. His domination was diminished inside the paint, and during his one year playing pro baseball, he looked very average. Different job, different skill set.

[1] Correlations developed by Dr. Joseph Montgomery, Washington State University, March 2004, using 2002-03 Kennewick student data.

In addition, we find that each instructor tends to target a certain quintile (20%) of students. When we take our 933 third-grade students for whom we have both fall and spring reading scores, we find that individual teachers create more growth among one quintile of students than among the others. In Kennewick, we consciously work at getting more growth for the lowest 40% of students.

While we are just beginning to identify ways to increase student performance by matching teacher strengths to student needs, it is very evident that improving the quality of instruction is an increasing focus within our district.

In our last chapter, Stephanie modeled many of the moves that earned her a black belt in instruction. The kind of great instruction resulting in high growth is hard to define, but we know it when we see it. Or do we?

During a summer session at the Harvard Institute of School Leadership in 2002, approximately a hundred educators including our leadership team viewed and analyzed a videotaped high school lesson. Our assignment was to evaluate the quality of instruction. The results were so "all over the place" that our only consensus was that the teacher had a well-managed classroom. If our Harvard leadership team could not agree on whether or not they were seeing good instruction, what sort of *uniform* expectations were the rest of our administrators providing to our teachers?

Back in Kennewick, we formulated four questions to guide a systematic district-wide approach to the professional development of instructional leaders.[2] The questions were:

1. As administrators, how do we heighten our focus on instructional leadership?
2. Is the district leadership team focused on teaching and learning?
3. How do we help each other recognize clear purpose, engagement, and rigor to achieve results in instruction?

---

[2]For an expanded version of these concepts, see Paul Rosier, " Why Instructional Leadership Must Be Our Craft," *Leadership Information* 2, no. 4 (Fall 2003): 3-8, School Information and Research Services, in conjunction with the Washington Association of School Administrators.

4. What knowledge, skills, and leadership behaviors will help teachers increase the academic performance of all students?

Out of these four questions, we established four major activities:

- Instructional conferences for all administrators
- Learning walks
- The two-ten goal
- Literacy coaches at middle and high schools

Now in our second year, the initiatives keep morphing as we find better ways to do them. Here is Kennewick's current version:

Instructional Conferences. We hold these conferences five times a year and run three sessions at each conference so that all of the district and building administrators and teacher-leaders (elementary district reading instructors from each elementary school, literacy coaches from middle and high schools) from our 21 schools can attend. We determined that the best method for learning about quality instruction would be to study our best teachers. Groups of 40 administrators view and discuss a previously videotaped lesson in a seminar-type arrangement.

Based on the work of Anthony Alvarado and Elaine Fink (former New York District 2 administrators), our directors of Elementary and Secondary Education led the instructional conferences and facilitated presentations that involved high rigor and high engagement. Jim Huge and Connie Hoffman, our Gates Foundation consultant-coaches, were invaluable in molding and modeling the conference process. Split-screen views showed both the instructor and the students simultaneously. We studied whether the purpose of the lesson was clearly maintained throughout the lesson. We analyzed the results of the lesson in terms of student behavior as well. That is, could the students do what the teacher intended for them to do at the conclusion of the lesson? When students were interviewed, did their experience of the lesson correspond with intended learning?

High rigor, high engagement, and clear lesson purpose should yield high student results. This model, which is an adaptation of a variety of principles coming from authentic instruction, teaching for understanding, student-centered instruction, and constructivist teaching is only "observable in about 17% of classroom lessons," according to Gates researcher Jeffrey Fouts and his associates. "The other 83% of the lessons observed may have contained some elements of constructivist teaching, but as many as one-half of the lessons observed had very little or no elements of constructivist teaching present."[3]

Instructional Framework

Purpose:	Teacher intentionally plans and instructs for student achievement of essential learnings.
Rigor:	Each learner is appropriately challenged as the teacher moves students to higher levels of thinking.
Engagement:	Teacher and student actively participate in the learning and are focused on the lesson.
Results:	The intended learning is achieved.

An important aspect of each instructional conference is using reflective questioning to engage teachers in conversations about their practice. This methodology allowed us to look beyond classroom management. The viewing is followed by a discussion of probing and open-ended questions such as:

- What are the students being asked to do?
- What makes the materials relevant and challenging?
- How is the instruction rigorous?
- What is the evidence that it is challenging, i.e:
  - What was the result of the instructor's questions?
  - How were the questions varied to get different results?
- In what ways does the instructor vary the students' activities?
- How are students expected to interact with each other as well as with the teacher?

[3] Jeffrey T. Fouts, Carol Brown, and Gayle Y. Thieman, *Classroom Instruction in Gates Grantee Schools: A Baseline Report*, September 2002. Retrieved at http://gatesfoundation.org on May 5, 2004. Dr. Fouts is former senior researcher and executive director of the Washington School Research Center at Seattle Pacific University.

- Are the students engaged at a "ritual" or "supposed to" level or on an "authentic" and "actually interested" level?

Principals were encouraged to use a coaching model that utilized reflective questions like, "What did you learn by teaching this lesson?" and, "How will that influence your next lesson?" instead of a consulting model, which tends to ask, "Why did you choose to present that point the way you did?" as well as make evaluative statements. (See Appendix C for a list of the leadership standards.)

IF Initial Achievement + Growth = Ending Achievement,
AND Growth = 17% (purpose, rigor, and engagement)

THEN it should follow that

Initial Achievement + 17% (purpose + rigor + engagement) = Ending Achievement

While growth relationships are complex, this analysis suggests how significant variations in student academic growth can occur between instructor classrooms where purpose, rigor, and engagement are present 17% of the time versus classrooms where they are present 70-85% of the time.

Ted Mansfield, the veteran Ridge View Elementary principal who was the first to introduce Core Knowledge[4] west of the Mississippi, watched a high school teacher present math concepts at the first Kennewick conference. He concluded: "She wasn't bad." At the third conference six months later, when he watched the same teacher teach another demo lesson, he commented, "I was surprised at how much she had improved her purpose. Her focus was much clearer." Then Greg Fancher, director of Elementary Education, informed the group that they had just viewed the same videotaped lesson shown at the first conference.

[4] The Core Knowledge® Foundation was founded by E. D. Hirsch, Jr., professor emeritus at the University of Virginia. The foundation can be reached at 801 East High Street, Charlottesville, VA 22902; Phone: (434) 977-7550, Fax (434) 977 0021, www.coreknow@coreknowledge.org. Kennewick Core Knowledge schools are Ridge View, Vista, and Washington.

Ted recalls, "It took Greg quite a while to convince me they hadn't re-taped anything. It was the same lesson, seen this time through very different lenses." Our principals have learned a new set of skills by which to appraise the instructional element of the TAG loop.

Learning Walks. Our learning walks are a spin-off of Alvardo and Fink's work called "walk-throughs." Conducted at least once each year at each school, the group is composed of three to four principals joined by several central office administrators. The host principal gives an overview of his or her school. Small clusters of administrators then visit three to four classrooms for 15 or 20 minutes each, looking for the purpose of the instruction, levels of student engagement, and lesson rigor. After the learning walk, the administrators debrief for an hour. That gives principals a chance to learn from each other, share about teaching and learning in their schools, and write a short "thank you" note to the classroom instructors, commenting on positive aspects of the purpose, rigor, engagement, and student learning they observed.[5] However, observations during the learning walks are for the increased learning of the observers and are not tied to formal teacher evaluation in any way.

Two-Ten Goal. Learning walk time counts toward the two-ten goal. Each administrator is expected to spend two hours a day or ten hours a week on instructionally focused activities, 60% of which are to be direct classroom observations. Many principals, particularly our elementary principals, were already doing this.

For others, especially at large middle and high schools, their first response was, "What do we get to take off our plate?" While some things have been removed—such as a few district reports — the real change is in attitude. We choose to do with our time what we think is important. If student learning is the most important function of schools, then instruction is where we focus our time and attention. Administrators at each school developed a list of "look-fors" that are used during these observations.

Literacy Coaches. This concept developed out of a district-wide math coach model we had been using for several years and a plan used

[5] For more information on this strategy, see Rosier, "Why Instructional Leadership Must Be Our Craft."

by the Lancaster Pennsylvania School District. In 2001, a cadre of literacy coaches was selected in collaboration with the Kennewick Education Association for teacher-leader roles. District policy required literacy coaches to meet weekly with principals to review the status of students below the 50% percentile and to plan building-level professional development. In addition, the literacy coaches met regularly with the classroom teachers to enhance literacy instruction in middle and high school. These two moves created momentum, and literacy became high priority in the secondary schools.

"At Southgate, we hire a couple of substitutes for a morning. Two teachers and I go around to other classrooms in our building. After each class, we write thank-you notes, including some things we learned during the observations. We spend the final hour debriefing, using reflective questions to explore the rigor and engagement in what we saw. Initially there was a palpable reluctance to teach in front of their peers, but then it changed to the excitement athletes or musicians experience before a big performance. Great energy!"

— Le Fulfs, Principal, Southgate Elementary,
President 2001-02,
Assoc. of WA School Principals

The combination of the instructional conferences, the learning walks, the two-ten goal, and the literacy coaches has resulted in four significant improvements.

First, the "talk" among administrators has shifted to instruction and away from management and athletics. Talk is the best cultural indicator of focus. Shifting administrative focus to the support of classroom instruction is like a new coat of paint on an old house. The walls are still the same, but everything looks, smells, and feels different. After a while, we started to function differently because experienced administrators, like Ted Mansfield, were seeing differently, more keenly, more astutely.

Second, Kennewick now has general agreement on what constitutes quality instruction and what evidence supports it. Rigor was the big winner. Teaching to the edge of what students understand without frustrating them is absolutely essential for high growth. Administrators and teachers are looking for better ways to engage students and to make sure the purpose of the lesson is clear and maintained. Everyone still expects good classroom management, but now they look beyond it.

Third, the videotaped instructors have become almost famous. They are local celebrities in our 1,400-person organization. Every administrator knows them. They get over one hundred little "thank you" notes from all of the instructional conference participants. Segments of some tapes have been played during board meetings. Their classroom moves have been dissected like a Saturday night game film. They deserve their fame. They took real risks when it was not clear at the outset how safe this activity would be. Until we established ground rules to focus on what was being done well, it was a little dicey. Instead of railing against bad teaching (which historically has been fairly ineffective, we might add), we are now celebrating great instruction. This dynamic continues to create immense energy for change. Learning walks are now springing up at the school level, as principals and substitutes cover classrooms, allowing teachers to go on in-building walks. The building instructors, encouraged by the positive response to the videotaped instructors, view observations as a way to showcase their skills, instead of being critiqued and evaluated.

An outgrowth of the instructional conferences and peer assistance and review program (Chapter Ten) has been the development of alternatives when "unsatisfactory" is marked during formal evaluation. A specific plan of support and improvement is now in place. Measurability is key and clear steps are specified, like teaming with a senior teacher, observing other classrooms, or taking instructional classes.

The fourth element, which we call an "expectation of excellence," is more elusive and is best described by contrasting the past with the present. In the past, teacher evaluations rarely resulted in anything other than "satisfactory" being marked on the negotiated form. The rare "unsatisfactory" was nearly always grieved. Occasionally, a single principal would focus on a single teacher whose mediocre performance had either become too egregious to bear any longer or too public to ignore. The union and the district would then pit their resources against each other for the next two years, draining both organizations. The union would often prevail. However, the principal, whatever the outcome and even with legal support from the administration, would quietly and fiercely resolve not to repeat that experience for a *long* time. Over-all pressure and leadership for improvement through the evaluation process came from 5% of the administration and affected less than 5% of the certified staff.

Now, the isolated pressure from the evaluation process from a few administrators has changed to a district-wide expectation for excellence from nearly 100% of the administrators. The five-times-a-year training in purpose, rigor, engagement, and results has been kept alive by the two-ten scheduled use of time in the same way the weekly board workshops kept the elementary schools focused on the reading goal. A common district-wide vocabulary has emerged, and everyone, board members to para-professionals, use these new terms. Celebrating truly skillful teachers harnesses the power of great instruction that generates student learning.

We have always known that excellent instruction was critical. In fact, it is vital. Achieving at least a year's worth of growth in reading and math for all students (and catch-up growth for students who are behind) requires a high uniform level of quality instruction in addition to more instructional time.

> *Luck is where preparation meets opportunity.*
>
> — Old adage

Kennewick is not hoping to strike it lucky with charismatic principals and gifted teachers who happen to wander into the district. We have made our own luck by mobilizing the intelligence and will of a corps of educational leaders who see, communicate, and honor results-centered teaching. We concentrate on getting good data for our teachers, providing them with the best tools available, sharing the accountability for student-by-student progress, and celebrating our achievements. This expertise in educational excellence and instructional leadership, which is foundational for each of the four elements of the TAG loop, is the craft at which our principals excel.

CHAPTER SIX

Loving the Data: Diagnostic Testing, Teaching to the Deficiency, and Retesting

"In God we trust. Everyone else shows their data."

— Unknown

"At Lincoln Elementary," Angie Clark explains, "our class size runs from 22 to 28 students. We have a 150-minute reading block at first grade, 130 minutes at second grade, and 120 minutes at third grade. For reading, there are 16 regular classroom teachers K-5, and one and one-half reading teachers supported by two para-pros."[1]

Every Kennewick elementary school has one "district reading teacher" funded by the local property tax levy. At Lincoln, that is Angie. Six schools have two more reading specialists and two to four para-professionals who are paid for by federal Title I or federal-state pass through money. For example, Eastgate will get $364,000 and Amistad will get $257,000 of Title I funding in 2004-05. Lincoln will get none. Virtually all qualifying elementary schools in the United States get these funds.

"Before the Reading Goal, we were like utility infielders in baseball," recalls Angie. "If a first-grade teacher was out, we taught

[1] Para-eds and para-pros are para-educators and para-professionals who aid certified staff.

first grade. If the second-grade teacher had a district meeting, we taught second grade that afternoon. Smooth classroom management was a first-level priority, and reading remediation was just part of the process. If students didn't learn to read as first graders, there was always second grade . . . and third and fourth grade. But with the 90% Reading Goal, our role changed."

Reprinted courtesy Larry Wright and The Detroit News.

The leadership role of the district reading teacher and other reading specialists emerged gradually as grade-level reading standards became a priority. At first the focus was at third grade, but within a few years it extended to second grade, then first, and as early as kindergarten. The reading specialists took the lead in poring over student data, analyzing the effects of past interventions, charting the needs of students in the coming semester, and finding efficient ways to serve more students with the limited resources. After nearly a decade, unique building-level practices evolved that were unlike anything in existence in 1995. The practices revolved around data.

"We start our reading assessments in September," says Deborah Peterson, the district reading teacher at Vista Elementary. "We have some students who make summer surges, some with summer losses, and some who've just moved in our school boundaries. We test everyone. Our testing window is open until we get done. It takes us about three weeks. As district reading teacher, I test the first and second graders. Our other reading specialists test the other grades. We use whole-class tests where we can. Though it is not as accurate as one-on-one testing, whole-class testing is a lot faster."

Every school divides the testing responsibilities differently among its staff. The testing time frames vary as well. Years ago, testing at some schools did not finish until the end of October with remediation starting afterwards. Schedules were delayed to accommodate migrant students who dribbled in during September and October and started moving out in November and December. Now at Washington Elementary, testing is finished the week after Labor Day so remediation can start the following Monday. Schools like Lincoln and Cascade with less mobile populations test a little more selectively and rely more on spring scores.

"We looked everywhere," continues Deborah, "and we couldn't find anything that tested the 12 phonemic awareness sub-skills. Finally, I sat down and put together a series of tests. We've been using it ever since."

This can-do attitude of finding an existing tool or designing a new one permeates our elementary schools. Many of the Kennewick schools still use the phonemic awareness test that Deborah Peterson developed and shared. The Rosner is used heavily, and the McCracken is common as well. This series of tests forms a skill continuum. The tests not only measure where each student is, they also reinforce the importance of the skill continuum to the staff.

"Once we have the data," adds Claudia Glover, the district reading teacher from Washington Elementary, "we rank every student in order of ability. Then, we draw a line of demarcation. Students below the line get additional services. Students at or above grade level do not. Any students not likely to be at the 90% goal level get additional help."

The data analysis for grades K-5 takes about seven hours. Deborah, Claudia, and Angie take the lead at their schools. After they organize the data, they meet with the rest of the staff, verify that the teacher's classroom observations correspond with the testing results, and work out scheduling issues. Principals are also involved, comparing the student data with their own lists for each grade level. A system has evolved at each school that determines which reading specialists deal with which students, given the data and the teacher expertise available at each school.

One School's Reading Assessments, 2002-03
Deborah Peterson, District Reading Specialist
Vista Elementary

First and second graders start at the top of this list and test downward until they reach the limits of their ability. Third, fourth, and fifth graders start at the bottom of this list and test upward.

Phonemic Awareness Test—A to Z Book Test, given to Grade 1
Alternate A to Z Test, given to Grade 1 or 2

Letter Recognition and Letter Sounds Test—Grades 1-2, Grades 3-5 if appropriate

Vocabulary—McCracken for word recognition and vocabulary meaning—Grades 1-5

Fluency—Read Naturally or Open Court Fluency Tests—Grades 1-5

Comprehension—McLeod Cloze Procedure Test—CORE, whole class—Grades 3-5

Open Court Individual Reading Inventories (IRI)—Grades 1-2, or when test results are questionable

Phonics—Vista made, given to whole class—Grades 2-5.
Given individually to Grade 1 students in program

Phonemic Segmentation Test—CORE, given individually—Grades 3-5

"Remediation starts with phonemic awareness, moves to phonics, then accuracy, fluency, and comprehension," Claudia continues. "Students work on the phonemic awareness task in which they are deficient and graduate when they have mastered that task. Students who have difficulty with phonics often stay most of the year in our program. Otherwise, it's pretty well the same with accuracy, fluency, and/or comprehension. I diagnostically test, teach to the sub-skill, and retest to make sure they have mastered this sub-skill. Students stay in small group remediation until they have mastered the deficient skill."

In the past, remediation was process oriented. Reading specialists worked with students who were behind. If the students didn't catch up in reading this year, they might get more intervention time next year. Individual classes operated much the same way, and with little coordination between them. The consistent result was that some students arrived at the next grade level with gaps in their skills. Now, Washington and Vista progress through the basic skills very sequentially and with the support of the classroom teacher who emphasizes the same skills in the small group sessions during the individual reading block. Their students work on the same deficient sub-skill until they master it, then move on to the next one. Angie at Lincoln likes to layer the practice of several deficient skills into each day's intervention session.

Elementary Reading Sub-Skills

Phonemic awareness is the understanding that spoken language is composed of speech sounds. It is the ability to blend, segment, and manipulate sounds in spoken words. The developmental sequence begins at the word level (how many words you can hear in the sentence), to the syllable level (say "cowboy" without the "cow" = "boy"), and then to the phoneme level (say "clap" without the "l" = "cap"). There are 16 tasks to be completed by the end of second grade.

Phonics is putting the sounds to letters to form and identify words. There are about 45 phonics rules that help both read and spell words. Examples include "i before e except after c."

Accuracy is the number of words read correctly. Beginning readers often decode the first letters of a word but then guess, decreasing their accuracy. For example, "there" could end up pronounced as "that" or "the."

Fluency is usually equated with speed but reading specialists look for smoothness and expression as well as conversational speed.

Comprehension is attaching meaning to the words. One of the impacts of the whole-language movement was to accelerate getting young readers into the comprehension process as quickly as possible.

Table 6.1
Intervention Strategies at Lincoln Elementary by Grade Level for 2002-03

Intervention Strategies	Kindergarten	1st Grade	2nd Grade	3rd Grade	4th Grade	5th Grade
Standard Reading Block	100	150	150	130	140	130
Remedial Time	30	30	30	30	30	
1. Teachers work individually and in small groups w/ students	x	x	x	x	x	x
2. Reading specialists provide small group intervention	x	x	x	x	x	x
3. Accelerated Reader		x	x	x	x	x
4. Second Shot Reading				x		
5. Constant communication w/ home, reading specialists, para-ed	x	x	x	x	x	x
6. Read-alouds with parent and community volunteers	x	x	x		x	x
7. Para-eds work individually and in small groups	x	x	x	x	x	
8. Cross-grade tutors listen to students	x	x				
9. Waterford Reading Program	x					
10. Emphasize 20 minutes of reading w/ parent a day	x	x	x	x	x	x
11. Recess reading		x	x	x	x	x

"There is lots of communication now that did not occur a few years ago," Angie adds. "I talk to the classroom teachers all the time about each of their students that I see. We coordinate what we do, so if Tony is working on short *'e'* sounds with me, the classroom teacher is emphasizing it with him in the standard reading block as well."

The district reading and Title I teachers have unique positions within our elementary schools. They have no special salary arrangements. They have no positional authority. They are peers with their teaching colleagues. Their influence is based on their competence in achieving catch-up growth. For reading specialists, creating more than a year of reading growth during the year has been about falling in love with what the data show is working for their students and falling out of love with well-worn practices that don't work.

These teachers are prominent players in the TAG loop. They administer the diagnostic testing, provide leadership in determining proportional increases in direct instruction time, organize the interventional blocks, and do much of the actual teaching to the deficient skill or sub-skill in conjunction with the class room teacher. They re-test to see if the student made the necessary growth. They are clearly the "go to" people when it comes to leaving no child behind; but to a person, they resist being singled out in this way.

"We are all part of the team," they jointly insist. "No one can get this many kids to read at grade level by themselves."

And of course, they are right.

CHAPTER SEVEN

WHAT OUR ELEMENTARY PRINCIPALS ARE SAYING

"You can either fight assessment or embrace it. However, you cannot be a high-performance school without embracing assessment."

— Dave Montague, Principal, Washington Elementary

Lynn: What would you suggest to another principal or district about how to reach a 90-95% Reading Goal more efficiently?

Judy (Cascade): Patience! I don't think it's a quick thing.

Chuck (Vista): Everybody is at a different place. Every school has to do things differently to get to a goal that high. With some schools, it is tough to get the teachers to focus. New hires coming on need to hear: "This is the expectation."

Dave (Washington): I don't know how you can be a principal today without knowing what it takes for kids to read, what good instruction looks like, what problem solving in math and in the writing process look like. Teachers need to know that you know what you are actually looking for. Out of necessity, principals have to become involved in instructional training.

This chapter is an edited version of an extended conversation with the director of elementary education, Greg Fancher, two of the authors, Lynn and Nancy, and five of our Kennewick elementary principals.

Chuck: In the beginning, we need to be allowed to figure out how to best utilize the players we have, with their strengths and weakness. I couldn't take my specialists and do what Washington Elementary does because of the players that I have. I have to use my players differently. The down side of this approach, however, is that some schools aren't going to figure it out for a long time.

Greg: Rob came to Kennewick from Othello [a district 50 miles to the north] that was just starting into the accountability step with the state testing system. I know Rob's made comments before about how it was different.

Rob: (Amistad) A couple of years before my wife and I came, a principal up there told me there was no way he would ever go to Kennewick because of the 90% reading goal. From the outside, it looked pretty scary. Not only was I coming to Kennewick with its reading goal, but I was coming to a school that was nowhere near 90%.

Table 7.1
Kennewick's Elementary School Principals, 1995-2004

School	2003 Free or Reduced	2003 Minority Enrollment	2003 English Language Learners	Minority Enrollment	1995-1996	1996-1997	1997-1998	1998-1999	1999-2000	2000-2001	2001-2002	2002-2003	2003-2004
Amistad	76	67.7	47.2	39.7	Terry Barber				Rob Phillips				
Westgate	80	37.3	30.9	36.1	Joe Sullivan				Dorothy Fanning				
Eastgate	82	68.2	60.8	19.1	Linda Hardy							Mark Stephens	
Washington	54	25.7		33.3	Dave Montague								
Hawthorne	60	33	20.8	30.3	Gail Still							Craig Miller	
Vista	50	24.4		30.6	Chuck Watson								
Edison	73	58.6	43.4	45.3	Libby Herres			Doug Carl					
Lincoln	41	21.8		22.9	Mike Hepworth					Doug Campbell			
Canyon View	38	28.7		34.2		Bruce Cannard							
Ridge View	23	21.9	13.9	24.7	Ted Mansfield								
Cascade	35	14.4		35.6	B. Ding		Judy Long						
Southgate	20	12.2		29.6	Le Fulfs								
Sunset View	9	11		18.2	Terry Tanneberg						B. Mehlenbacher		

Nancy: So why did you come?

Rob: It was a death wish. [Laughter] No, actually, I knew Greg, and some other principals here, so it was easy to come.

Lynn: On the district level, we saw a big first-year jump in 1995-96 from 58% to 74%, but pretty flat growth for the next three years. What happened at your building?

Judy: I don't think this kind of change happens just because somebody says it is going to happen and then the next year—Presto! It takes a while, and we are still all doing it.

Chuck: It takes a while to turn the ship.

Judy: Yes, and we haven't turned that ship completely. We are all looking for bigger and better ways to do it. It takes a while to motivate so many people. A lot of people are going in different directions and have different mindsets. So you bring everybody together as best you can and try to get them all focused on the goal. It takes time. It doesn't happen overnight.

Chuck: I think over the years we've gotten better at understanding what it takes to teach kids how to read and how to break that process down by grade level, figuring out the grade-level expectations, and figuring out how to get all that organized. The climb you are seeing now took us two to four years to figure out. It takes even longer to get pretty good at what it takes to teach kids to read.

Dorothy (Westgate): It takes a while for teachers to let go of what they've done for years and years and years. I hear all the time: "How are we going to fit it all in?"

Lynn: What did the board and district office do that was helpful?

Dorothy: You started with reading. It was the right place to start. It's essential. I totally buy the third grade reading goal, because you can see that if students don't read by third grade it's so hard for them to be on level in fourth grade. And it just gets worse as you track them up further.

Judy: Making us report what we are doing, as much as I don't like that. It keeps the facts in front of us. It's a reality check.

Ted (Ridge View): Just moving to a single focus had an immense impact. No one realizes how many "initiatives" hit the elementary schools in the '80s and the '90s. We had a new flavor of the month all through both decades. One of our time-tested strategies was just to wait them out. In education, if you screw around long enough, it will go away.

Dorothy: The reading goal was permission to finally take something off the plate. When I can take something off my plate and add reading, it looks like a do-able thing. What I tell the parents is that if their children can't read leaving second grade, they will not be able to enjoy social studies and science all the rest of their lives.

Summary of what the central office and board did:

- Established reading as the focus.
- Set a clear and specific target, with measurements.
- Encouraged systematic realignment of time and resources.
- Trained administrators to be instructional leaders.
- Required reporting and monitored progress.
- Used board workshops to review building growth data over time.
- Built public support and parent involvement.
- Stayed the course for a decade.

Nancy: Dave, you've said that you think instruction is perhaps 200% more effective now then when you started years ago. What was the hardest piece of making that happen?

Dave: Well, I'll identify what's hard for me. Accountability. Accountability is not a lot of fun. We report to the board once a year, and I don't like to spend it explaining poor student performance. Yet, because of accountability we've improved 200%. Because people are accountable now, they're paying attention. They are looking to see what has happened. You're evaluating your program all of the time, because you don't want wasted time in your day. You want to make sure you are using the best program, because people are looking for the first time ever, not just principals but teachers in the classroom.

Chuck: Instructional leadership was the hardest, especially in the first four years of trying to meet the 90% Reading Goal. There is no way to fake spending 20-25 hours a week in the classroom and fake coaching teachers in advanced curriculum and instructional techniques. But I was hired at the beginning to manage a building. I sat in my office, moved paper, ran schedules, and handled parents. I got good at it. Taking responsibility for improving reading instruction and student reading scores didn't cross my mind. In a decade of going to principal conferences, I never heard it mentioned.

Difficult changes included:
- Becoming the instructional leader.
- Achieving staff buy-in and training.
- Analyzing data correctly.
- Reporting to board and community.
- Managing resources (i.e. time, materials, technology)

Judy: And parents. All of a sudden, parents are getting on board. They're looking at numbers. They are talking about accountability. They've always wanted it. They just couldn't put a name to it.

Lynn: So tell us about assessment and how you use assessment data.

Dave: You can either fight assessment or embrace it. However, you cannot be a high-performance school without embracing assessment. For years, "talk" was what was valued among school administrators. Good "talk" was what got promotions or recognition. Now it's results. The standard has changed to "Don't tell me about how good you are—show me your data."

Ted: We have parents complain that we test their kids too much. We tell them that their children are looking at a different future because of these tests. We look at the data; and when it tells us that something is wrong, we change. We grew beyond blaming the materials. It's not the materials. It's us.

"There is no point in testing if you don't look at the data, don't understand it, and don't change."

— Chuck Watson, Principal, Vista Elementary

Chuck: There is no point in testing if you don't look at the data, don't understand it, and don't change. High performance is impossible without each of these three steps.

Dorothy: I didn't come until 1999-2000, so coming on board at that point I had to learn about functional level testing in Kennewick. I think it's been a very effective tool. It's part of the reason scores are going up because you have data to actually track kids through grades. Also, the pre- and the post-tests allow teachers to self-analyze.

Rob: We look at trends. We don't look at a score this year or that, but at trends because there could be many different variables affecting the score with the kids. So I look at the trends and see if it's positive or if the scores are starting to tank.

Lynn: After assessment, what else works?

Dave: We think direct teacher instruction is what teaches kids to read. You can have a two-hour reading block; but if kids are reading silently or working individually on a ditto or doing word searches, this is not the best use of time because it is not reading instruction. Direct instructional time is too important to use as reading practice time. Kids *do* need to practice reading but not at the expense of reading instruction.

Chuck: In some grades, our struggling readers will spend over 75% of their day in reading instruction. You do not catch struggling readers up by pulling them out of their standard reading block for special remediation. Remediation time needs to be additional reading time.

Ted: It is important to figure individually for each student. They get the two-hour reading block in the morning, and some will get up to 45 minutes in the afternoon. Some go to a reading specialist at lunch. Some go after school for a few hours every week. We do whatever it takes to get the kids to the 90% goal. Intermediate readers probably get three and a half hours. I have never heard a child complain about that amount of focus on reading. I *have* heard mumblings from the adults.

---

[1] Westgate uses its "Clinton money" (for smaller class size) and special state funding (I-728) to hire two extra teachers who teach in the resource room.

Dorothy: At second grade, we have a special classroom with just twelve students and two teachers called the reading resource room.[1] It is only for students who leave first grade just beginning to understand reading but actually reading far below grade level. It has made a tremendous difference for these children. Without it, virtually none of these kids would pass the third-grade test. Seventy-five percent of them now do. Overall it accounts for 10-15% on our third grade test scores.

Nancy: That's great. Tell us more about the reading blocks. It sounds as if the content of the reading block is important.

Dave: Our reading block was 70% more effective the second year than it was the first year, and an additional 40% more effective the third year. There are no assemblies, no announcements, and no special programs during the reading block.

Chuck: We group by skill. Para-pros who, after six years of training are almost indistinguishable from our certified staff, teach the students who are at grade level in large groups. Kids who need instruction the most are taught by our best-trained, certified staff in small groups, often as small as four to six. You can't hide out in groups that small. The instruction is directed toward the specific needs of these kids—for example, phonemic awareness, phonics, fluency, accuracy, and comprehension. The groups are fluid, and students can easily move from one to another as they progress.

Critical instructional issues include:

- Good assessments and expert use of the data
- Generous reading blocks composed of small, fluid, skill groups
- Additional time for those behind, outside the reading block
- Emphasis on direct instruction rather than independent practice
- Focus on phonemic awareness, phonics, then comprehension

Judy: At Cascade, we have a two-hour reading block taught by our classroom teachers. The students who are the farthest behind get pulled out in groups of three to five students and taught by our para-professional tutors in 35-minute blocks. Much of our success comes from the evolution of these small groups, the 10-15 minutes of planning and supervision a day with them by our reading specialist, Caprice Olson, and a 20 minute meeting once each trimester with the tutors and the classroom teachers while the principal teaches. First grade used to be the only grade that taught phonics. Now we have realized that phonemic awareness and phonics is what works. It's amazing, if you teach phonics, what you can do with kids. It is also amazing when you give them one-on-one instruction in small groups. That is key. There are very few kids who don't want to learn to read.

Greg: It is almost like an army attacking on different fronts at the same time. Training is one front. People and materials are another front. Time is another. Part of the school's success is coordinating all of those issues. If you're not focused on time, you're not as successful as schools that are. A school that has just bought new materials and is focused on learning them isn't as successful as one focusing on all three. Moving into small groups really helps, but what is going on in those small groups is quite a bit different if you look at the class from the first year to the fourth year. We've really pushed teacher/group instruction. We don't want kids sitting and working by themselves. We want teachers in front of kids teaching the activities. I think that's a big piece of the directed instruction.

Nancy: So how do you keep morale strong when the going gets tough and before you see the successes?

Judy: We celebrate even the tiniest increase.

Dave: Celebrating as much as you possibly can has helped. There's a real fine line between pushing your staff, leading your staff, keeping the pressure on, and just wearing them out. In the last few staff meetings, I've been pounding them, and then I realized I needed to back off. Concentrate on the things that are really important. Back off on the things that aren't so important.

Judy: People take the statements that come from the board, or anybody that they see in authority, and micro-analyze them to the point that it's almost ridiculous. But when the board gives them a pat on the back — that is really a big deal. As far as the board workshops go, for the most part it's been pretty positive, and that has helped a ton.

Lynn: This is a people business. How do you lead, make decisions, and govern?

Dave: Your ability to get *anything* done is directly related to your relationship with your staff.

Ted: Having the right people is everything. You get loyalty by giving loyalty in relationships. Unity in a faculty happens because everyone knows what's going on. You've got to build trust. Everyone has a say; but since it's my responsibility, I have a bigger say. The principal has veto. There's a fine line between shared decision making and abdicating your responsibility. We rotate team leaders. We live or die as a team. You're only as good as your weakest teacher.

Dorothy: You have to develop a way to make decisions as a building that stay made. We have a very good site team that guides all of the discussion and information gathering on school issues and brings it to the staff. Their bottom line is student achievement. The site team works very hard to make sure everyone is on board. It works well for us.

Greg: As I look back, Paul Rosier said it's not going to happen without leadership. I believe that now. You have to have someone calling the shots a little bit. I think you have to have a balance between top down and bottom up. Leadership must provide vision and direction. Staff needs to help with the action plan. Leadership can't do all of it, but I don't think that an approach that involves some top-down direction is bad.

Ted: It's never going to happen bottom up.

Dave: Something I think is vital is to clean up the talk. Whining is very contagious and very difficult to stop. But the opposite is also very contagious. When *I* stop whining about accountability and talking positively about it in staff lounge, the whining stops. It's the same among principals. At our first meeting on the Reading White Paper, people started talking negatively, and that really influenced my attitude about it. If people sat around a table and had a negative attitude about it when you came in, you probably had it when you left because that stuff is contagious.

"The success of the 90% Reading Goal could be analogous to The Perfect Storm. *A lot of conditions came together in a unique way. We had stable board members who had done their research. They established a priority with a standardized measurement tool and an accountability system. This priority didn't waver.*

"The superintendent was knowledgeable and influential. He set a compassionate yet consistent course. The adversarial relationship between administration and union softened and became more cooperative. The elementary director was respected, became a reading expert, and offered continued support and direction.

"The senior principals took a positive and supportive stance with their staffs and peers. Within two years, a target school reached 90%, providing credence to the belief that it was indeed possible.

"All of this created a momentum and systemic nature that would now be more difficult to stop than it was to start."

— Chuck Watson, Principal, Vista Elementary
Washington State Administrator of the Year, 2002

Rob: Years ago, I had several teachers who were excellent instructors and who consistently had the kids' best interest at heart. In the process of changing to a new curriculum more aligned to what our state was testing, feelings were hurt and conflict among the staff developed, spilling into our reading scheduling. The result, from my point of view, was that every new suggestion or alternative for our school team was blocked. These teachers needed to make a decision on whether or not Amistad was right for them. After some open and honest conversations, they decided that our teaming plan wasn't right for them. We needed to have that difficult conversation to create the right environment. These are good teachers, and they're successful in their new schools.

Lynn: In concluding these interviews, it should be evident how critical building level leadership is. In Chapter One, we emphasized the importance of excellent leadership, excellent instruction, and excellent assessment systems as precursors to effective use of the TAG loop. Jim Collins may have said it best in his book on how good companies become great companies in *Good to Great*. Each of the great companies worked seriously at getting the "right people on the bus, the right

people in theright seats, and the wrong people off the bus."[2] Much of Kennewick's success has come from getting the right principals at the right buildings.

Kennewick Elementary Administrators, 2003-04

Front left: Brenda Mehlenbacher, Judy Long, Bruce Cannard, Greg Fancher, Mary Pruitt, Dorothy Fanning, Peggy Gregory. Back left: Dave Montague, Chuck Watson, Ted Mansfield, Doug Campbell, Rob Phillips, Le Fulfs, Craig Miller, Mark Stephens, Doug Carl. Absent: Jo Ann Hare, Maria Henrickson

[2] Jim Collins, *Good to Great* (New York: Harper Business, 2001), 41.

CHAPTER EIGHT

The Board and Superintendent: Policy, Governance, and the 90% Reading Goal

---

"You must maintain unwavering faith that you can and will prevail in the end, regardless of the difficulties, AND at the same time have the discipline to confront the most brutal facts of your current reality, whatever they might be."

—Admiral Jim Stockdale
Vietnam prisoner of war

Kennewick has invested eight years, almost a whole generation for students, in a relentless focus on achieving its 90% reading goal. We think we've finally discovered what works: instructional leadership, superb teaching, and excellent testing which assures annual growth and the four-phase TAG loop: (1) diagnostic testing to identify sub-skill deficiencies, (2) proportional increases in direct instructional time, (3) teaching to the deficient sub-skill, and (4) retesting to be sure the skill has been learned that assures catch-up growth.

But we made a lot of mistakes along the way.

This chapter explains how we crystallized our 90% goal—although since the federal government has mandated the 95% reading and math goals in No Child Left Behind that process will not be as necessary as some other pieces. What might be more useful to you is identifying some of the mistakes we made—pitfalls you can avoid—and describing what kept us focused and determined during some discouraging stretches.

January 1995

"It's time to think really radically."

The words hang in the air. Paul Rosier (pronounced "ROE-zhure") is speaking. Kennewick's Superintendent of Schools stands 5 foot 11 inches. His black hair is combed straight back. His leadership style is stirred, not shaken.[1]

A two-hour district-wide meeting on reading has just ended. The lists of reasons why students don't read better fills two portable whiteboards. Written at the top of the first board is the new proposed district goal: "90% percent of our second graders will read at grade level in the next three years." Those words are also hanging in the air. About 100 stunned elementary teachers file out of the room. The school board is more than pensive.

Thirty years earlier, Rosier was teaching as part of an elementary team on a Navajo reservation in Arizona. Navajo students typically scored in the 16-20th percentile on standardized reading tests, but the elementary team decided to change that. They identified barriers limiting effective reading instruction and spent the next decade improving the curriculum, instructional structure, and their own instructional skills. Students who came to first grade speaking only Navajo were, by fifth and sixth grade, scoring at the national average in reading and math and two years above comparable reservation schools. Young Rosier wrote his dissertation on the process and published it in 1980, thinking that he and his colleagues would be inundated with inquiries.[2] The results? The U.S. Bureau of Indian Affairs sent out a team to investigate for testing fraud. Nationwide, a total of three other educators wrote, wanting to know more.

---

[1] Dr. Rosier's coauthors successfully resisted his strenuous attempts to edit this chapter.
[2] Paul W. Rosier, "A Comparative Study of Two Approaches of Introducing Initial Reading to Navajo Children" (Ed.D. dissertation, Northern Arizona University, April 1977).

There are heroes in war, in sports, and even in politics. There are few heroes in education. Every educator knows there is little upside in thinking radically and a whole lot of downside.

1995-96

The reading goal was still hanging in the air in February 1995 when a District Reading Committee formed and tried to decide where to start. By May, the district piloted the Northwest Evaluation Association reading tests that measured students' growth at the beginning and end of a school year from third through tenth grades with startling accuracy. These tests could be scored in-district in less than a week with the scores reported as raw scores, as grade-level equivalents, and as national percentiles.

In July, the Kennewick District Strategic Planning Committee cautiously adopted the slightly modified goal that 90% of our *third* graders would read at or above grade level by the spring of 1998. After a significant internal discussion between principals who were suggesting that the cut-score on the test be set as low as second grade sixth month and board members who were lobbying for the third year ninth month, the standard was set at the third grade fourth month — in other words, the level at which students should be reading during December of their third-grade year. This level corresponded roughly to the 44th percentile.[3]

From August through October 1995, the four school board directors up for reelection campaigned on the reading issue. All of them won by significant margins. In November, the board designated $500,000 of levy funds for the reading goal. In December 1995, the superintendent and the board issued a draft of its seven-point Reading White Paper (see Appendix B) to provide more impetus to the reading committee,

[3] The standard was set at 194 on the Northwest Evaluation Association RIT scale. In 1995, this point was the 44th percentile. After NWEA's renorming in 2002, a RIT of 194 became the 37th percentile, although the higher than normal focus on growth by NWEA schools suggests that it may still be the 44th percentile nationally. Dr. Richard Allington has recommended that the 45th percentile is an appropriate place to set a grade-level standard versus the 25-30th percentile suggested by G. Reid Lyons, Jack M. Fletcher, Joseph K. Torgesen, Sally E. Shaywitz, and Vinta Chabra in "Continuing the Discussion," and "Reply to Lyon and Colleagues," *Education Leadership,* March 2004, 86.

stalled over committee letterhead, split over how to adopt a single reading curriculum without alienating everyone who wanted a different district-wide program, and generally united in their expert opinion that this job couldn't be done.

> *"The governance model has changed. Boards set policy with the advice and consent of the superintendent. The superintendent operates the district with the advice and consent of the board."*
>
> — Anne Bryant, Executive Director National School Board Association; Paul Houston Executive Director, American Assoc. of School Administrators, NSBA National Conference, New Orleans, April 2002

By January 1996, a year had passed without much progress except in perhaps three of the district's 13 elementary schools. Dr. Rosier and the board held the first of what became annual workshops at each elementary school.[4] Minutes of the workshops circulated to all the other elementary schools, highlighting schools and principals who were on the move. In February 1996, the board released its final draft of the White Paper authorizing some of the radical thinking that Paul Rosier had called for. The White Paper handed over the primary responsibility and accountability for the goal from the district office to the elementary principals.

The strategy worked well. No school wanted the board, the central office, or some committee to choose its reading curriculum. The lack of a centrally imposed program provided a period of effective experimentation. The board chose to ride out the turbulence of different programs, waiting for convergence to emerge from experience.

The White Paper also included the data from the Northwest Evaluation Association (NWEA) of the district's third graders from the fall of 1995. These raw scores, issued by school but without naming them, had painful lowlights: 13% of third graders read at a kindergarten

[4] At these weekly workshops, the board opens its regular meeting, clears off the consent items in about five minutes, and turns the time over to the school's principal. He or she introduces the presentation and goes through a series of 10-12 PowerPoint slides prepared by the district office which the board requested beginning in 1999. The slides show historical growth and achievement data for grades K-5. Most of the building's teachers attend the meeting, present about 70% of the workshop, and highlight their recent curriculum innovations. By the end of 2003-04, the board had met with each elementary school each year for a total of 104 workshops. Appendix D reproduces the slides that Washington Elementary used in its 2003-04 workshop.

level, 14% at a first grade level, 16% at a second-grade level. The highlight was that 57% were reading at or above grade level.

Many of our professional educators, from district officers to classroom teachers, were initially stunned by the White Paper and the data. The shock turned to anger, and the anger to resolution. Earlier emotional outbursts about district meddling gave way to determination and productive efforts. Staff training began shifting from the choice of individual teachers to building-wide training in the same reading program and strategies for teaching deficient skills.

An unpublished second part of the Kennewick District Reading White Paper explored the possibilities inherent in involving parents with their children's literacy from birth. In December and January, Dr. Rosier and board members visited surrounding districts, organizing an area-wide coalition that encouraged parents to read with their child 20 minutes a day from birth. In May 1996, Mario Moreno, U.S. Assistant Secretary of Education, visited the Tri-Cities (Kennewick, Richland, and Pasco, with a combined population of 165,000) to kick off the newly organized Mid-Columbia Reading Foundation, our nonprofit corporation under Nancy Kerr's direction. Nancy, a high school educator with deep community roots and a gift for mobilizing volunteers, set twin goals:

- Encouraging parents to read aloud with their child 20 minutes a day from birth.[6]
- Supporting schools in their efforts to have 90% of the students read at or above grade level by third grade.

The NWEA tests in the spring of 1996 came back with good news: a district wide score of 74%. We were jubilant. We had gambled, and nearly two years of focus had paid off. The $500,000 earmarked for the reading goal from a levy passed in March 1996 hadn't yet hit the system, and staff training sessions were barely starting. Nevertheless, we were already up 16 points. What would happen when instruction actually got aligned? Our elementary teachers began working even harder. This was the good news.

[5] See Lynn Fielding, Nancy Kerr, and Paul Rosier, *The 90% Reading Goal* (Kennewick, WA: New Foundation Press, 1998), Appendix C, p. 172.

[6] Over time this objective has been also been stated as: "Assuring that children enter kindergarten with literacy skills typical of five year olds."

1997-99

The bad news came a year later in the spring of 1997 when the district-wide scores dropped to 70%.[7] Because we are tough in Kennewick, we simply redoubled our efforts. In spring 1998, the target year for reaching the goal, our scores climbed one solitary point to 71. The math was simple. At this rate, we'd hit the target in 2016 — just about the time our first graders would be completing their junior year of college — if they made it that far.

"As a district, we simply didn't know how to teach 90% of our students to read to our standard by third grade. We had thought it was a matter of doing more of what we were already doing, a matter of working harder. It wasn't."

— Paul Rosier

Dr. Rosier began assuring nervous principals that it was superintendents, not principals, who got fired when board goals weren't met. The board assured the superintendent that we were in it together for the long haul. Boards can play the outside critic or the inside team member. The first role is easy but not very productive. Trust is higher, more information is shared, and better decisions get made when the board chooses to help develop and implement solutions, holding itself to higher standards of accountability as well.

As the 1998-99 school year began, we finally said it out loud for the first time. As a district, we simply didn't know how to teach 90% of our students to read to our standard by third grade. We had thought it was a matter of doing more of what we were already doing, a matter of working harder. It wasn't. We had reached the limits of working harder, and we weren't even close. We had to figure out what we didn't know.

So what kept us in the game?

[7] It usually takes us at least a year to shake out our testing bugs to provide uniform assessments. Some of our assessment people think that the spring of 1996 scores were reported higher than they should have been, suggesting that the first year was a couple of points too high. Thus, all three of the first years would be in the low 70s.

The Iowa Lighthouse Study

Most candid educators say school boards rarely make a difference in student academic achievement. Many superintendents provide minimal board training and limited access to data on student achievement, personnel, and budget. The intent is to minimize the board's impact on the district, especially if board members are divided, contentious, ill-informed, or temporary (in office only two or three years).

In a first-of-its-kind study, the Iowa Association of School Boards analyzed school boards based on quantifiable, reliable measures of student achievement. "School boards in high-achieving districts are significantly different in their knowledge and beliefs than school boards in low-achieving districts," says Mary Delagardelle, Iowa School Board Association leadership development director. The full report of critical differences among school boards became available in the spring 2004 at www.ia-sb.org/studentachievement/. Here is its summary of results.

- School boards in high achieving districts consistently expressed the belief that all students can learn and that the school could teach all students. This "no excuses" belief system resulted in high standards for students and an on-going dedication to improvement. In low-achieving districts, board members had limited expectations and often focused on factors that they believed kept students from learning, such as poverty, lack of parental support, or societal factors.
- They were far more knowledgeable about teaching and learning issues, including school improvement goals, curriculum, and instruction, assessment, and staff development. They were able to clearly describe the purposes and processes of school improvement efforts and identify the board's role in supporting those efforts. They could give specific examples of how district goals were being carried out by administrators and teachers.
- They used data and other information on student needs and results to make decisions. The high-achieving boards regularly monitored progress on improvement efforts and modified direction as a result.
- They created a supportive workplace for staff. Boards in high-achieving districts supported regular staff development to help teachers be more effective, supported shared leadership and decision making among staff, and regularly expressed appreciation for staff members.
- They involved their communities. Board members identified how they connected with and listened to their communities and how they focused on involving parents in education.

First, the Reading Foundation under Nancy Kerr's leadership was succeeding spectacularly in its goal of keeping the importance of reading to children from birth in front of the public. According to a professional survey conducted in our community in 1999, 97% of parents supported the 90% reading goal, 98% believed that reading 20 minutes a day to their child from birth was important, and 74.5% reported regularly doing so.[8]

"It took several years for principals to get the focus off demographics, which they could not control, and onto curriculum, increased time, and quality of instruction that they could control."

— Ed Frost, Kennewick School Board

Second, the data showed that some schools had made such amazing forward leaps that we couldn't abandon hope. Southgate, a low-mobility and low free or reduced-price lunch school, jumped from its initial baseline of 73% to 92%. Sunset View, with even more favorable demographics, had also moved from 70% to 90% and was holding in the mid-80s. Even Vista, with a 39% free or reduced-price lunch count achieved the goal in spring of 1998, with three other schools in the high 70s or low 80s.

The workshops at every elementary, middle, and high school focus the board and administrators on academic growth. Gone are the meetings where 80% of the time is wasted plodding through policy language that has little real impact or could have been handled in a tenth of the time. Gone are meetings devoted to a parade of extra-curricular or special program presentations.

Third, we were beginning to see patterns. While school scores were bouncing around, making principals insist that each class was unique, we could see that most schools averaged 13 or fewer RIT points of annual third-grade reading growth. The whys and hows of that pattern were something we could work with.

Fourth, we realized that we could make fairly accurate predictions about each school and the district for spring scores based

[8] Harris Survey, "Parent Questionnaire Component," 1999 for Kennewick Schools. The district has run the survey every two years as part of its "Customer Satisfaction" process begun in 1997. The Harris Company currently serves 200 school districts nationwide. Its offices are located at 135 Corporate Woods, Rochester, N.Y. 14623 and its Educational Research Division can be reached at (800) 919-4765.

on fall scores. Of the fall scores, the following percentages would make it to the goal by the spring:

> 95% of the students who were nearly grade level in the fall and with normal growth would reach our standard, plus,
> 25% of students who were a year and a half behind, plus
> 5% of those more than a year and a half behind.

This was our first cut at the formulation of "annual growth" and "catch-up growth" that would later develop.

The Reading Foundation, the growth in some schools, identifying the limits of growth at third grade when time was kept constant, and our ability to use data to make accurate growth predictions all *helped* keep us in the game. But what actually *kept* us in the game were the workshops. By 1999, the board and superintendent had spent an hour and a half to two hours in each of 52 elementary school workshops over the last four years. We knew the data, the principals, the buildings, many of the faculty, and the differences in their programs. We could clearly see the desperate need to teach reading every time we looked at the struggling middle and high school students scores. No one was willing to declare victory (or defeat) and go home.

> *"In organizations, goals erode because of low tolerance for emotional tension. Nobody wants to be the messenger of bad news. The easiest path is to just pretend there is no bad news, or better yet, "declare victory"—to redefine the bad news as not so bad by lowering the standard against which it is judged."*
>
> — Peter M. Senge[9]

And no one was willing to slide the institutional focus of our strategic plan to some lesser goal.[10] Middle and high school administrators made encouraging and supportive noises but were secretly relieved that the elementary schools were consuming most of the superintendent and board's attention.

---

[9] Peter M. Senge, *The Fifth Discipline: The Art and Practice of the Learning Organization* (New York: Doubleday Currency, 1990), 153.

[10] For Kennewick's District Strategic Plan, 2003-04, see Appendix E. The superintendent reports quarterly on progress made on each item in the strategic plan. The progress report has developed into our primary communication device about most strategic plan objectives and also serves as the basis for the superintendent's performance pay. A copy of the district's 1998 strategic plan is Appendix E in Fielding, Kerr, and Rosier, *The 90% Reading Goal.*

Table 8.1
Percentage of Kennewick School District Third Graders Reading at or above Standard, Spring 1996-2004

School	1996	1997	1998	1999	2000	2001	2002	2003	2004
Washington	72	72	68	78	**94**	**96**	**99**	**94**	**98**
Cascade	78	79	72	83	88	**91**	**99**	**96**	**93**
Vista	83	73	**90**	79	80	**93**	**91**	**95**	**94**
Southgate	**92**	80	81	86	88	82	**90**	**93**	**91**
Ridge View	80	69	78	88	79	84	**94**	**90**	**92**
Hawthorne	69	62	62	78	73	87	**90**	**92**	**80**
Canyon View	71	66	78	65	83	76	**90**	**90**	**90**
Sunset View	82	86	**92**	85	84	87	89	**95**	**93**
Lincoln	79	75	73	85	87	86	78	**99**	**92**
Westgate	58	55	47	51	57	49	55	76	82
Eastgate	53	55	52	40	53	54	67	68	80
Amistad	66	65	55	52	44	47	51	65	80
Edison	66	68	71	54	53	55	53	46	74
District	**74**	**70**	**71**	**72**	**77**	**78**	**82**	**86**	**88**

We persisted. Getting better data was our first significant response in figuring out what we didn't know. Under our current system, we were data blind before third grade. We could not see what was happening at second grade, first grade, or kindergarten. We decided to extend the NWEA test down to the end of second grade after our assessment director told us about another district that had successfully done so. Some principals complained bitterly about "yet another test." The board was sympathetic but firm.

With the second grade tests, our 1999 spring second-grade test scores jumped about six points district-wide above what they had been at the beginning of third grade for the prior two years. District administrators were surprised (and a little chagrined) when one second-grade teacher in the district emphatically declared, "We could have made these kinds of gain earlier if you had given us these tests earlier."

In the fall of 1999, we added the incoming kindergarten assessment that appears in Chapter 21. In 1999, the state mandated a second-grade developmental reading assessment (DRA) that we administered in the fall of 1999 and the spring of 2000. We added reading assessment at first grade during the winter of 2000 as well.

2000-01

Now we had a nearly seamless assessment system in place. By the spring of 2000, it was apparent that the extra six points of second grade growth had carried into third grade. When we added our average growth of 12-13 points to it during third grade, we jumped five points overall to 76%, our first significant growth in four years. It was also in the spring of 2000 when Washington Elementary really hit its stride, articulating clearly what it was doing and then instituting the four powerful steps of catch-up growth later labeled the Targeted Accelerated Growth (TAG) loop.

> *"If your view of academic achievement corresponds with the volumes of published data about poverty, you would have predicted that Sunset and Southgate would maintain the highest percentage of students reading at or above grade level and that Washington, Vista, and Hawthorne would be among the last to do so."*
>
> — Dan Mildon

This genuinely was good news. After three years of flattened scores, we seemed to be doing something right. Nine schools scored above 76%. The elementary director credited better staff training. The principals noted the improved faculty morale, enthusiastic parents, and community support. The board pointed to the movement in scores in 1996 and again in 1999 following new assessments. Yet from May 1996 to May 1999, the average scores of our four lowest schools had actually decreased 11.5 points, offsetting the gain made by nine other schools. We had four schools at or below 55% with a 20-point gap between them and the top nine schools.

By the fall of 2000, the board workshops began to seriously explore the impact of increasing instructional time. Our higher performing schools began reporting how they had increased direct instructional time per student in proportion to how far behind grade level the student was. We asked for reports about reading time in the elementary school workshops. Unsurprisingly (but unhelpfully), almost all of the schools reported spending 85% of their time in reading-related activities. Scores inched up one point to 78% in the spring of 2001.

2001-03

In the fall of 2001, we asked a better question and got better data. Instead of asking about "total reading time," our strategic plan requested October and February reports of "direct reading instruction minutes," specifically excluding reading in the content areas and practice time. What became clear is that there were large ranges in instructional time at first through third grade. Not only were standard blocks different, but some schools were front loading, with more time in first grade than in third, and were more flexible in increasing catch-up time.

One of the most powerful decisions a board makes is to determine what is on its agenda and how it uses board meeting time. Another powerful decision is to focus on how instructional time, the district's most valuable and costly resource, is being used.

The "focus" part of the Time and Focus Report asked how schools used the additional time. The NWEA pinpoint diagnostics told each teacher, child by child, what he or she needed to know. Teachers reprioritized the additional time to focus on those skills. For example, if Tony scored below grade level in reading and the subtests indicated weakness in fluency, then Tony's catch-up time focused on fluency.

The obvious message imbedded in the superintendent and board's request for Time and Focus Reports on direct instructional minutes reinforced the questions in the workshops. Less than oblique references emphasized the obvious jumps in scores of Vista, Ridge View, and Washington after these schools adopted proportional increases in direct instruction, diagnostic testing, instruction targeted to the deficiency, and retesting as a primary strategy for catch-up growth.

During 2001-02, our four low-performing schools, for various reasons, did not adopt the strategy of proportional increases in instructional time and its targeted use on deficient sub-skills. Superintendent Paul Rosier, Assistant Superintendent Marlis Lindbloom, and Elementary Director Greg Fancher were meeting with them monthly. Still district elementary reading scores climbed 4% more in the spring of 2002, reaching a district average of 82%. Seven schools met or exceeded the 90% goal. In fact, Washington Elementary had reached a truly amazing height of 99% in the spring of 2002 when all but one-third grader reached the goal.

By the fall of 2002, the Time and Focus Reports showed that every elementary school but one had increased direct instructional time and was using the additional time in a targeted way. Only one of the four lower-achieving schools still grimly clung to its 80-minute daily reading program. In the spring of 2003, its scores, which had dropped precipitously from 71% in 1998 to 54% in 1999 because of an influx of English language learners (ELLs), sagged to a dismal 46%.

"Are your board's academic policies effective? Compare the district's reading and math test scores ten years ago with those from last year. Have the policies resulted in significant improvement? Board members' primary duty is to enact and implement the academic policies in their district that lead to student success. Social, financial, and athletic issues should claim board agenda time only after academic issues have been attended to."

— Lynn Fielding

Meanwhile, below-grade-level students at Washington, where 54% of students qualify for the federal free or reduced price lunch program, and Vista students, with 50% free or reduced price lunch, were getting 180-210 minutes a day. The scores from those schools had topped 90% since the spring of 2001.

Just as important as the extra 40-100 minutes a day for third graders was the accumulation of extra time during kindergarten, first, and second grades in canny schools that were tracking progress of each child each year. (See Tables 3.2 and 3.3.) District elementary reading scores climbed 4% more in the spring of 2003 to 86%.

The Targeted Accelerated Growth (TAG) loop had captured the essential elements of annual growth and catch-up growth. In the fall of 2002, we began requiring Time and Focus Reports for students below the 50th percentile in reading and math in middle and high school. We also simultaneously required principal scheduling reports, showing which lagging students in middle and high school were getting extra classes in math and reading.

Kennewick has nearly reached its district goal of 90% of its third graders reading at or above grade level. It is also closing in steadily on the federally mandated goal of 95%. In the spring of 2004, while this book is being written, we had targeted 89%, expecting to hold onto the 15 percentage points of cumulative district gain in the last five years while gaining 3 percent more. We held on to our prior gain and added 2 percent more.

Questions can be directed to:
Lynn Fielding at
lynnfielding@hotmail.com
and Paul Rosier at
rosipa@ksd.org

We are still struggling with the daunting problems of mobility and English language learners. Often the schools with the highest mobility rates are the schools with the greater numbers of students learning English as a new language. We are searching for effective strategies to address the academic needs of students who move frequently. We are exploring ways to help our non-English-speaking populations to come to school bilingual, leveraging the first five years when it is easiest to acquire a second language. We have also begun to implement the TAG loop at our middle and high schools. (See Chapter 17.)

Dr. Rosier has not aged noticeably over the last eight years. His hair is still black, undyed, still combed straight back. Dr. Rosier is still thinking radically. With the passage of ESEA (2001), perhaps thinking radically is no longer a luxury. Perhaps it is the new leadership style. Perhaps it is what is necessary to deliver on the promise.

CHAPTER NINE

GETTING TO THE GOAL FASTER: CENTRAL OFFICE REFLECTIONS

"We like to think we follow our beliefs. In reality, our beliefs follow our experience."

— Paul Rosier

Lynn: So what do you remember of the beginning of the 90% reading goal?

Greg: I'll tell you a little story. Dr. Neil Powell was our curriculum and instruction director. All of his experience was in high school; and after we set the goal, he came down and said, "I don't know much about elementary reading. Will you do this?" It was only my first or second year, and I was still green. I said, "Sure, okay."

This chapter is based on an interview with Dr. Paul Rosier, superintendent and Greg Fancher, director of elementary education, conducted by Nancy Kerr and Lynn Fielding, February 2004.

We really didn't know what we were doing when we started. I look back now and think how ridiculous it was. The first thing we did was form a committee. The committee talked about letterhead for the 90% reading goal and how to communicate to the elementary schools. Everything we talked about was pretty superfluous kinds of stuff and not very much got done.

The real first turning point was when we got our functional-level test results[1] and really got to look at objective data. It was the first big driver in what we did. I can remember going to Paul and saying, "How do I go to a building and say, 'Your program is not working. . . . We need to do something to change it'? As an outside person, how do you do that?" He kept saying, "You just show them the data and show them objective information about their school. You are not making any judgments. You just show them the data." And that's what we've become really good at — just showing them the data.

Another thing that's really interesting is the extent to which people eight years ago didn't believe we could be where we are today. Everybody uses the words; but when we're going to measure it and look at it by classroom, by school, and by district, people were really hesitant and really nervous about it. I think that, because of the progress we've made, we've changed that belief system. Now people believe we can do it. We *can* get to 90%.

Paul: We like to think we follow our beliefs. In reality, our beliefs follow our experience. Until you change your behavior, you cannot really change deep, embedded beliefs. You may say things on the surface like, "All kids can learn," or "All kids can learn at high levels," but in the back of your mind you're saying, "Ah, no, no, no, no . . . That's not what my experience tells me." So you're just mouthing the words, because it's politically acceptable.

It's part of what we're dealing with right now with limited English-speaking kids. The belief statement is that these kids don't learn English very fast, and it's going to take six to eight years. That's what people believe, because that's what their experience tells them. What we're trying to do now is get people to go in and really hit the English hard to see if we can't get kids to acquire English at a much

> *"Until you change your behavior, you cannot really change deep, embedded beliefs. You may say things on the surface like, 'All kids can learn,' or 'All kids can learn at high levels,' but in the back of your mind you're saying, 'Ah, no, no, no, no . . . That's not what my experience tells me.' So you're just mouthing the words, because it's politically acceptable."*
>
> — Paul Rosier

[1] The Northwest Evaluation Association conducted Kennewick's first round of functional-level reading tests in September 1995. They were tabulated by school by grade span and attached to the December 1995 District Reading White Paper.

higher level and much earlier than they did before. So we're asking our ELL (English language learner) people to behave differently than they believe. That's really what we asked people to do in reading too. Behave differently than they believed.

Gradually what our reading teachers found from their behavior is that their belief system wasn't very accurate. The belief system today is that 90% is possible. Look at the schools that hit 99%. So 90% has sort of become the norm of what we can do. A poll in 1996 would have shown overwhelmingly that 90% is not possible, because that is what their experience had told them. "Could I do a lot better?" meant, "I really wasn't doing things very well." So you protect yourself with your belief system.

Greg: To finish the committee piece, we ended up disbanding the committee because that wasn't the way to attack the problem. Just as Paul said: In every profession, people tend to protect what they are doing because they believe what they are doing is the right thing. We had to find other ways to get people to examine what they were doing. That's when we started with four different training models for people to choose from, and then narrowed it down to two so they could really look at their practice and figure out what direction they needed to head.[2]

The other thing that we did, tactically, was to not say, "What you're doing is bad," but "How do you get one step better at what you're doing? What's the piece that you add?"

Nancy: What else did you do?

Greg: Another thing that we discovered was that supplying training to our folks was only one piece of what they needed. The schools that went through CORE training did okay; but until they got materials that were Open Court or Open Court-like, they couldn't implement the training. So what we learned was that the training was a critical piece of the whole game, but you have to have the right tools to implement the knowledge and skills acquired in the training. At first we took a piecemeal approach. We tried to buy this phonics kit to do this piece of CORE and that

[2] The two systems were Consortium on Reading Excellence (CORE) referred to in footnote 4 of Chapter 2 and First Steps, which are no longer used in the district.

vocabulary kit to do that piece of CORE and it didn't work. We needed to provide our teachers with the whole package.

It goes back to what Dr. Kame'enui[3] says, "Teachers cannot be the conductors and composers of the curriculum. The job of the teacher is to conduct the curriculum in a way to benefit all kids."

Lynn: Anything else?

Greg: We've talked about training and materials. The third thing that we've learned is implementation. The implementation phase is really important on a couple of levels.

One level is to provide training for the principals. We had a daylong training session for principals so they would know what Open Court looks like when they're observing their classrooms.

On the next level—training the teachers—we brought the Open Court people in to do demonstration lessons and small-group work with teachers, so they could get their questions answered. That was our traditional approach: to train before the teachers got the program, and then not train much afterwards. In 2000, we brought Open Court back after the teachers had been using it, because teachers have their best questions after they have used the program for a while. That's when their questions are really going to affect their instruction, because they've had experience with it. Before you've used it, you don't even know what your questions are. By the way, we insisted that our lowest performing schools change to Open Court in the 1999-2000 school year.

Another really interesting thing has happened. We have kept harping on the fact that you have to have a K-5 program. As we have moved to issues of instruction and doing learning walks with principals, we've asked them how what happens in first grade affects what happens in second grade and then what happens in third grade. How are those things connected? We've really gotten everybody to see the need for a

[3] Dr. Edward J. Kame'enui (pronounced come-ME-new), Department of Special Education, University of Oregon at Eugene, is one of the 17 members on the writing committee for the National Research Council's *Preventing Reading Difficulties in Young Children*. In addition, Kennewick Schools contracted with Dr. Kame'enui to provide an analysis of the strengths and weaknesses of each of Kennewick's elementary school's reading programs pursuant to its strategic plan for 1999-2000.

very structured program, which is why even some of our most resistant schools have decided they need to have that kind of a K-5 structure provided by Open Court, so they can build upon what happens grade upon grade. Every one of our schools now runs a basal program K-5. A basal series is necessary to get the materials, support, and structure to build high-performance programs. We have found that it's necessary in order to have a reading program that truly builds and is connected from grade to grade.

Lynn: So what programs are the schools using?

Greg: Nine elementary schools use Open Court, two use Harcourt Trophies, one uses MacMillan and one is using Scott-Foresman.

Nancy: Why were some schools more resistant to changing than others?

Greg: The most resistant schools were schools that traditionally had the highest scores and that had reached the 90% reading goal early on. They felt good about what they were doing and didn't see a need to change. When they used our earlier strategy of looking at their assessment data to see what it was telling them, it told them they were doing pretty well.

The pressure came when other schools with way more mobility and much higher free or reduced lunch counts started to do as well as the high-scoring schools. Then they had to look at what they were doing a little more carefully. That's my guess, just from talking to folks. That's my story and I'm sticking to it.

Nancy: Are people working much harder today?

Paul: I think the difference isn't how hard people are working today; the difference is how much smarter and more strategically they are working. Changing beliefs is required to do that. First, you have to believe reading is so important that you'll give it the time necessary to do the job. You have to believe that it is more important than anything else in the curriculum.

Second, the strategy or idea that we can teach reading in the content areas is probably not true. We can reinforce what we do in the content areas; but if instructors are not teaching it formally, it's rarely going to be taught in the content areas. I don't think so, anyway.

Third, everywhere we increased the amount of direct instructional time significantly; we made significant improvements in reading RIT scores. Sunset View has probably, in some respects, changed the least.

Lynn: So how did you focus the schools on instructional time?

Greg: Getting schools to focus on time was fairly simple after we got the hang of it. The first time we asked schools to report on the time they spent on reading was during the fourth year. We asked for total reading time and, because 85% of public school curriculum is delivered by reading, that's what we got back: They said they were spending 85% of their time on reading. Well, the second year we asked a better-defined question, and the report identified only direct reading instruction time. That's what we really wanted to know.

The Time and Focus Report (Table 3.1) not only monitors the amount of instruction time, it also focuses on kids who are falling through the cracks. When a student was in the 20th percentile and getting only 105-120 minutes of direct instruction, it was very obvious that this situation needed to change—and it did. All the principals knew that those reports weren't going to stay on my desk. Paul Rosier, Marlis Lindbloom (Assistant Superintendent of Curriculum and Instruction), and the Board of Education were going to be going over them as well.

Nancy: If we were starting over, knowing what we know now, how long would it take us to make this kind of growth?

Paul: If we could start today and if we could take all that we have learned today with the people that we have, we could make pretty significant growth pretty rapidly. It takes time to learn, time to integrate that learning into effective instructional experience, and time to change your beliefs. If you look at what limits you in what you're doing right, most often it's the parameters you set based on your experience and beliefs.

It's also going to depend on the leadership team in the district. Probably the best example I know of a leader who got things moving fast is Vickie

Phillips of Lancaster, Pennsylvania.[4] What Vickie Phillips did there, in the four-year period, is pretty impressive. She started with only 20-25% of her kids reading on grade level.

Her community was initially less than responsive, so she took 10 students, went down to Rotary, sat eight of them down, and said, "These two kids are reading at grade level. Now, what are we going to do with the other eight?" That really got the community's attention.

She decided she had to have the teachers with her so she brought the union president in on a full time salary but spending half her time on curriculum instruction, much like Jan's involvement here with our association.[5] Vickie brought in some outside assistance that she knew would help, a team much like our Bill and Melinda Gates Foundation contractors. Vickie knew that her focus was going to be elementary literacy first, and her district put a major focus on kids learning to read in kindergarten. This is a lot of progress in a single year.

Knowing what we know now — what we've learned in eight years — we could have done it in maybe half the time, but getting the training, increasing instructional skills, acquiring the testing systems, and learning how to use the data all takes time. It doesn't happen overnight.

You might think that the leading edge of change in our district would occur at our upper-end schools where change was easiest, or at our lower-end schools where they might be willing to try anything because they had nothing to lose. But that wasn't the case. The leading edge was at middle-tier schools where the conditions of leadership, willingness to team, and fewer distractions all came together. Knowing that now, I would have worked harder on enhancing those conditions that encourage change: excellent leadership, excellent instruction, excellent assessment system, and the TAG loop. We would have moved the right people into the right positions quicker, gotten Open Court to our low SES schools quicker, extended our testing system, and figured out the TAG loop faster to catch up those who were behind.

---

[4] Dr. Vicki L. Phillips became the State Superintendent of Public Instruction in Pennsylvania in March 2003

[5] Jan Fraley has served as the Kennewick Education Association president from July of 2000 to the present. See Chapter 10.

CHAPTER TEN

UNION LEADERSHIP PERSPECTIVES

In the late 1990s, the Kennewick Education Association (KEA) changed its nearly exclusive union focus on member services to member services within the context of increased student academic achievement. The new focus facilitated school wide staff training, scheduling changes necessary to increase instructional time for students who are behind, and increasing flexibility in time within the contract day. Teachers became involved in school decisions through site councils. This chapter discusses how that change occurred, how the Eastern Washington Network facilitated the change, how the risks taken by union leadership changed their paradigm, and how increased levels of trust were developed and maintained.

Lynn: So what were you doing when the 90% reading goal was announced and what are you doing now?

Wish: In 1995, I was vice president of the Kennewick Education Association. I am currently Uni-Serve representative for the southeast part of Washington for the Washington Education Association (WEA).[1]

This chapter is based on a conversation with the authors, Greg Wishkowski, and Jan Fraley, past and present presidents of the Kennewick Education Association (KEA) respectively, in March 2004.

Jan: I was a counselor in a middle school and am currently KEA president.

[1] Wish, as Greg Wishkowski is commonly called, was chair of the English Department at Kamiakin High School, Kennewick School District (1980-97), KEA president (1997-2000), and is now Uni-Serve representative for the southeast part of Washington for the WEA. Jan Fraley has served as KEA president from 2000 to the present and piloted a series of innovative and cooperative initiatives with the district including the Peer Assistance and Review (PAR) program.

Nancy: Do you still remember any reactions to the goal?

Jan: Sure! It immediately made people mad. "The board is telling us what to do again." "Another top-down decision." It was so much pressure and nobody believed initially they could get there. Yet it caused a lot of creativity, and people tried new things. When success started occurring, it was easier for people to believe. We celebrated reaching the 90% goal, but we also celebrated annual growth. People may say that we will never get there; but if you celebrate the successes, they will keep working incredibly hard.

Lynn: So what was the management-labor context of the goal?

Jan: We were working in partnership with the district and the Eastern Washington Restructuring Network. Paul Rosier was very much involved and the network was a big focus for the union. The union was really separated, as it often is, into many different camps or factions. Some of the members were pro-reform and pro-education and part were into the positional and adversarial bargaining that had been our pattern for a number of years. Sometimes in large districts of 3,000-5,000 members, constituency groups become so fragmented nothing moves. Kennewick's union wasn't so large that it left us fragmented totally.

Wish: The network experience was critical. We had a series of meetings facilitated by Steve Paulson and Pat Dolan.[2] One thing that set the table for me on a real deep and personal level was our conclusion to do business differently in education, to support our members properly, and also secure employment for them over the long term.

The network was based on a reform model and co-directed by a WEA member on sabbatical. It was pushed in Eastern Washington. Later, it singled us out for hits within our own state association, because we were doing business differently. When I work with districts outside Kennewick, I still argue for some of the practices we learned. But the network is gone now—disbanded during the 2001-02 school year—and

---

[2] Steve Paulson was the executive director of the Eastern Washington Restructuring Network and a Washington Education Association (WEA) employee on sabbatical. The WEA funded his position with the network. W. Pat Dolan is an international consultant on organizational change and the author of *Restructuring Our Schools: Our Primer on Systemic Change* (Kansas City, KS: Systems and Organizations, 1994).

I'm a little worried about that. It gave us some real momentum. I believe that the Kennewick School District retains vestiges of some of those processes that function at a pretty high level.

Nancy: How was the network organized?

Paul: The network consisted of 21 school districts in the eastern part of the state of Washington. We met every month for about four years. We started out with a keynote speaker at 1:30 on the first day, stayed through the evening, and worked until noon the next day. Some of our speakers were Carl Glickman, Pat Dolan, William Bridges, Tony Alvarado, Elaine Fink, Bob Chase, and Linda Diamond.[3] We went through collective exercises that helped us to identify the reality we had and envision the reality we would like to have.

Wish: You don't do anything without ideas. If you can focus more on ideas and less on current problems, then you can always grow.

Jan: We did "interest-based bargaining," and we had training. We practiced how to work cooperatively with each other, to tell the truth, and to trust that the other party would be honest with us. That doesn't mean all teachers were on the same page—but we had to learn to take some risks, shut the door, and trust that what happened in that room would stay there. We accepted that we would each do our jobs in the controversial times. But we could shut the door and be honest with each other.

Wish: Maybe the most important focus was captured by our pact that we were going to do what was best for students in Kennewick. We decided we were going to work together on some fundamental educational issues. Both sides risked a lot to make that move. It was a risky environment. I was in meetings with the school administrators when they were personally attacked. I was shocked at our behavior. The administration was pretty stoic. It was very adversarial and very

---

[3]Carl Glickman is the author of *Revolutionizing America's Schools* (San Francisco: Jossey-Bass Publishers, 1998). William Bridges is the author of *Managing Transitions: Making the Most of Change* (Reading, MA: Perseus Books, 1991). Bob Chase was then president of the National Educational Association and was encouraging collaboration and student academic achievement. Linda Diamond was the executive director of Consortium of Reading Excellence, (CORE). Tony Alvarado and Elaine Fink were top administrators in New York City's District 2.

defiant, but people saw because of the training that the reform was here to stay. Enough of our work force believed in the change to tip the balance. But that was a crucial time.

Lynn: What was the impact of the network on instruction?

Wish: The transition to high performance instruction requires some decentralization. Decisions have to be made by the people on site who are most affected by them. This is a transition that every district faces. Healthy districts work their way through it.

Jan: We are doing a lot of transitions such as using site councils, developing teacher-leaders, operating the PAR [Peer Assistance and Review] program, instructional councils, and learning walks.

Paul: The site councils were pretty impressive at Kamiakin High and Southridge. We had a real setback at Kennewick High where mutual levels of distrust delayed the process for about five years. Things happened pretty well at the middle schools although they were not as heavily into instructional improvement as the elementary schools. In the last few years, we've started to look at how to support instruction beyond content emphasis—how we look at instruction in total in the district and how we can raise the bar.

Jan: Some of the varied reading programs used throughout the district aren't consistent, so we're reverting to programs that are more consistent between different buildings.

Paul: There is still a lot of latitude within the buildings about how to apply the programs.

Wish: That doesn't surprise me. Common sense says you decentralize, find the programs that work, and then come back together. A group that can do that is a healthy organism.

Jan: Another transition that Kennewick District has made is to give teachers an increasing voice in their schools. The teacher-leader program instituted in the summer of 2002 means that there are many teacher-leaders in the buildings now and many different avenues by which they can take leaderships roles. They feel valued. I think teachers need to be involved in the whole process. If they're not part of the process, they could very well defy the process. The best possible way is to involve all of the parties. So when teachers become leaders and are seen as leaders, there is greater buy-in. I think that's the direction we have traveled during this entire process. It started with the network, and I've seen it change and really grow over time.

Nancy: Following up on your comment with the emerging teacher-leader, what happened last summer?

Jan: Each summer, all of the central office administrators and principals typically go on a retreat before school starts. Last summer, the administration opened the retreat to all of the literacy coaches and a teacher representative from every school. Since then, the same group attends all of the instructional conferences scheduled throughout the school year. The summer retreat is no longer an administrator retreat; it's a leadership retreat. To me, that was a big change.

Paul: The network, with the support of the WEA and KEA, gave us latitude on how to approach instructional issues like the reading goal. It opened the door so that we could start to do things such as teacher involvement in the instructional conference process. We've always had teacher-leaders in the buildings but they are emerging into a stronger position now. Another thing we did was to establish the PAR program for new teachers. The district and the KEA committed to helping new teachers succeed, so it made the PAR program an official joint operation.[4]

Lynn: Then KEA applied for the NEA/Saturn Award for the PAR program in 2002?

Jan: The Kennewick Education Association and the Kennewick School District were one of six districts nationwide to receive national NEA-Saturn/UAW Partnership Awards. Saturn's description of the award is that it recognizes a bold union-management partnership that improves the quality of public education at the K-12 and post-secondary levels.

[4]The Peer Assistance and Review (PAR) program is a joint Kennewick School District –KEA program to assist teachers during their first two years in the profession. Three full-time master teachers, funded by the local levy, provide initial orientation, and thereafter demonstrate, observe, and conference with the new teachers about classroom management and instruction as well as advise the PAR management panel about their progress.

We were fortunate to win. We had some visitors from the NEA who followed our consulting peer educators around. They also came to a PAR panel meeting and listened to some really tough, very frank, honest, confidential conversations about some of the new teachers. They seemed fairly surprised with our discussion of the problems, the things being done well, and the directions we were going. I feel good about that too. The district and the association didn't come with a model and get married to it. Our model moves and changes to fit needs.

Nancy: Tell us about the learning walks.

Wish: The cooperation between Jan and Paul on the learning walks is causing the WEA horrific problems throughout the state in terms of district and labor relations, because now there are all of these teams doing learning walks/ walk throughs in other districts. But they're using them for teacher evaluations—for negative accountability. It's a good practical way to look at instruction and it builds strong teaching, but it's being inappropriately applied as a quick fix for the state WASL tests. It's really hurting a lot of teachers in other districts. Though it's a good practice in Kennewick where it is applied with 10 years of cooperation and leadership and with a continuous focus on academic goals, it goes awry elsewhere.

Jan: You cannot by-pass the process—planning together, conversations, and collaboration—and just go straight to the product: in this case, the learning walks. I've stood up many times and said. "Yes, we can do learning walks, but they cannot be tied to evaluations." Because my reasons were heard and respected, we've pulled all of these teacher-leaders forward as great examples and experts. As a result, our teachers have tried to improve their own instructional skills by watching others and learning from them. Our focus is "What can I take back to my class?" not "How is this going to reflect on my evaluation?" I participate in all the elementary and secondary learning walks that I can possibly shoehorn into my schedule.

Lynn: Can you think of two or three places where we would have had tougher sledding with the 90% reading goal if it hadn't been for the cooperative relationships between the union and administration?

Wish: Paul is very good about understanding Maslow's hierarchy of needs. I think the district has been very good about taking care of the basic needs first, as preparation for changing to the higher-level stuff. Some examples are our insurance pool, meeting health care needs for members, the PAR program, and opening building budget information to the membership. When we say, "Members are hurting over here," the district winces a little but it doesn't say "no."

In my current role, other districts don't understand that if teachers are in survival mode you are never going to get the 90% goal. Kennewick has new-teacher support through the PAR program, teacher-leaders to provide on-going, in-service learning, and learning walks, because the district has taken care of its teachers. It's met some of the basic economic and resource needs. People have to have a living wage.

> *"Consider, for example, the following puzzle. I give you a large piece of paper, and I ask you to fold it over once, and then take that folded paper and fold it over again, and then again, and again, until you have refolded the original paper 50 times. How tall do you think the final stack is going to be? In answer to that question, most people will fold the sheet in their mind's eye, and guess that the pile will be as thick as a phone book, or if they're really courageous, they'll say that it would be as tall as a refrigerator. But the real answer is that the height of the stack would approximate the distance to the sun.... As human beings we have a hard time with this kind of progression, because the end result—the effect—seems far out of proportion to the cause....We need to prepare ourselves for the possibility that sometimes big changes follow from small events, and that sometimes these changes can happen very quickly."*
>
> — Malcolm Gladwell, *The Tipping Point*

Jan: Third-year teachers are saying, "I don't know if I can do this the rest of my life. This is really tough." Because the union can go to the bargaining table and take care of some of those needs, it's a little less stressful in Kennewick to be a new teacher and deal with the tremendous pressures in education.

Wish: The district probably won't get to the 90% reading goal if teachers jump ship at five to seven years. It makes sense to make it easy for them to stay.

[5]Malcolm Gladwell, *The Tipping Point: How Little Things Can Make a Big Difference* (Boston: Little, Brown and Company, 2000), 11.

Nancy: It is certainly about people. When we lose our people, we start all over again.

Jan: And right now the people are talking to each other. There is not as much isolation in classrooms. People are sharing in teams, sharing on grade levels and curriculum levels. Sometimes they combine classrooms to accomplish projects. There's a lot more talk, a lot more sharing of good ideas. Classrooms are opening up.

Wish: My sense is that districts need a crystal ball to see what will happen in the future, so that they can take steps to prevent certain types of chaos from happening. Good leaders look toward the future. I see pressure points and tipping points all over the place in educational change. I tell my districts that the bomb is there and the fuse is lit, but administrators are not paying attention to it. The Kennewick Board always keeps its eye on the 90% reading goal, but lots of things have happened to maintain that focus.

Jan: Always look at unintended consequences.

Wish: Membership can be a tipping point. One tipping point is that our recent survey shows that members believe their workload increased 40% this year. Well, 40% plus or minus a couple of points. That is a tipping point. I'm concerned about charter schools, which we see as a real threat. Jan has a volatile membership of 900 people. They could go one way or another on any important issue and when they go, you'll lose them—and you lose them for a long period of time. We know that a terrible labor situation sits in the community for 30 years. That is what keeps me up at night at times. And how do you manage that? So much is at risk.

Lynn: If I were to summarize—the relationship between administration and the union is a supportive cocoon around the high academic achievement goals. Without the cocoon, it's tougher to maintain high performance. People's attention moves away from instruction and moves back to "terms and conditions of employment" issues. Is that close?

Jan: You have to look at where you focus your energy. We could focus our energy on conflict, but that doesn't buy us much. When the administration can understand the teachers' needs, and the teachers can look at the pressures that are on administrators—then we can share. Then our whole scope is larger, and we don't have to fight as much. There will still be some battles that we'll have to work through. But nobody hates each other, because there is a foundation of respect.

Nancy: Paul, you've had administrative experience in different districts and different states. How did you manage to move this relationship in Kennewick forward?

Wish: It is either because of his Colorado luck or because he is very, very, smart.

Paul: Why can't I get anyone to buy the "very smart" theory? [Laughter.] Seriously, you have to have a basic belief that this goal is important and that concentrating on getting results together will work. If you push your way through and are successful, the organization will say, "We hate the SOB, but look at what we are achieving." But the minute the success slows down, you know what's going to happen. If we can figure out how to move together in a collaborative way with administrators, boards, parents, and staff, then the process will keep going. Our strategic plan may be less of a collaborative document, but it has been a unifying and driving force for the district.

Lynn: Most of America's 15,000 school districts will not participate in a 20-school district network like we did. What do you suggest for them?

Wish: You can't jump over a lot of the processes like many school districts try to do.

Jan: In the beginning, we had to go slow to go fast. We had to have the initial planning and the initial conversations before we could start moving at any speed. Today, it looks as if the Kennewick School District is really picking up its pace; but in the beginning, we had to go slowly and have all of the conversations that you have as a president with the district. It starts with conversation. "What is best for the kids?" We always have to ask each other that and challenge each other to keep focused on our reason for being in education. That vision has to be somewhere in all beginning conversations with the district, union, and school board and in all of those anchor agreements.[5] We had to get over things.

Wish: Give me a light-handed facilitator and a retreat situation that allows for such questions as "What is your current reality?" and "What do you want your future reality to look like?"—so that labor and management talk about what they want to build. Read books together that facilitate discussions about team building and more democratic decision-making.

Jan: Paul was great about going out and visiting all of the schools. Every classroom every year. What a commitment to teaching! People have collections of little notes from him after his Monday morning visits. They frame them. We got better at communicating jointly together.

Lynn: Specifically, what are some of the things that you had to get over?

Jan: We couldn't hold grudges. Of course, we started out with huge trust issues. People had to take risks and be honest. Before we got that piece worked out, the main strategy was to hold information back and not tell it all. Then you could bring a piece of it out eventually, at a point when you could use it as a weapon. We had to get beyond that. But I actually don't know *how* we got beyond using information as a weapon. We just did.

There are a lot of processes that the union and teachers are invited to attend. The union was invited to participate in strategic planning, network programs, the bond and levy elections, the summer institute at Harvard for the last three years, and the physical facility planning committee. The budget process is pretty open.

Paul: It really comes back to the board, the superintendent, and the union leadership being willing to take the time. It's just like a marriage. You'll have your ups and downs. There are times you're going to do

---

[5]The anchor documents are derived from W. Pat Dolan, *Restructuring Our Schools*. The anchor agreement in Kennewick was between the board, association, and administration, and it formalized our decision to agree to collaborate, to decentralize, to create local site councils, and to provide for building-level variances in contract language.

something that hurts the other side. And usually what happens immediately is that everybody retreats to an entrenched position. If the leadership allows you to stay in that position, you're stuck. So you have to force yourself back out. You have to forgive one another and continue to collaborate and work with one another. Either party can destroy that relationship. That hasn't happened in Kennewick. When I can see where the administration has caused a problem, all I have to say is, "We're not going to do this any more," and it's over. It's the same thing from the KEA side. All Jan has to do is say, "We're not going to do this any more," and it's over. Neither one of us is storing up the bad memories to unleash at the next moment of crisis.

When you get to the bottom line, it's relationships, relationships, relationships. That is what it is. That's what it's always been.

CHAPTER ELEVEN

Reading Foundations: Engaging the Community

"If everyone were to take the Reading Foundation's advice and read to a child 20 minutes a day, we would revolutionize education in our state."

— Gary Locke, Governor
State of Washington, 2002

"A local Reading Foundation encourages parents to read daily with their children," explains Nancy Kerr, president of the National Children's Reading Foundation. "From birth to kindergarten, a child who is read to at least 20 minutes a day absorbs 600 hours of structured language. With this wonderful daily experience, most children will acquire the pre-literacy skills essential for learning to read. They also learn to love books and are eager to become good readers."

The message of the Reading Foundation is simple. "The most important 20 minutes of the day. . . read with a child." Community Reading Foundations skillfully reinforce this message everywhere within their member school districts. Public service radio and TV announcements feature governors, judges, and local sports celebrities promoting the message in English and Spanish. Posters in businesses, static-cling signs on car windows, and reader boards display the 20 minutes a day slogan, as do highway billboards. Newspapers, willing allies investing in a generation of future readers, provide supportive editorials and features. The message appears on restaurant tray liners, balloons at community parades, and baseball game programs. It appears on summer reading activity calendars, campaign-style lapel buttons, "Books for Babies" materials[1] in hospitals, and booths manned by volunteers at community events. One foundation has transformed a transit bus into the "Story Bus," carrying the reminder throughout the community 18 hours a day. Another foundation has a life-size mascot and co-sponsors the "Read-Aloud House" with their regional library. By the time a child starts kindergarten, parents have heard the reading message at every age and stage of their child's development.[2]

The message works. The community easily recognizes it. Parents remember it. In a customer satisfaction survey conducted for the Kennewick School District in 1999, 98% of parents had heard the message. The recognition was sustained at 99% in 2001 and 99.2% in 2003.

> *"Last year there was a town meeting in our area for citizens to ask legislators questions. One person stood up and started complaining about teachers, schools, and test scores. A voice from the audience called out, 'Are you reading with your child 20 minutes a day?' In other words, are you part of the solution? Teachers deserve and need that kind of support from their communities."*
>
> — Nancy Kerr

"The advantage of the message, of course, is that it involves parents early on," points out Courtney Shrieve, executive director of the South Sound Reading Foundation in Washington. "We know that children who have involved parents are much more likely to function at or above grade level from kindergarten on. We aren't asking parents to teach their child to read. But by just reading aloud every day, parents build their child's phonemic awareness, vocabulary, and love of reading. The power of a parent with a book can change our schools."

In the past, public schools either discouraged parents from teaching pre-academic skills or were reluctant to share the specific skills

[1] In spring 2004, the Utah Reading Foundation assembled 20,000 baby back packs for hospitals, and distributed 250,000 summer reading calendars in English, 20,000 in Spanish and 15,000 in a Native American language. The Mid-Columbia Reading Foundation has provided Books for Babies packets at four area hospitals for the last six years. South Sound Reading Foundation provides parents with a book, information and a diaper bag at their baby's six month check-up.

[2] Lynn Fielding, Nancy Kerr, and Paul Rosier, *The 90% Reading Goal* (Kennewick, WA: New Foundation Press, 1998), chap. 9, shares a pot-pourri of about 150 creative ideas that the Mid-Columbia Reading Foundation used to spread the message to the community.

needed for school readiness. But in this time of limited resources, school districts are seeking help in new, nontraditional ways. Reading Foundations are proving to be powerful partners in that process.

> *"If you want your children to be brilliant, read them fairy tales. If you want them to be very brilliant, read them more fairy tales."*
>
> — Albert Einstein

The No Child Left Behind legislation, with its measurements and reporting mechanisms, has school districts focused on and seeking things that will help show progress. Schools are asking: How do we get other people helping us, especially parents? In these days of increased accountability, we need all the help that we can get.

As of spring 2004, there are nine Reading Foundations serving 656,484 students in 116 school districts in four states. Three other regions are in the process of launching their foundations. The National Children's Reading Foundation provides a common 501(c)(3) tax-exempt umbrella, organizational support, and a library of resources for the executive directors.

"One of our elementary principals came back from a conference with a copy of *The 90% Reading Goal,*" recalls Scott McDonald, executive director of the Treasure Valley Reading Foundation in Idaho. "I read the chapter on the Reading Foundation and thought, 'If they can do it there, we can do it here.' It took us a year and a half to get the core districts signed on and ready to go. The local organizational phase of a Reading Foundation seems to take forever . . . but it doesn't. Never, never, never give up. This is the part that takes time and two or three resolute persons. But the actual legal organization is a snap. The National Reading Foundation takes care of the incorporation, by-laws, and 501(c)(3) tax-exempt status filings for a fraction of the cost and time that it would have taken us. Then things take off. Before the end of the year, we had 10 school districts as members; and during the second year of operation, we had 16 districts as members."

"Reaching families in 10 counties requires mass marketing," continues Scott, "We've handed out 200,000 *Read to Me* brochures, sent home 25,000 newsprint magazines, run hundreds of ads on TV and radio,

Table 11.1
Reading Foundations, 1998-2004

Entity	State	Date Formed	Districts Served	Students Served
The National Children's Reading Foundation	WA	1998	-	-
Washington State	WA	2000	-	-
Mid-Columbia	WA	1996	11	42,000
Eastern Oregon	OR	1998	11	14,000
South Sound	WA	2001	10	41,000
Treasure Valley	ID	2002	16	56,000
Mini-Cassia	ID	2002	2	4,500
Lewis County	WA	2003	13	14,000
Utah State	UT	2003	40	477,800
North East Washington	WA	2004	1	184
Twin Harbors	WA	2004	12	10,000
Total			116	659,484

and acquired and handed out 74,000 free books to low-income families in just two years. School districts have never done this level of advertising. It's foreign to their nature."

"Utah State has a leveraged and dynamic Reading Foundation, thanks to help from the National Reading Foundation," adds Chieko Okazaki, cofounder of the Utah Children's Reading Foundation. "It took a lot of up-front work. I encourage fledgling foundations to be prepared to take the necessary time to find like-minded people and develop strong partnerships. But after all our work, it is so gratifying to hear the message coming out of the governor's office. Now we have billboards, media ads, educational materials and partners statewide reminding families that success for children starts in the home when parents understand that the most important 20 minutes of their day is spent reading with their child."

From birth to five, a child's brain is wiring itself to hear the distinct sounds and syllables within words and absorbing the grammatical patterns of language. This is a critical stage. Reading aloud exposes children to a richer vocabulary as well. The average child enters kindergarten familiar with approximately 5,000 words. Most parents and teachers don't realize that the normal child's book has 17% more "rare" words than the conversation of a college graduate.

"The best geographical base for a Reading Foundation is neighboring school districts within a common media market. The Reading Foundation model has been successfully replicated in areas of various demographics and diversity," says Brad Dell, executive director of the Washington Children's Reading Foundation. "Getting multi-district buy-in requires a small group of champions to patiently enlist the support of dues-paying school districts. Then the creative good-will of community members generates fantastic ideas and opportunities. Partnerships and collaborations are key components of effective Reading Foundations. The community courageously commits to assure every child learns to read and help every parent raise a reader."

Each Reading Foundation is guided by local leadership, in concert with community values, in developing its strategic plan. The local Reading Foundations collect $1-$2 per student per year from the member districts to fund basic overhead costs. The executive director rallies community donations and in-kind services to achieve the goals established by the board's strategic plan.

Once the districts commit, the citizen leaders serve as the first executive committee. They incorporate under state law and expand the board. The board is composed of 16 to 20 respected citizens representing a cross-section of the communities including newspaper publishers, TV and radio station owners, legislators, business leaders, together with one or two prominent superintendents and school board directors. The board hires an executive director with a strong public relations and marketing background, whose primary job is to manage a long-term media and community education campaign.

"At its core, the Reading Foundation is an idea about commitment. It exists because a visionary group of educators—joined by their peers, business leaders, and members of the media—understand that we must enable every child to succeed if we, as a society, are to succeed. And in order to succeed, children must learn to read early and learn to read well."

— Nolan Curtis, President
Mid-Columbia Reading Foundation, 2003

Executive directors participate in monthly conference calls that provide training and facilitate networking. The affiliation agreement provides for sharing collateral materials so that media scripts, printed pieces, promotional designs, and program ideas developed by one affiliate are available to other affiliates.[3]

Comments Jim Swan, executive director of the Lewis County Reading Foundation, "As a new executive director, the advantages for me are obvious—immediate support, proven ideas that work, tips on implementation, and access to the pool of common resources. The *Organizational Handbook* is packed with useful information."

---

[3]Available services and resources for affiliated Reading Foundations include the *Organizational Handbook*, media "PSAs," PowerPoint presentations, website access, brochure and newsletter templates, vendor lists of baby packets, artwork for posters, brochures, stationery, buttons, etc.

Our website at www.readingfoundation.org showcases national and local affiliates' activities, as well as board membership and community and business partners. Parents will discover information on child development and children's book titles, as well as links to other literacy-based organizations.

"We are here to help you give the children in your community a good reading foundation," Brad Dell offers. "Families and communities are the foundation of this effort. Please contact us on-line or at (509) 735-9405 for further assistance of additional information."

Your inquiries are welcome.
Nancy Kerr at
nkerr@readingfoundation.org

(888) 668-8952

CHAPTER TWELVE

THE FACE OF A CHILD

"We never really leave our non-reading children behind. We may forget about them, but we are chained to them socially and economically. Like a ship and its anchor, we must either lift them up or drag them along behind us."

— Lynn Fielding

Our statistics, growth charts, and figures reveal only part of the toll of low literacy. Another part occurs deep in the hearts and minds of our children. Tony and Mindy, two composite children reflecting thousands of recurring real life stories, put a human face on that impact.

Tony and Mindy Now

Fourth graders are eight going on nine. They weigh between 40 and 70 pounds. They come in a vast array of sizes, shapes, and skin shades, talents, interests, and skills. Tony is one of them, and he can't read. Actually, he *can* read, but he reads on a first grade/sixth month level. Right now, he is staring blankly at his science book. It's from a national publisher, carefully written on a fourth-grade level.

> **So scientists believe that there never was any water on the moon. The moon is a dry, airless, and very barren place.**

This is what the sentence looks like to adults like you and me with high school diplomas. It's what the sentence looks like to Mindy, sitting next to Tony. To Tony, who struggles to decipher "See the cat," the sentence looks like this:

> **So scxxxxxsts bexxxve that there never was any wxxer on the moon. The moon is a drx, axxxss, and very bxxxn place.**

Or, more realistically, because we adults fluently recognize the repetitive x's and other letters, it really looks more like:

> **So sci¬näts be??¥?ve that there ne?er was any w*&??er on the moon. The moon is a d*?, a?+?°áá, and very b?¥¥?n place.**

Tony doesn't like science. Science is very hard. Math and social studies are hard too. Tony knows that he can sit much longer and work far harder than Mindy, but that he still won't get it.

Mindy gets it. She just looks at the pages and gets it. Tony doesn't know why. He doesn't know that Mindy's parents have read with her at least 20 minutes a day since birth and still do. The happy accumulation of alphabet letters around the crib, singing nursery rhymes, focusing on beginning and ending sounds in words, talking constantly, pointing out the "S" on STOP signs, daytime reading, and bedtime stories have banked a solid investment of more than a thousand hours in Mindy's literacy skills before she came to school. These activities have hard-wired her brain in a literacy-efficient way.

> *"Young children most familiar with nursery rhymes were top readers three years later, regardless of intelligence or economic circumstances. Children with reading difficulties often showed insensitivity to rhyme."*
>
> —P. E. Bryant [1]

Literacy and Brain Functions

Tony doesn't know that part of his brain isn't working effectively. A nickel-sized area just behind and above his left ear should be converting the visually perceived shapes of letters to brain signals similar

[1]P.E. Bryant, L. Bradley, and J. Crossland, "Nursery Rhymes, Phonological Skills and Reading," *Journal of Child Language* 16, no. 90 (1989): 407-8.

to auditorally generated sounds. It isn't.[2] It hasn't had enough stimulation; and compared to Mindy's, its neurological wiring is inadequate. Without the ability to convert letters smoothly to sounds, the rest of Tony's perfectly adequate brain, eyesight, hearing ability, and recognition of objects provide little help for him to read. Another part of Tony's brain, located toward the front and normally used in comprehension, is trying to compensate for the inadequate letter-to-sound conversion process. But using the front part of the brain requires a huge effort, and Tony quickly wearies of the task.

Tony doesn't know that a series of simple parenting activities for a few minutes every day could have assured that he would fluently and instantaneously convert letter shapes into sounds. Rhyming, singing, and clapping exercises would have effortlessly taught Tony how to hear the beginning, middle, and ending sounds of words. Simply talking to him a lot and asking him simple thinking questions would have extended his reasoning and increased his vocabulary, so that he reached kindergarten with the same skills as his five-year old friends.[3] Instead, he came to kindergarten with a new shirt, a bright smile, and his parents' eager hopes for him, but with the pre-literacy skills typical of a two or three year old. Mindy, with the same bright smile, new top, and parents' eager hopes, arrived with the skills typical of a seven year old.

Why Tony Stays Behind

A kindergarten class focusing on social skills was fine for Mindy, since she had spent her preschool years in an environment saturated with visual and oral language. Mindy is one of the 17% of American third graders who are reading on the first day of class at a seven- to eight-year-old level. And, unlike Tony, Mindy spends a lot of her free time with books. She thinks she is reading for pleasure—and she is—but she is silently adding more vocabulary and concepts. She is reinforcing and strengthening the neural networks that increase her fluency and extend her comprehension.

[2]Sally Shaywitz, *Overcoming Dyslexia* (New York: Alfred A. Knopf, 2003), chap. 7, "The Working Brain Reads," 71-89.

[3]Simple age-appropriate exercises taught with good parenting skills from birth to five would eliminate a high percentage (although not all) of the struggle with phonemic awareness that a great many students in the public schools wage against great odds that they will never catch up with their peers.

Tony desperately needs to make catch-up growth in reading. He doesn't know—and neither do his parents—that a kindergarten curriculum that did not focus on letter recognition, phonemic awareness, and phonics has robbed him of valuable literacy learning time.

Tony's school district considers assessment to be a useful exercise beginning with fourth graders. As a result, Tony's teachers have virtually no incoming kindergarten tests,[4] no kindergarten data,[5] no yearly beginning and ending reading assessments for the first, second, and third grades, and no specific diagnostic assessments for those who are behind.[6] Tony's teachers rarely group by skill level in any part of their class, [7] use 30-minute daily pullouts as their primary intervention, and do not team well together. They have not learned how to be nimble and creative in cutting less valuable curriculum to free up more time, in creating smaller groups, or in matching student instructional needs across grade-level classrooms.

Tony needs 180-240 minutes of direct reading instruction a day instead of the 60-minute, three-reading-level groups format that gives him 20 minutes of direct reading instruction a day in his group. It works just fine for Mindy, but he needs extra time focused on the precisely diagnosed sub-skills in which he is deficient. He has needed this individualized intervention since kindergarten, and has needed it with increasing urgency in first, second, and third grade as well. What help he's getting now in fourth grade is too little and too late.

There have been few, if any, adjustments in the classroom reading process as a result of his failure—or the failure of the 10 other children in his class who read a year or more below their grade level. It was not until January 2002 that federal legislation required his school to baseline the numbers of students reading below state standard and to progressively reduce that number each year. Most of the No Child Left Behind pushback from the school is resistance from adults who don't

---

[4]See Chapters 20 and 21.

[5]Quick and reliable assessments of phonemic awareness that can be administered in less than 20 minutes include the Test of Phonemic Awareness (TOPA), Roswell-Chall, Yopp-Singer, and the Rosner. A simple letter and sound recognition assessment appears in Chapter 21.

[6]See Chapter 6.

[7]Leveling by skill is grouping students of similar ability based on identified need only during reading or math instruction.

want to change, adults who ignore the hope inherent in changing the system for students like Tony. That would be true hope. Instead, Tony's school is pinning its hopes on the chance that Tony will "develop" into a reader.

Tony doesn't know any of this. What Tony *does* know is that he's dumb. Dumb at science. Dumb at math. Dumb at social studies. He gets the same message every day in every class.[8]

Actually, Tony is a bright kid. He has an above-average IQ, good reasoning skills, and a strong work ethic. But part of his brain needs specific exercise. He started in kindergarten two to three years behind his peers, and there is no way that he can catch up in 60-80 or even 120 minutes a day. He has already figured out that there is not a lot of correlation between working hard and doing well. And he's right. When a child doesn't read, there is virtually none.

So during fourth grade Tony is reading at a first-grade level and Mindy is reading at a seventh-grade level. Few educators or parents talk about the six-year spread, because so few are aware of it.

Tony's parents would be devastated to know that he cannot read. They are only moderately concerned when the teacher tells them that Tony is a little behind but will catch up. They remember being a little behind, too.

But Tony's teachers, despite their practiced reassurance and genuine hope, are concerned. They know he is struggling to read. They accurately predict—as most elementary teachers can—that Tony probably won't make it through high school.

Later

For Mindy, dozens of doors are opening. Now, and into middle school/junior high, she is roaming the Web and instant-messaging with three or four of her friends at a time. In school, there are young writer contests and science fairs; there are field trips where she reads labels

---

[8]K. E. Stanovich, "Matthew Effects in Reading: Some Consequences of Individual Differences in the Acquisition of Literacy," *Reading Research Quarterly* 21 (1986): 360-407.

next to paintings and instructions for interactive exhibits. There are class and student body offices for which she makes speeches, accelerated and enrichment programs, band, and chorus.

Poverty is generally a symptom, not the cause, of poor reading skills.

These doors remain closed for Tony. Tony needs to read to use the computers for anything except video games. In numerical terms, Tony has read about 800,000 words in his lifetime outside school. Mindy has read about 14 million.[9] He is behind—not only in reading, but in virtually everything else also. His sixth-grade curriculum does not deal with letters, sounds, and word attack skills. The curriculum and the teacher's instruction are about nouns, verbs, topic sentences, and six-trait writing.

Gradually Tony finds ways to resist. He comes late, cuts class, misses a day (or two or three) of school a week. What does it really matter? It's no fun anyway. His principal talks about his problem almost exclusively in terms of attendance. "We cannot teach them if they aren't here," he says. And of course, he's right. Yet no one focuses on his reading.

Tony can't keep up with Mindy's crowd so he seeks out those more like him—those who space out homework and ridicule the "geeks" and "nerds." He figures he's not getting it anyway so why not break his pencil lead off inside a lock, leave his homework home, ride the buzz of the little white pills, flaunt some gang insignia, or hang out where he fits in a little better. The principal's office is not so bad, really. He has been there a dozen times already. Mindy hasn't been there once.

Much Later

By high school, Mindy is still on cruise control. At fifteen, she still reads three grades above grade level, is involved in student

[9]At the fifth grade, children at the 90th percentile read 2,357,000 words per year from newspapers, magazines, and books versus 134,000 words per year for those at the 20th percentile. R. C. Anderson, P. T. Wilson, and L. G. Fielding, "Growth in Reading and How Children Spend Their Time Outside of School," *Reading Research Quarterly* 23 (1988): 285-303. Those numbers have been multiplied by six, assuming that this relationship holds true from fourth grade through ninth grade. Mindy's total is derived by multiplying 2,357,000 words per year by six years and Tony's by multiplying 134,000 words per year by six years.

government, plays sports, writes for the school paper, sings in the choir, and has practiced taking the SAT each year since eighth grade. She can't imagine not going to college.

Tony, on the other hand, is reading at a sixth-grade level. He's sitting in heterogeneously grouped classes and getting slaughtered. He failed two classes first semester and is flunking another one in his second semester. He suddenly realizes he isn't moving along automatically from grade to grade like in middle school. His counselor tells him that he won't graduate in four years if he doesn't buckle down. He really hits the books after that, but he can't cut it.

The six-year gap between Tony and Mindy since kindergarten hasn't changed much. It has just become more obvious. Tony and Mindy have both made nine years of growth. Tony's growth moved him from the skills of a three-year-old to the skills of a sixth grader as a high school sophomore. Mindy's growth moved her from skills of a seven year old to those of a high school senior or college freshman as a high school sophomore.

The competitive difference seems to surface everywhere except P.E. and metal shop. Mindy got 1250 on her SAT and is sorting through college applications. Tony, like many other minority kids his age, scored below 800. Even if he got into a college under some preference, he is still four to six years behind Mindy. And he still has to get the credit hours to graduate. "I'm good with my hands," Tony tells himself. "I'm sixteen, and I'm outta here."

Tony has low skills. Low employment skills generally pay minimum wage if they pay at all. Tony lacks the reading ability to qualify for any apprenticeship programs. He finally gets a GED, but it doesn't get him very far. Even the military has found that a GED is more or less equivalent to an eighth-grade skill level.[10]

---

[10]To pass the GED, persons must achieve a minimum score on five multiple-choice sub-tests (usually 35) and an overall score of 225 although the standard differs state to state. The GED is distributed by the General Educational Development Testing Service located at One Dupont Circle NW, Suite 250, Washington, DC 20036. Originally developed for returning war veterans, the Department of Defense no longer accepts the GED as equivalent to the high school diploma, finding that GED holders performed similarly to high school non-completers. John Pawasarat and Lois M. Quinn, *Research on the GED Credential and Its Use in Wisconsin 1986*, retrieved on May 5, 2004 from http://www.uwm.edu/Dept/ETI/pages/serveys/each/gedres.htm.

Tony's friends suggest a little shoplifting, a few random purse snatchings, and the occasional daytime home theft to help out. Tony's going for it. It is one of the few doors that have opened for him.

It's Now Again

By the time Mindy is graduating from a four-year college, Tony has drifted in and out of a dozen jobs and a few jails. He tried an electrical and a refrigeration apprenticeship but couldn't handle the reading. He looked at community college but stopped when he found he would have to pass four remedial English and math classes before any of his credits started to count. He has a couple of really cute kids from various relationships. Of course, he spends almost no time reading with his children or helping them learn to recognize alphabet letters, shapes, or sounds. There are lots of reasons: time, distance, money, and the fact that Tony is raising his kids the way he was raised.

So these cute kids will go to kindergarten knowing only one or two alphabet letters, unable to hear and repeat beginning or ending sounds of words, and having heard someone read aloud to them less than 40 or 50 hours total. They will go with skills typical of three or four year olds, not ready to read. At kindergarten they meet their own Mindys who have been talked to, reasoned with, and read to daily from birth, and the cycle will start again.

And So We Conclude

Add up the other disadvantages for all of the other Tonys. What if some, or even most, of their language experiences are not in English? What if they can't sleep at night, because someone is screaming in the next room, or worse? What if they have only one parent part of the time? What if there is no clean, quiet place to do homework, or never a safe place to put it after it is finished? What if there isn't a dad or older sister to help with a science project? What if no one ever goes to parent-teacher conferences?

All of these problems will make it harder to overcome Tony's non-reading handicap. Yet the real handicap is still that Tony cannot read well.

If a child cannot read, she or he bears the consequences mostly alone—embarrassment now, intensifying frustration with each school year, and an adulthood of limited options. We all know someone who struggles—sometimes in open frustration, sometimes in silent shame—with poor reading skills. It may be a fifth-grader who refuses to bring her schoolbooks home to complete her assignments. It may be an uncle who always asks his wife to read the newspaper headlines aloud. The fact is that 20% of adults in America age sixteen or older today cannot read well enough to review a pay stub and write down the year-to-date gross pay or write a letter about an error that appears on a credit card bill. [11]

We never really leave our non-reading children behind. We may forget about them, but we are chained to them socially and economically. Like a ship and its anchor, we must either lift them up or drag them along behind us. It is time we teach our Tonys to read.

[11] *Data Volume for the National Educational Goals Report*, Vol. 1 (Washington, DC: U.S. Government Printing Office, 1995), 122.

PART TWO

The National Story

Is No Child Left Behind a plot to replace public schools with charter schools, vouchers, or worse? Can we simply wait it out? What business do the feds have telling states or local districts what to do? These are a sample of questions circulating among educators today. Part Two answers these questions by:

- Providing a historical perspective of this educational reform and why it's not going away (Chapter 13).
- Explaining achievement (where students start and end each year) versus growth (how much they learn in between) and how to build reports that show both achievement and growth (Chapter 14).
- Exploring how other industries use standards, why student achievement standards are new to education, and how they vary from state to state (Chapter 15).
- Examining elementary achievement and growth reports (Chapter 16).
- Examining middle and high school achievement and growth reports (Chapter 17) and,
- Showcasing a testing system that provides accurate annual growth and achievement data in affordable formats (Chapter 18).

At an average adult reading speed of about 300 words a minute, including sidebars, kickers, and footnotes, and spending five minutes on each data figure, you can read Part 2 in 57 minutes.

CHAPTER THIRTEEN

Achieving Adequate Yearly Progress

"Ten years ago it was visionary to assure that each student read at or above grade level by third or fourth grade. Today it is the law. Ten years from now it may be a civil right."

— Lynn Fielding

We find ourselves in the midst of our third major educational reform in a century.[1]

The first educational reform started in 1900 and lasted for about 30 years. During those three decades, the school year increased from 144 days to 173 days.[2] The average number of days a student was absent from school decreased by 19 days. Enrollment in grades 6-12 grew 15 times faster than elementary school enrollment.[3] High school graduation rates increased from 6.3% to 28.8%[4] and the number of four-year college degrees granted rose from 27,410 to 122,484.[5] This educational reform

---

[1] Willard R. Daggett and Bendict Kruse, *Education Is NOT a Spectator Sport* (Schenectady, NY: Leadership Press, 1997). Daggett is president of the International Center for Educational Leadership, 1587 Route 146, Rexford, NY 12148; (518) 399-2776; fax: (518) 399-7607; http://www.dagget.com.

[2] U.S. Bureau of the Census, *Historical Statistics of the United States, Colonial Times to 1970, Bicentennial Edition, Part 1*, p. 375, Series H, 520-30.

[3] Ibid., p. 368-69, Series H, 412-32.

[4] Ibid., p. 379, Series H, 598-601, calculated as a percentage of 17 year olds.

[5] Ibid., p. 386 Series H, 751-65.

occurred in the context of a noisy social and economic transformation. In 1892, just 18% of the population voted.[6] By 1920, the 19th Amendment added women to a voter pool previously limited to those who were male, literate, 21, and property-owners—and the decision-makers increased to about 25%[7] of the population. In 1913, the 16th Amendment authorized wealth redistribution through the federal income tax. Other changes included a world war, major population shifts from rural to urban, and an economy that tipped from agriculture to heavy industry.

Table 13.1
Educational Profiles in the United States, 1900-30
Change in Percentages

	1900	1930	% Change
Average school year in days	144	174	
Average days missed per student	45	30	
Net days attended	89	144	161%
Elementary students in thousands			
Public	14,984	20,556	
Private	1,147	2,255	
Total	16,131	22,811	141%
Secondary students in thousands			
Public	519	4,399	
Private	111	341	
Total	630	4,740	752%
% of high school graduates	6.3%	28.8%	
Number of college degrees granted	27,410	122,484	467%

[6] U.S. population in 1892 estimated from census population table retrieved on June 22, 2004, from http://www.census.gov/population/censusdata/table-2/pdf. Number of voters for 1892 presidential election retrieved on June 13, 2004 from http://www.uselectionatlas.org/uspresident/frametextj.html. Voting population (12,068,037) divided by total population (65,626,246) equals 18%.
[7] Voting population retrieved on May 28, 2004 from http://clerk.house.gov/memberselectionInfo/1920election.pdf. 1920 population retrieved on May 28, 2004 from http://www.npg.org/fact/us_historical_pops.htm. Voting total (26,368,528) divided by population total (106,461,000) equals 24.7 %.

Our second major educational reform began as millions of service men and women returned from World War II and the Korean conflict. College enrollment skyrocketed from 2 million to 6.9 million students.[8] The growth resulted in accelerated construction at virtually every institution and a near doubling of the community college system. Both construction and enrollment were initiated and sustained by federal legislation and funding.

We are now in the third major educational reform. During the 1980s, nearly every state raised its graduation requirements. The 1990s saw another radical shift, as virtually every state adopted legislation that mandated testing. The legislation generally set minimum achievement standards, required elementary, middle, and high schools to baseline the number of students at or above the standard, and expected an increasing number to reach the minimum standards. This near-uniform action was unprecedented in the prior 50 years. In 2001, the first step was taken to standardize these reforms by the passage of the Reauthorization of the Elementary and Secondary Educational Act (ESEA).

The third reform is also occurring in the context of loud, bitter debates about major social and economic transformations. Pressures from businesses operating in global markets fostered the beginning of this reform in 1983. By the mid-1990s, entry-level jobs required higher reading skills than the lowest 40-50% of our high school students. It is not that public education is doing worse than it had previously. It is simply that the job market now demands higher minimum verbal and math skills to find employment than it does to go on to college.[9] The focus of the third revolution is not more degrees or even higher skills for the top quartiles. The focus is on getting our lowest performing students to acquire the minimum reading and math skills of the near-average student. It is the reality of leaving the Industrial Age and entering the Information Age.[10]

The issues of this third educational reform are fairly simple: Large numbers of our students are a long way behind.

[8]Ibid., p. 382, Series H, 700-15.

[9]Daggett and Kruse, *Education Is NOT a Spectator Sport*, 13-14.

[10]In 1993, computing was the third largest industry at $360 billion a year, surpassed only by autos, oil, and accounting for 25% of all capital equipment purchases. "The New Computer Revolution," *Fortune*, June 14, 1993, 56-57 and *Businessweek*, Nov. 1933, 22.

How do the reading abilities of these four groups compare? Our D students have not yet achieved the reading skills as 10th graders that our A students acquired as third graders.

Suppose we could sort all the students at each age and divide them into four equal groups based on reading or math ability. We could sort and divide them in many other ways as well. For example, we could divide them into four groupings based on effort, improvement, attendance, or a combination of these factors. However, to illustrate the focus of this third educational reform, our grouping is solely on the basis of the students' ability to read and do math at third grade. Suppose we call the top quarter of these students the A's, the next quarter the B's, the next quarter the C's, and the lowest quarter of students the D's.

How do the reading abilities of these four groups compare? Our D students do not achieve the reading skills of third-grade A students until ninth or 10th grade. Our C students are slightly better off. Our C students acquire the reading skills of the third grade A students when they are eighth graders, as Figure 14.1 in the next chapter will illustrate.

A comparison of math skills yields similar results. Our D students acquire the math skills as ninth graders that our A students acquired as third graders. Our C students acquire the math skills of the third-grade A students during sixth grade as Figure 14.2 will illustrate.

The focus of this reform is on our C and D students—this 40% of students who are a long way behind.

There has always been a gap between the top and the bottom students. Ten decades ago, when 93% of students didn't finish high school, the gap was even wider. Yet, the goal of this reform is not to eliminate the five-to-seven year gap between the quartiles.[11] The objective of business, the intent of the state and federal legislation, and the result of the reporting mechanism is to raise the skills of the lowest two quartiles to a minimum level.[12] Like the Civil Rights Act of 1964,

[11]Most of the state minimum standards are not set at the 70th or 90th percentiles. They are being set nearer the 50th percentile, where a typical, average student usually scores, although a few state standards also range as low as the 9th -18th percentile (Colorado for 4th-10th grade reading) and as high as the 75th, 80th, and 89th percentiles (Arizona, South Carolina, and Wyoming respectively for eighth-grade math).

[12]Increased student achievement, education's new paradigm, was created in the mid-1990s by legislation passed in the 50 states. The legislation set minimum standards in core subjects, baselined the number of students at or above the standard, and articulated the expectation that progressively more students each year would be at or above the standard. Its fundamental design, copied by the federal ESEA of 2001, focuses attention and resources on students in the lowest two quartiles.

the Clean Air Act of 1970, and every other major piece of legislation, the ESEA will need technical corrections and adjustments. (Appendix F contains some of our suggestions.) But the primary focus has been established.

Despite fussing and some world-class whining by those with a vested interest in the good ol' days before educational accountability, this reform is not going to fade away. Its relentless focus on the lowest performing students did not happen by chance at either the state or the national level. "Waiting it out" or even significantly changing the current law won't work for three reasons:

Economics: Students in our current lowest 40% simply will not have the skills to be self-sufficient in tomorrow's economy. Manual jobs are being taken over by technology or are being exported to locales where goods can be produced for a tenth of the U.S. minimum wage. Most post-high-school entry-level jobs require higher reading skills than college classes in higher education.[13] Society has legitimate needs for employees with basic academic skills and expects schools to produce them. That pressure will not diminish.

Racial Inclusion and Social Equality: Our educational goal of racial inclusion is at odds with our social goals of equal treatment for those with similar measurable achievement. If college admissions and business employment mirror our K-12 academic achievement, a majority of ethnic minorities are tacitly excluded from universities and from higher paying jobs. Conversely, if college admissions and employment mirror the nation's actual demographics, large numbers of more academically prepared Caucasians are displaced by less-prepared minorities.[14] In both

[13]Willard R. Daggett is completing a multi-year study of the Lexile reading level of each standard job classification with levels of high school and college reading proficiency funded by the U.S. Department of Labor. Preliminary findings indicate that the required Lexile difficulty of most entry-level jobs exceeds that required by most freshman college course work.

[14]"The employer hiring the typical black high school graduate (or the college that admits the average black student) is, in effect, choosing a youngster who has made it only through eighth grade. He or she will have a high school diploma, but not the skills that should come with it. . . . The most recent NAEP study reveals that blacks nearing the end of their high school education perform slightly below white eighth-graders in both reading and U.S. history, and perform significantly worse in math and geography. In math and geography, indeed, they know no more than white seventh graders." Abigail Thernstrom and Stephan Thernstrom, *No Excuses: Closing the Racial Gap in Learning* (New York: Simon & Schuster, 2003), 13. The NAEP Data Tool is available at http://nces.ed.gov/nationsreportcard/naepdata and provides a great deal more information than is available in the published volumes reporting assessment results.

scenarios, the sense of injustice and resentment are real. These forces will continue to fray the fabric of our society unless and until we raise achievement in the lowest two quartiles—the two quartiles with most of America's ethnic minorities.

Legislative Power: For decades, U.S. educational associations have successfully lobbied for increased funding with virtually no accountability. Beginning in the mid-1980s, higher education got hit with the accountability movement. By the mid-1990s, state and national legislatures finally linked public K-12 educational funding to the requirement that progressively more students would achieve minimum competency levels each year. Legislatures can and have threatened to reduce funds, but their most potent lever for change is publicly identifying schools and districts that fail to make consistent yearly improvement. It is not likely that legislators will abandon these powers and relatively newly found tools.

We predict, given the global economic pressures, that the education race of the 21st century will resemble the arms race of the 20th century in most of its important aspects. After the initial educational goals are reached in 10 years, we will see continued escalation for the next 30 years. The outcome of the global economic contest, with inevitable military consequences, will hinge on the education race.

It is becoming more critical that we deliver on the promise of public education. The interaction of economics, racial inclusion versus social equality, and legislative power guarantees a relentless, need-driven emphasis on rescuing the lowest 40% of American students who are two or three years behind. The goal is to catch them up, so that they can perform at the level of our average students.

You've probably got some questions. Here are the four we hear most often when people encounter these statistics:

1. Are the lowest 40% really two to three years below grade level?

They are, and they are this far behind in virtually all districts unless yours is truly unique. The only exceptions seem to be tiny rural schools where parents value education and have no mobility, and the gated, self-contained upper-class suburban districts. Otherwise, these struggling students are behind when they start, and most of them stay behind. Unless your district is a genuine anomaly, Part Three of this book describes how 40% of your state's and district's students will enter kindergarten with the academic skills of three and four year olds.

2. Doesn't America's vaunted educational system assure that these children make annual growth?

Generally it does. However, adding a year's worth of growth to the 6+ year range in initial reading and math skills merely assures that the 6+ year gap stays firmly in place for each subsequent year.

3. Every school has remedial programs. Don't these programs get the lagging students up to speed?

We wish the answer were "yes," but for most children, the data say "no." *Annual* growth occurs in most of our schools, but very little *catch-up* growth occurs. (See Chapter 14.)

Reauthorization of Elementary and Secondary Educational Act (2001)

Every six years since 1965, the federal government has reauthorized the Elementary and Secondary Educational Act (ESEA). The most recent reauthorization, called the Elementary and Secondary Educational Act of 2001, passed the House and Senate in a highly bi-partisan action with 90% of all senators and representatives voting for it. The President signed it on January 8, 2002, and it became Public Law No. 107:11 commonly known as No Child Left Behind. Originally introduced in 2001 as HR 1, it passed the House by a vote of 381-41 and passed the Senate by a vote of 87-10. Contrary to widely held perceptions, more Democrats than Republicans supported the bill. In the House, 183 Republicans and 198 Democrats voted in favor with 33 Republicans, 6 Democrats, and 2 independents opposed. In the Senate, 43 Republicans and 44 Democrats were in favor with 6 Democrats, 3 Republicans, and 1 independent opposed. For the roll call vote, see http://senate.gov/legislative. Bill summary and status information is at http://clerkweb.house.gov.

The three-year range between the midpoint of the lowest quartile and the "average student" is not an abstract piece of educational trivia. The Elementary and Secondary Educational Act Authorization (2001) has deposited the consequences of that range on district doorsteps. It requires that we create catch-up growth for these students on an unprecedented scale. As boards, superintendents, building administrators, teachers, and parents, we will spend most of the next decade dealing with it.

Here is how it will work. Each state is required to set a series of fixed (or criterion-based) standards in reading and math. Suppose your state sets its fourth-grade reading standard at what is now the 50th percentile and you just happen to have one student at each percentile (a statistical improbability in real life). For purposes of illustration it means that, historically, out of your 100 fourth-grade students, 50 students will achieve the standard this year and 50 will not. Under ESEA requirements, you must get roughly five *additional* students at or above this standard *each* of the next 10 years, at which point, all of the students will be reading at grade level.[15] The progressively increasing numbers of students who must reach the standards is called making "adequate yearly progress."

In most districts, the first year should be relatively easy. The five students closest to the goal are in the 45th to 49th percentile. Using our rough rule of thumb, the 45th percentile students are about $5/13^{th}$ of a year behind. They will need three to four months (5/13 times 9 months equals 3.5 months) of "catch-up growth," and merely aligning the curriculum to the test will get them to the standard.

The second year becomes more difficult, especially if students come into fourth grade reading at the same level as they did the prior year. The second year, this statistically symmetrical district must not only get the five students in the 45th to 49th percentile to the goal, but also boost the five students in the 40th to 44th percentile to the goal. The bottom students in this second wave of students are about seven months ($10/13^{th}$ time 9 months equals 7.1 month) behind and must make normal

[15]Ninety-five percent of students must be tested; 100% of those tested must pass by 2013, effectively setting a 95% goal and effectively excluding most of the learning-disabled students who are physiologically unable to reach normal standards. Each state provides its own assessment and sets the standards or cut-scores on elementary, middle, and high school achievement, usually at the 4th, 7th, and 10th grades. Each grade must report four categories for nine disaggregated groups of students. The four categories are whether adequate yearly progress was made in (1) reading, (2) math, (3) whether 95% of students took the test in reading, and (4) whether 95% took the test in math. The nine student categories are All Students, Asian, Black, Hispanic, Native American, White, Limited English Proficiency (LEP), Disabled, and Disadvantaged. The four categories multiplied by 9 groupings of students equal 36 cells. The 37th cell is attendance in elementary school, attendance at middle school, and the graduation rate for high school.

A Useful Reminder from Another Industry

In 1975, Los Angeles cowered under a brown greasy cloud. A new word, "smog," was coined to describe the air-borne pollutants that prior industry practices and legislation had allowed to accumulate. Denver, Houston, Miami, Baltimore, New York, and every other major metropolitan area were no different. We were breathing brown air, and we wanted better.

Individual states passed clean air standards, and in 1978 the federal Clean Air Act passed. Most of the automotive and heavy industries rose in protest. They alleged that America had caved in to those determined to destroy Detroit. Hundreds of thousands of jobs, from mining in Colorado to smelting in Tennessee, would be affected as well as the assembly-line jobs in Michigan. It was economically impossible to build a car or a plant that could meet the emission standards. Life as we knew it would end.

The furor of the debate is a distant memory now for most of us. Detroit did not die. Reasonable legislators modified truly impossible provisions. The air is not perfect in our great cities, but it is greatly improved. Yet the industry efforts to place profits over our lungs still rankle.

In 2004, we are passing through the same phase in education reform. Thirty percent of our students don't graduate. Many of the students who do graduate have the reading and math skills of eighth and ninth graders. We want better.

State and national educational organizations must decide whether to lend their agendas, keynote conference speakers, publications, and resources to fixing the problem for students, or whether to pour their energy into opposing the change in the industry.

Three decades from now, this educational reform will be a distant memory. Public education will not be destroyed. Fewer educators than autoworkers will lose their jobs. Truly unworkable legislative provisions will be modified. After all, our children and grandchildren should achieve minimum levels of literacy and math competencies. Along with breathing clean air.

annual growth plus seven months of catch-up growth—a little more than a year and two-thirds of growth in a single year. This achievement will be difficult unless their growth spurt starts before fourth grade.

The third wave of "adequate yearly progress" students (the 35th-39th percentile) begins a full year behind their classmates. The fourth wave (the 30th–34th percentile) is about a year and a half behind.

The pattern's long-term consequences in the fifth and subsequent years are pretty clear. Kindergartners who start out at or above the standard are in good shape if they make normal annual growth.[16] But students who start out below the standard must make more than normal annual growth in the school year. The school system has to find ways to assure that growth. By the second year, the limits of growth achieved during the assessment year (usually grades four, seven, and ten) have been reached. The extra margin of catching up has to come from somewhere else—and logically, the only place is growth at each prior grade for each prior year.

Percentile	Years Behind
37th	1 year
24th	2 years
12th	3 years
1st to 5th	Rarely achieve 50th percentile

4. So just how much catching up are we talking about to get students who start out in the 5th–10th percentile up to the 50th percentile set by the state in our example?

The strategy of focusing resources on just the students closest to achieving the standard, while ignoring those who lag even farther behind them, guarantees a collision with the mandated requirements. All the students will also be tested as sixth, seventh, or eighth graders and 5% more each year must also reach the standard.

The answer is the bad news mentioned earlier in this chapter. Students in the 12th percentile are more than three academic years behind "grade level." In the next 10 years, each grade has to get more efficient at catching students up, because making one year of annual growth plus three additional years of catching up is virtually impossible except for extraordinary students in extraordinary circumstances. This is the focus of the third educational reform.

[16] However, students who enter at or near the standard, make annual growth, and then move from a low-standard state to a high-standard state may find themselves two to three grade levels below the new state standard.

CHAPTER FOURTEEN

Understanding Achievement Versus Growth

"There is an important yet subtle difference between student achievement and student growth. Educational leaders today must be mindful of both."

— Nancy Kerr

In Chapter 13, we used "achievement measures" to compare the scores of our hypothetical A, B, C, and D groups on reading and math tests at the end of each year. Achievement measures use end-point measures, like reading scores at the end of a grade or GPA at the end of a semester. "Growth" measures, on the other hand, compare the amount of progress that the A students or the C students make between two end points—from the fall to the spring of a school year, for example. Most studies focus primarily on achievement, occasionally on growth, but rarely on both.

This chapter explains the difference, presenting national reading and math graphs that combine views of both achievement and growth. They show intriguing patterns from second through 10th grades that likely mirror the growth and achievement patterns of students in your district. These graphs are easy to understand and are central to the concepts in this book.

National achievement and growth scores in reading and math show the gradually increasing scores of our nation's A students (our highest 25%) and the gradually increasing scores of our D students. The two in-between lines show the achievement and growth of the B and the C students. (See Figures 14.1 and 14.2.)

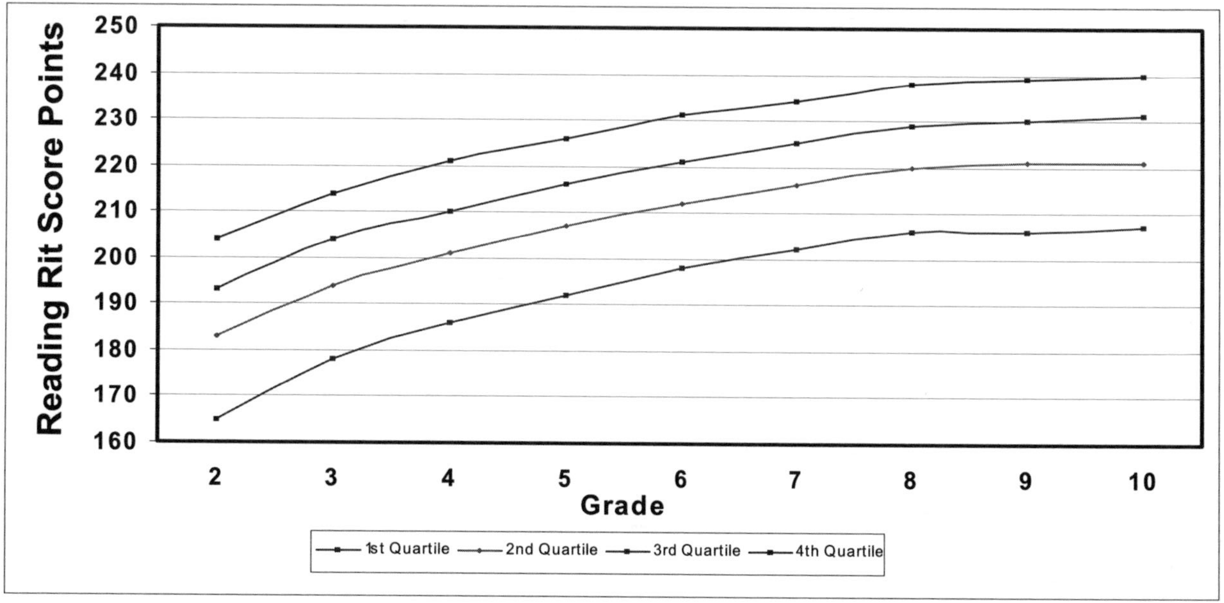

Figure 14.1. The Six-Year Range in National Growth and Achievement Reading Scores. This graph shows the average reading scores of 1.3 million students nationwide from second to 10th grade using high to low quartiles (25%). The top line on the chart is the average reading score of the top 25% of students at the end of each grade. The bottom line is the average reading score for the bottom 25% of students. There are 6+ grade levels between them. For example, students in the top quartile scored 214 RIT points in third grade while students in the lowest quartile do not score 214 even in 10th grade. Most students of all abilities grow 5-8 points each year. The data indicate that those who are behind in second grade generally stay behind. Constructed from data provided by the Northwest Evaluation Association's nationwide testing.

Here are some observations that can be drawn from these reading data, several of them counterintuitive:

1. The Six-Year Reading Span: There are six years of normal academic growth between our statistical D students and statistical A students at each grade level. Starting at a RIT score of 165 at the end of second grade and growing on average seven points a year, the D students should score 204 in about six years, when they are in eighth grade.[1]

Try this simple exercise. Using Figure 14.1, put one finger on the top quartile at second grade where these students are scoring 204 RIT points. Slide your finger horizontally across the chart following the 204 level until the line of the lowest quartile students intersects it just before the end of eighth grade. That is when second graders in the lowest quartile finally read at the same level as second graders in the highest quartile. If you repeat the exercise at third grade, it is evident that, even at 10th grade, the D's do not reach the level of the third-grade A's. The flattened growth in middle school increases the length of time it takes these students to reach the point where their top peers were seven full grades earlier.[2]

2. Annual Reading Growth: Students in all four quartiles make 36-42 points of growth in reading from grades two to 10. Students at the bottom actually gain more points. Students in the lowest quartile score 165 RIT points at the end of second grade. In elementary school, they grow about seven points each year. In middle school, their growth drops to five points and further drops to a single point in high school.[3]

Students at the midpoint in the top quartile score 204 points at the end of second grade. Like students in the lowest quartile, they also achieve seven points of growth on average per year in elementary school, about five points each year in middle school, and a single point per year in high school.

[1]204 points (the top quartile at second grade) less 165 points (the bottom quartile at second grade) = 39 points difference. 39 points divided by 7 points of growth a year is 5.6 years.
[2]This 40% of students do not *speak* two or three years below grade level, and we often assume that students with grade-level speaking skills have grade-level reading skills as well. Speaking skills are not a good indicator of reading skills. In fact, students with poor reading skills often develop better than average speaking skills to mask their reading deficiency.
[3]In elementary school, the growth is 13, 8, and 6 RIT points for the third, fourth, and fifth grades respectively. In middle school, the annual growth is 6, 5, and 5 RIT points for the sixth, seventh, and eighth grades respectively.

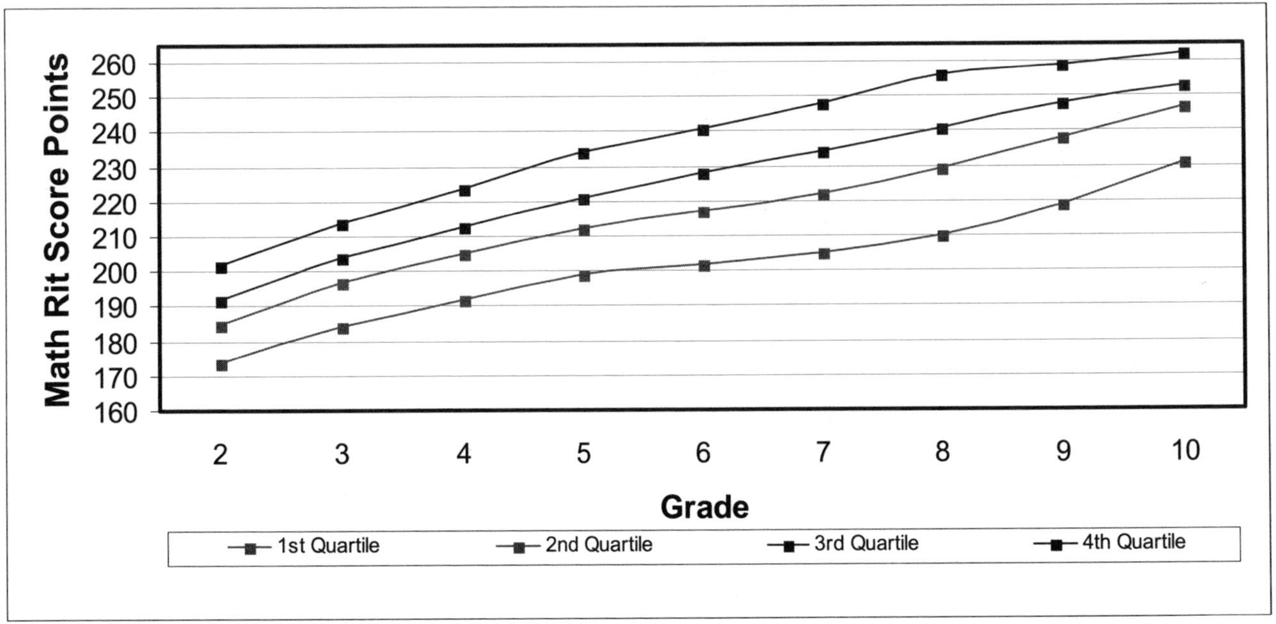

Figure 14.2. The Four-to-Six Year Range in National Growth and Achievement Math Scores. This graph shows the average math scores of 1.3 million students nationwide from second to 10th grade using high to low quartiles (25%). The top line in the chart is the average reading score of the top 25% of students at the end of each grade. The bottom line is the average math score for the bottom 25% of students. There are 4+ grade levels between them. For example, students in the top quartile score 202 in second grade while students in the lowest quartile do not score 202 until sixth grade. Most students of all abilities grow five to eight points each year. The data indicate that those who are behind in second grade generally stay behind. Constructed from data provided by the Northwest Evaluation Association's nationwide testing.

As the near-equal average growth among all of the quartiles suggests, public schools are very effective at creating annual growth in every quartile. Students in each quartile not only can learn, but on average they learn at nearly equal rates.

This fact suggests another important point. Public schools do not create the gap between quartiles in reading, nor is there any evidence that they add to the gap in reading for students in grades two to 10. Part Three explores where and how this gap is created.

> *"Public schools do not create the gap between quartiles in reading, nor is there any evidence that they add to the gap in reading for students in grades two to 10."*
>
> — Lynn Fielding

Figure 14.2, "The Four-to-Six Year Range in National Achievement and Growth in Math Scores," mirrors the same startling information provided for reading. Some observations that can be drawn from the math data are:

1. The Four to Six + Year Span: The span in math is similar to the span in reading. Put one finger on the top quartile at the beginning of second grade where the average student score is 202 RIT points. Slide your finger across the chart following the 202 level until the line for the lowest quartile students intersects it. That achievement occurs four years later, at the end of sixth grade. If you repeat the exercise at third grade, following 214 across, the D's match the A's achievement midway through ninth grade, some six years later.

2. Annual Math Growth: In math, students in the top three quartiles average about 60-62 points of growth from second grade through 10th grade while students in the lowest quartile average 57 points. The lowest quartile of students lose about three points overall. There is an important difference, however. In reading, the yearly variations in growth between the A, B, C, and D groups were tiny. In math, the D group steadily slips two to four points a year during elementary school and middle school. This decrease results in a cumulative 18-point loss—or almost three years—by eighth grade. What appears to be a sudden burst of growth in ninth and 10th grade may well be the result of the D students dropping out, a phenomenon that generally occurs during the freshman and sophomore years. The low quartile math growth is especially critical for minority students who are disproportionately represented in the lowest quartile.

Again, NWEA's national math achievement and growth scores suggest that public schools do not create the gap between quartiles in math. However, the scores do indicate that public schools slowly add two to three years to the gap at the lowest quartile during elementary and middle school.

3. Catch-Up Growth in Math. The catch-up growth issue is the same in math as in reading. The C and D students must make annual growth plus catch-up growth equivalent to two to three years. The focus of the ESEA legislation is to catch up students who are below your state's minimum standard. The whole reform process can be characterized as assuring that all students make "annual growth" and that low quartile students make catch-up growth in significantly increasing numbers.

These insights lead us to the following conclusions.

- It is imperative for students in the quartiles below your state's ESEA standard to make annual growth. Consistent annual growth is an absolute prerequisite before systematic catch-up growth can occur.

- Students who enter first grade with the emergent reading skills of three- or young four-year olds (three years below grade level) have to make one year of normal growth and one year of catch-up growth *in each of the first, second, and third grades* to catch up by third grade.

- The students who are three years behind in math at the end of third grade must make *two* years of growth *every year* to catch up by the end of sixth grade (one year of normal growth plus one year of catch-up growth).

- Poor readers typically are poor math students as well. Even students who are initially ahead in math will start to fall behind if they read poorly because there are more words than numbers in math textbooks, and the explanations become more complex as the curriculum advances.

- Catching up gets harder, not easier, with each year that passes. Before third grade, students learn to read. After third grade, students read to learn. The dynamics for literacy acquisition change abruptly at fourth grade.

- Making catch-up growth in middle school is perhaps twice as hard as doing it in elementary school and even harder in high school. The curriculum, master schedules, limited expertise in reading instruction by language arts instructors, materials, and student motivation all work against catch-up growth, especially when it must be double or triple the annual growth.

The 95% reading and math goals are "achievement" measures, in that they measure the number of students at or above the minimum standards set by each state. Yet it is the "growth" measures that allow schools to calculate what it will take to catch each student up. Planning for growth requires being able to calculate how much additional time is required on which deficient sub-skill for how many students.

Just as kittens, calves, and pigs don't grow fatter just by weighing them, students do not acquire skills just by testing them. Chuck Watson said it well: "There is no point in testing if you don't look at the data, don't understand them, and don't change." The point of good achievement and growth data is to use them for informed policy and decision-making.

Chapter 15 discusses state standards, where they are being set, and what you need to know about them to create necessary growth for your students. Not all states have set their standards at the 50th percentile. In fact, chances are that your state has not. The next chapter explores the state standard-setting process and suggests that you be aware of where reading and math standards have been set in your state.

CHAPTER FIFTEEN

STATE STANDARDS

"Our ultimate goal is improving student achievement, not just setting standards."

— Edward B. Rust, Jr.
Chairman, Education Task Force,
Business Round Table

Almost every industry has uniform standards. Each adoption has a convoluted history but far-reaching impact.

Railroads and railroad steam engines were invented in 1829. For the next 60 years, the distance between the rails ranged from as little as two feet in upper New England to five feet in the South, to the old New York & Erie's six-footer.[1] Locomotives and train cars had to be specially built for each little train company. Freight and passengers had to be taken off and reloaded every time it was necessary to move into an area with a different track width. Four different track systems entered Richmond, Virginia, and Philadelphia in 1861, but not one connected

[1]Freeman Hubbard, *Encyclopedia of North American Railroading* (New York: McGraw-Hill Book Company, 1981), 127; see also Albro Martin, *Railroads Triumphant* (Oxford: Oxford University Press, 1992). Delightful stories about railroads include a fairly credible hypothesis that the size of the most advanced transportation system known to man—the Saturn rockets—was determined by the width of two Roman horses. The story goes like this: The rockets, built by Thiokol in Utah, were transported to Texas by railroad. The rocket width was limited by the width of the current railroads and the tunnels they passed through. The current gauge of railroads of 4'8½" in turn, stems from the width of the stone "gutters" the Romans built in many of their roads to pull 10-15 carts linked together. And how wide were the "gutters"? Wide enough for a pair of horses. So the width of the Saturn rockets was determined by the width of two Roman horses 2000 years ago.

with another. After the Civil War, most companies used the northeastern standard of 4 foot 8½ inches. Federal legislation finally required that the system become uniform by 1893. In the preceding months, some 9,000 miles of track, covering a distance equivalent to that from New York to Los Angeles and back, was moved 3 ½ inches closer together to meet the federally imposed standard.

Likewise, the threads on shafts and bolts have been around since Archimedes in 250 B.C., running wine presses and water pumps in Greece, printing presses in A.D. 1400 in Germany, and fastening together all the pieces of the Industrial Revolution for the last 200 years. For decades, each threaded bolt was handmade, with its nut simultaneously fabricated as a unique matching pair. Then in 1797, Henry Maudslay created a lathe in England that made it possible for threads in metal to be cut rapidly, repetitively, and with incredible precision. He was frustrated by the endless trouble and expense when complex machines had to be taken apart, and their bolts and nuts were intermixed. For this reason, Maudslay standardized the taps and dies within his shops, so that any nut he manufactured would fit any of his bolts of the same size. Huge gains in efficiency and interchangeability resulted, paving an accelerated path for the Industrial Revolution. By 1841, the British adopted a national standard proposed by Maudslay's pupil, Joseph Whitworth. The United States adopted a slightly different standard and continental Europe a third. The U.S., British, and Canadian systems were not completely unified until 1956.[2]

In a similar fashion, the personal computer industry struggled with its standards from its inception in 1975. In 1981, IBM entered the PC market, publishing a small book of its specifications to allow the purchase of uniform software and hardware parts from multiple vendors.[3] Despite a variety of valid concerns, producers like Texas Instruments, Phillips, NEC, ITT, Hewlett Packard, Olivetti, Sperry Rand, and a host of tiny producers adopted IBM's standards as their own. Hard drives from different manufactures could now plug into different PC systems. Microprocessors, computer chips, and software programs could be designed for more than one system, and even power cords

[2]Robert E. Green and Christopher J. McCauley, eds., *Machinery's Handbook* (New York: Industrial Press, 1996), 1635.

[3]Daniel Ichbiah and Susan Knepper, *The Making of Microsoft: How Bill Gates and His Team Created the World's Most Successful Software Company* (Rockling, CA: Prima Publishing, 1991), 88.

would all fit. Uniform standards made a powerful industry out of what had previously been small and very diverse firms.

In each case, as standards are established, craftsmen within each industry railed against the uniformity. The industry experienced an initial retooling cost, and industry visionaries prepared for the greater efficiencies. The rest of the population wondered why it hadn't been done much earlier.

Despite the rhetoric about "high" and "low" academic standards in public education, actually setting minimum reading and math standards at elementary, middle, and high school levels is brand-new. In the 1950s and 1960s, the focus was on "seat time" or minutes of class time. States reimbursed school districts on the condition that they provided some minimum amount of teacher-student contact time like 375 minutes each day for at least 180 days a year. Even today, most students receive diplomas upon completion of a minimum number of high school class hours (seat time) in certain required subjects plus a few electives, with a D- minus or better, regardless of their achievement level (what they know and are able to do).

As a result, universities relied on ACT and SAT tests as one of the few uniform available measures of academic ability to determine college admission.

In 1990, states began to develop legislation using basic assessments of core subjects, setting minimum standards on the assessments, base lining the number of students achieving the minimum scores in the first year, and expecting an increasing number of students to reach the minimum each year thereafter.[4]

The ESEA 2001 (see Chapter 13) incorporates this model and allows states to set their own standards, determine which years to

---

[4]Prior to this round of legislation, New York was unique in requiring minimum standards from its graduating high school students. The historical New York Board of Regents, a board that predates the Revolutionary War, urged the establishment of a system of common schools as early as 1784. An 1877 statute authorized the regents to give academic examinations as a standard for high school graduation which they did. Starting in 1978, New York used a parallel system of a less demanding high school competency exams leading to a high school diploma and the regents' exam which could result in a regents' diploma. In 1996, the regents' exam was redesignated as the general testing standard for high school graduation.

conduct assessments, and set reading and math minimums on those assessments for the selected years. The major federal limitation is that there be at least one assessment in each of the three grade ranges (3-5, 6-8, and 9-11). Assessment authorities typically refer to general statements of what students should know or be able to do as "standards" and refer to the required minimum scores on the tests as "cut-scores." However, most educators and parents refer to the state test minimums as the "standards," and we will do the same here.

Given the inexperience and freedom of states in the setting of minimum academic standards, the wide range in standards should come as no surprise. The discrepancies surface, and states often reset or adjust their standards after a few years of experience—either to a more realistic level or to "smooth out" standards set at levels inconsistent with other years.

In the 2003 edition of *Testing the Testers*, its annual study of state accountability systems, the *Princeton Review* used the National Assessment of Educational Progress (NAEP) as a uniform standard to determine the "easy" and the "hard" graders. By comparing the percentage by which student proficiency on the state exams on eighth grade math exceeded that on the NAEP, the *Review* was able to determine where states had set their standards relative to each other. The study results appear as Figure 15.1. States that set their standards high, according to the *Review*, were designated "Tough Graders." They included, in descending order of "toughness":

1. Louisiana
2. Arizona
3. South Carolina
4. New Hampshire
5. Washington
6. Vermont
7. Massachusetts
8. Kentucky
9. Wyoming
10. Colorado
11. D.C.
12. Utah
13. Alaska
14. Wisconsin

In addition to the *Princeton Review*, the NWEA also completed a comprehensive analysis of 16 states, comparing where each fixed its standards at each grade level for reading (Figure 15.2) and for math (Figure 15.3). While the actual NWEA and state assessments differ in

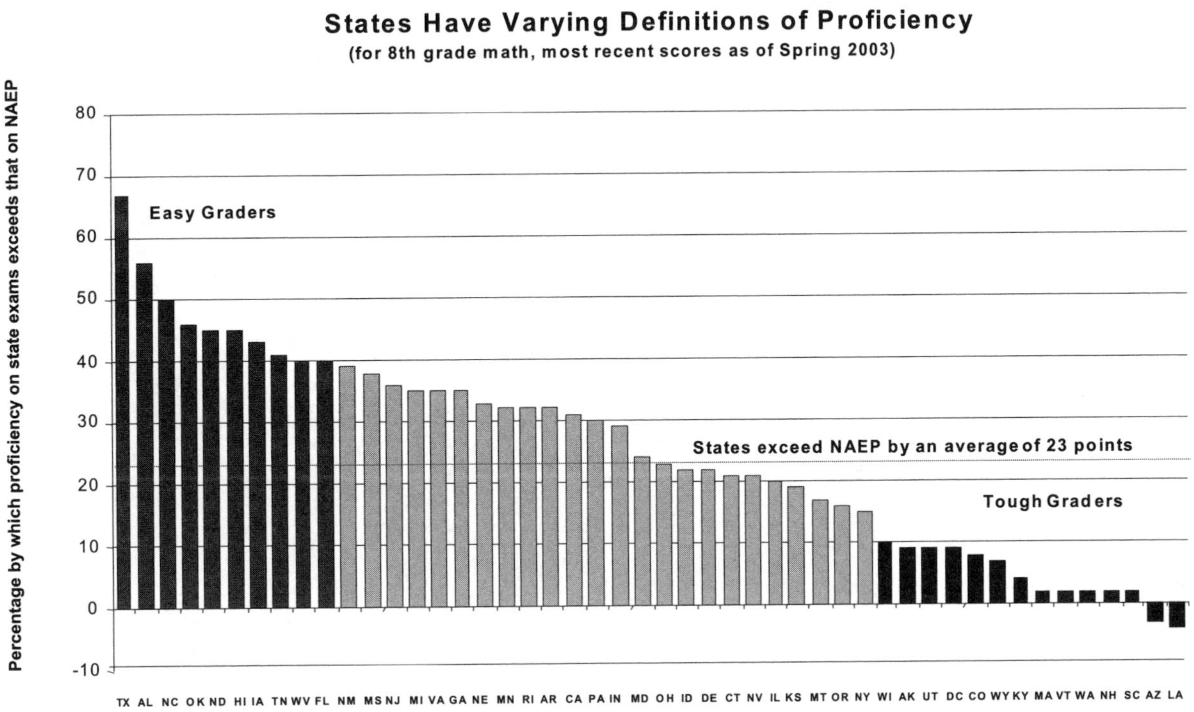

Figure 15.1. Varying Definitions of Proficiency for Eighth Grade Math, Spring 2003. Source: *Princeton Review*, "Testing the Testers" (Princeton, NJ: Princeton University, 2003), used with permission.

test type and complexity, the percentile ranking of students passing each test remains fairly constant.[5]

Both studies agree that Wyoming, South Carolina, and Arizona have high standards. The NWEA places California and Pennsylvania ahead of Oregon. Most notably, according to the NWEA's work, Colorado has set its eighth-grade math standard at the 31st percentile, the lowest of the 16 states in the NWEA study, and probably closer to the "easy" than the "tough" graders. The discrepancies highlight the infant nature of national standards. Even with the significant differences, these two studies are currently the best available.

Board members, superintendents, and principals should understand where their state standards are set and why they may be reset. There are four benefits in understanding where these standards are set. They provide:

- A sense of whether your state standards are extremely low, extremely high, or internally inconsistent and therefore likely to be changed.
- Ways to estimate the standards for the grades that the state does not test.
- Ways to calculate how far behind groups of your students are.
- Some idea regarding whether increased numbers of students passing at the third- and fourth-grade level, but failing at the seventh- and eighth-grade level is due to learning differences or due to the bar being set disproportionately higher.

For example, if your state has set its math standard at the 89th percentile, as Wyoming has done, only 11% of students nationally will pass. If 35% are passing (even though 65% are still failing), this is still fairly impressive. At the 89th percentile, however, all three-bottom quartiles must shift upwards. The bottom quartile must improve by as much as five normal years of growth, suggesting that Wyoming may

---

[5]NWEA sets these equivalencies using the most accurate predictors of three models. It first used simple linear regression to predict state scores from RIT scores. It then identified the passing level as the RIT value most likely to result in achieving exactly the passing level on the state test. In the second model, it used a regression model with a quadratic factor to account for the departures from linear relationships that were often observed to further refine accuracy. The third model, the state's passing status (pass/not pass) was treated as a test question that was calibrated to the RIT scale to identify the passing level.

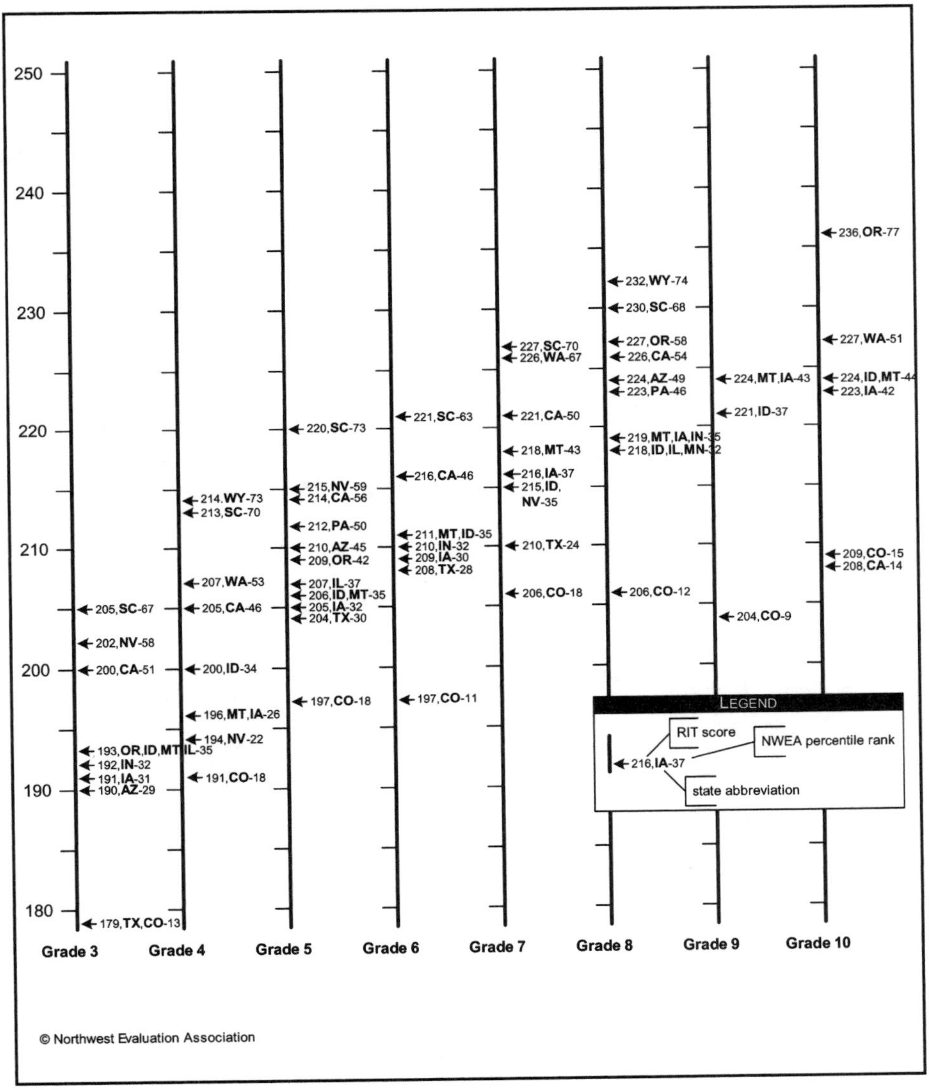

Figure 15.2. NWEA: Where Sixteen States Set Their Reading Standards, Locations on the RIT Scale

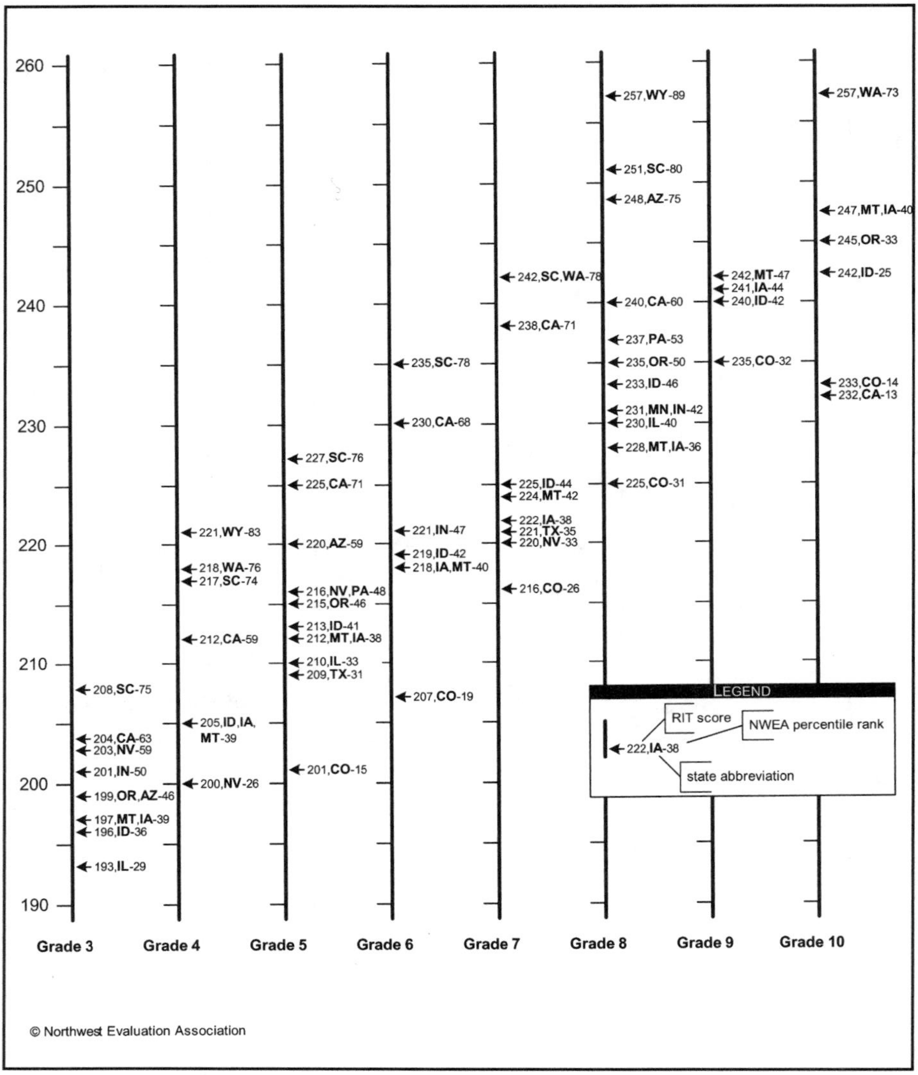

Figure 15.3. NWEA: Where Sixteen States Set Their Math Standards, Locations on the RIT Scale

start looking at pre-kindergarten interventions. Another alternative is that Wyoming standards might be lowered, because this educational revolution is not about increasing the top end as much as bringing up the lowest 40-50%.

Another example is California, which has set its reading standard between the 46-54th percentile for K-8 but has dropped it to the 14th percentile in high school. The 14th percentile is a little above the average fourth-grade level. Increasing numbers of students passing the reading standard at grade 10 will primarily result from the bar being set four grades lower at 10th grade than at eighth grade. California educators may reasonably expect backlash from employers and parents pressing for a more reasonable standard—like that which forced a readjustment in Texas in 2003.

A third example is Washington State where reading standards were initially set at the 53rd percentile at fourth grade, at the 65th percentile at seventh grade, and at the 51st percentile at 10th grade. Washington educators should expect that their seventh-grade standard would eventually be smoothed downward in relationship to their fourth and 10th grade standard.

A clear understanding of your state's standards will go a long way in helping superintendents, boards, and principals set district growth targets at each grade level and create the internal mechanisms to monitor and assure the achievement of adequate yearly progress.

CHAPTER SIXTEEN

ELEMENTARY SCHOOL GROWTH REPORTS

"When we want improvement, and we keep doing the same things and keep getting the same results—who, really, are the slow learners?"

— Dave Montague, Principal, Washington Elementary

Research data need to be put in formats that ordinary people can understand–ordinary people who not only lack Ph.D.s in statistics, but also cannot conceive of wanting one. Ordinary people like principals and board members, legislators, parents, and even kids. Only when data are understandable, are they usable.

Most of us have never seen growth data, especially growth data over time. Normal achievement data when viewed over a number of years also show growth. They show whether we are getting better or whether we are just getting the same results as the previous year. This chapter shows some ways to view growth data in simple formats that do not depend on statistical constructs.

Most of us do not want to repeat the mistake of the 1980s and 1990s. We had two decades of debate, staff training, new curriculum, and intense lobbying for increased funding with almost nothing to show for it. We had virtually no increase in student reading and math growth during those two decades. There is no point in heading down that road again under the impression that we will leave no child behind on it.

Figure 16.1 is a way to look at Washington Elementary's transformation in reading during the last seven years. Each box in each column represents a student. The number inside the box represents the RIT points the student grew during the year. Each year has a set of five columns of boxes which are numbered from (1) to (5). The columns represent the national quintiles (students divided into five groups by achievement) in which these Washington Elementary students started at the beginning of the year. Column (1) for each year shows the students in the first quintile (the lowest 20% of students) in the fall. Column (2) for each year shows the students who were in the second quintile (those from the 20-40th percentile). The same pattern continues for the third, fourth, and fifth quintiles.

Running horizontally across Figure 16.1 is a heavy black line. The system is working for students who are "above the line." All "above the line" students have made at least annual reading growth (8 points of growth measured on the RIT scale). However, if students are in the lowest two quintiles (lowest 40%), they have to make annual growth plus catch-up growth. So to be "above the line," each low quintile student must make at least double annual growth (at least 16 points of growth). Each set of five columns is for the subsequent year, showing the pattern of growth at Washington for third grade from 1996-97 to 2002-03. Appendix G has a simple summary of how these charts can be made in Excel.

The changes in growth for students and within quintiles, demonstrated by Washington Elementary, mirror what every school or district must do to go from poor to good or from good to great. Some comparisons worth noticing are:

1. **Lowest 40% of students nationwide:** At the beginning of third grade at Washington Elementary in 1996, there were 39 students in the bottom 40% of all students nationwide. There were eight students in the lowest quintile and 21 more in the second lowest quintile. By 2002-03, there were only 15 students in the lowest two quintiles; 5 in the lowest quintile and 10 in the second quintile. This kind of progress at earlier grades is key.

2. **The lowest 20% make at least double annual growth:** Not only does the total number of first quintile students decrease each year as first and second grades create more growth, but

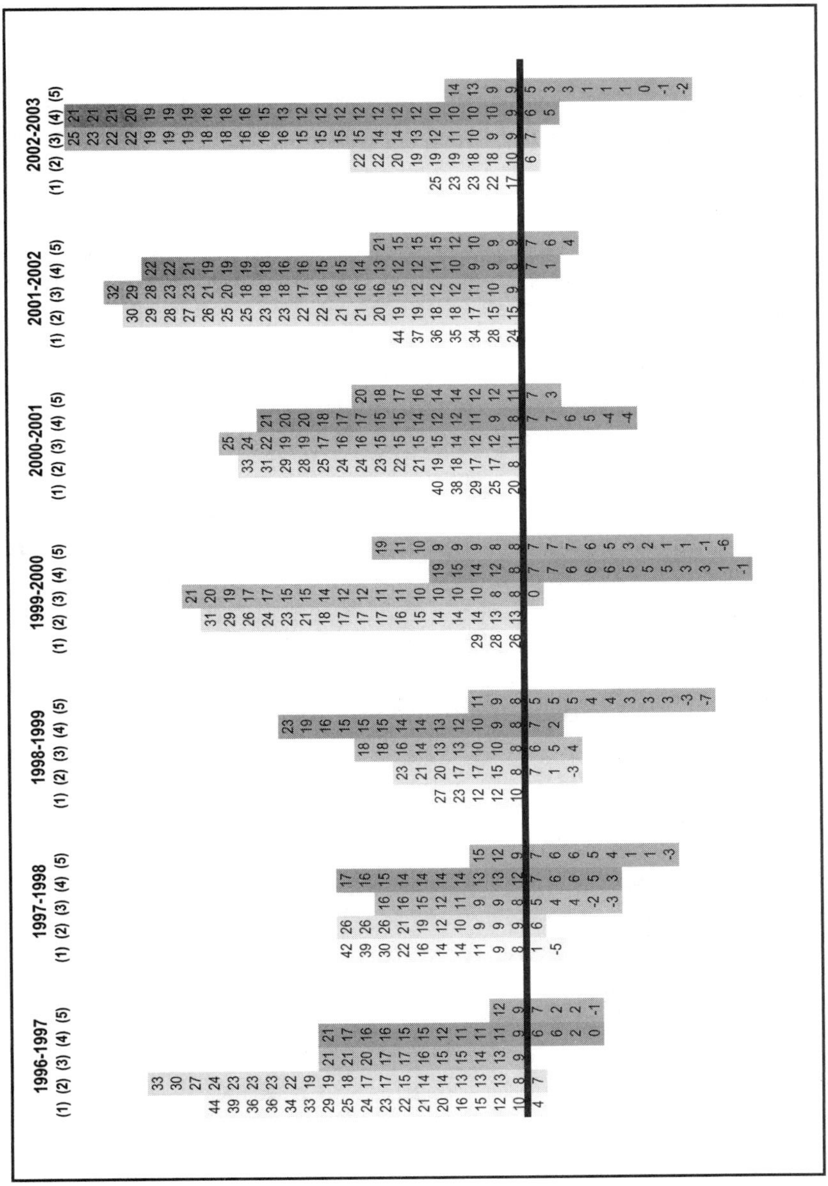

Figure 16.1. "Above and Below the Line" Growth Report for Reading by Student by Quintile at Third Grade at Washington Elementary, 1996-2003.

more and more students as third graders make double annual growth. By 2000-01, virtually all-first quintile students made at least double growth.

3. **More students in the top 60%:** The numbers of students in the third, fourth, and fifth quintiles steadily increase over time at Washington.

4. **Lack of annual growth in some top students:** Some students in the top 20%, reading at a fourth-to-sixth grade level, do not make annual growth. While some of these students are already reading on a sixth and seventh grade level, Figure 16.2 illustrates lower growth that can inadvertently occur in upper quartiles by focusing resources on lower-performing students.

Figure 16.2 is constructed in the same way as Figure 16.1 with a few exceptions. Each box is a student. Each box is in the column corresponding to the student's national quintile at the beginning of the year. The number in the box is the growth each student made during the year. The difference between Figure 16.1 and 16.2 is that, to be "above the line" in Figure 16.2, a student must have scored at least 8 RIT points no matter what quintile he or she is in and that the sets of columns show comparative growth at each of the 13 Kennewick elementary schools during the single year of 2002-03. Some observations that have policy and administrative ramifications are:

1. **Few "below the line."** Ten schools had three or fewer students in the lowest two quintiles that were "below the line." This means that all but three or fewer students made annual growth in reading at third grade in 2002-03.

2. **Similarities between different schools.** Cascade, a school with 37% free or reduced-price lunch eligibility and no English language learners, has about the same number of students in the lowest 40% as three schools with a markedly higher profile of economic need: Eastgate (82%), Amistad (76%), and Edison (73%).

3. **Reading periods.** Does Cascade's shorter reading and remediation period at the second grade result in more students arriving at

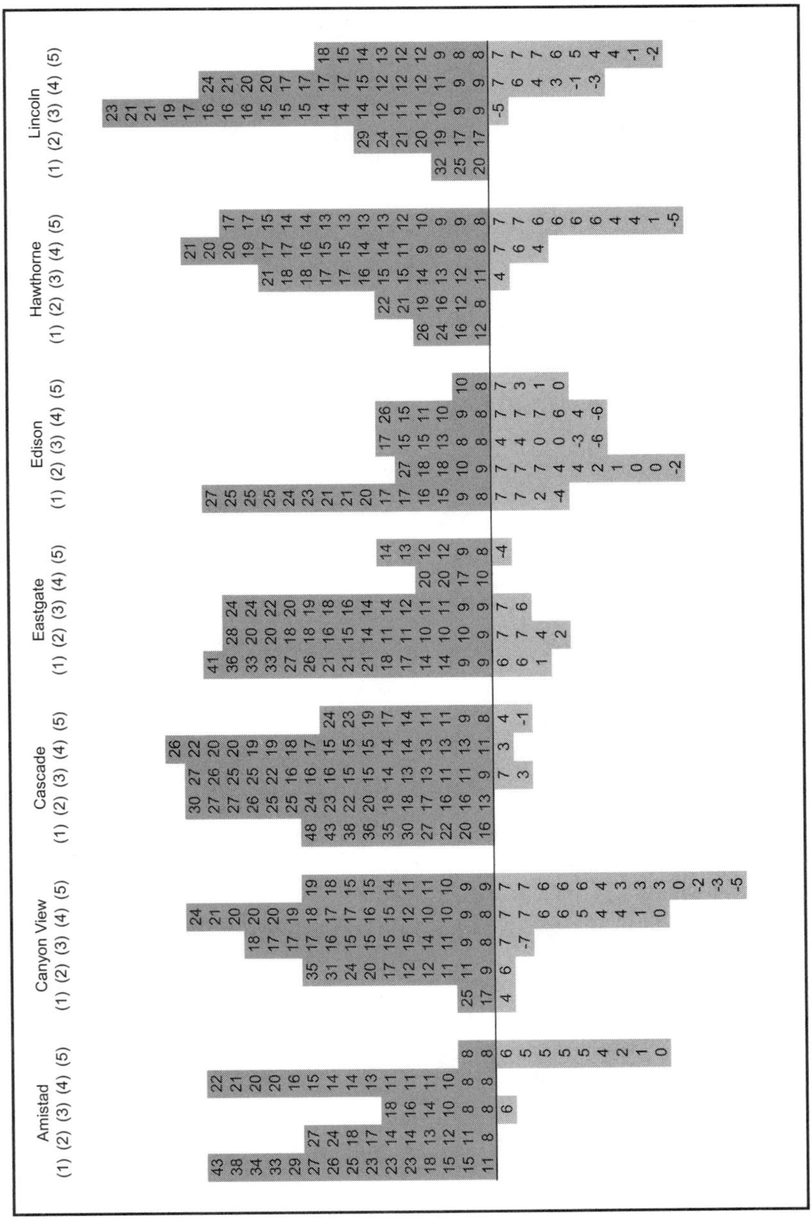

Figure 16.2. “Above and Below the Line” Growth Report for Reading by Student by Quintile at Third Grade at Kennewick's 13 Elementary Schools, 2002-03.

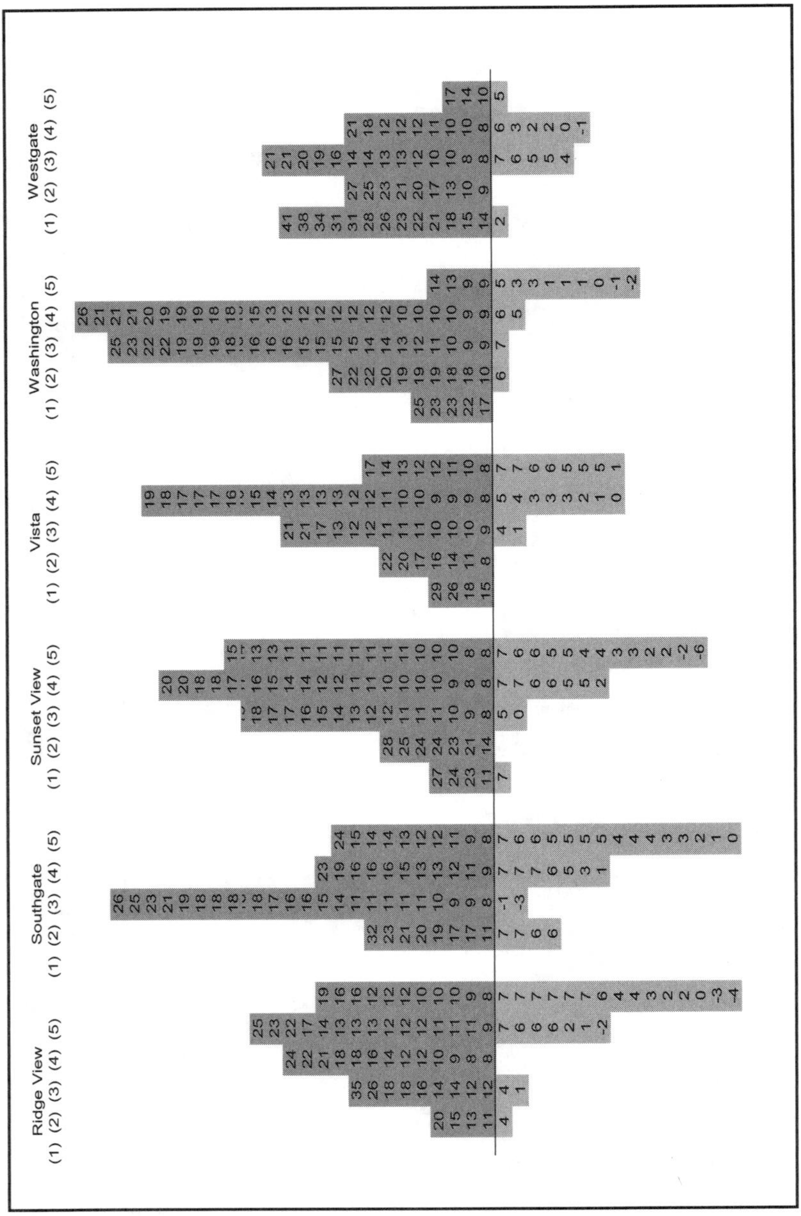

Figure 16.2. (Continued)

at third grade in lower quintiles? Slow rates of growth at first and second grade over two or three years will result in larger numbers of students far below grade-level targets, making it a more difficult task to catch up during third grade. Cascade has reached the 90% goal for the last three years in a row. It makes truly spectacular growth in its lowest two quintiles at third grade with its reliance, unique in the district, on one-on-one, some paid and some volunteer, non-certified tutoring.

4. Growth data. When students are in the lowest quintile in third grade, they are two years behind and must make triple annual growth to reach the minimum achievement level of the 90% goal. Without ever seeing the achievement data, it is evident from the growth information that most of the 30 students at Edison in the lowest two quintiles could not have reached the 90% reading goal in 2003. The good news is that growth jumped at Edison in 2003-04, resulting in 74% of Edison students reaching the goal in the spring of 2004.

The "Above or Below the Line" reports allow policy makers and administrators to see patterns at a glance. Non-statisticians can see the relationships almost as fast as the statisticians. Individual students are not lost in the averages, and individual classrooms can be analyzed in the same format.

These reports allow administrators and policy makers to verify at a glance whether there is numerical evidence that consistent annual growth in all students and catch-up growth in the lowest quintiles of elementary school students are occurring.

To achieve a near 90% at or above standard, Kennewick's elementary schools have created a growth pattern where nearly all students achieve annual growth (except some students in the high quintiles) and nearly all students in the lowest quintiles make double annual growth or more. Fifteen percent of students in the lowest two quintiles in Figure 16.1 made less than annual growth (7 or fewer RIT points of growth), 56% made one to two years of normal growth (8 to 15 RIT points of growth), and 29% made two or more years of normal growth.

Table 16.1
A Comparison: Kennewick and National Reading Growth at the Lowest Two Quintiles at Elementary Grades

	Kennewick	National	National	National
Grade	G-3	G-3	G-4	G-5
Quintile	Q 1-2	Q 1-2	Q 1-2	Q 1-2
More than two years growth	29%	31%	21%	15%
Between one and two years growth	56%	38%	30%	36%
Less than one year growth	12%	21%	28%	32%
No growth	3%	10%	15%	16%
Total	100%	100%	100%	100%

Note : National growth data for grades 3, 4, and 5 are based on about 25,000 students at each grade. Data provided by NWEA. Used by permission.

The national reading growth data shown in Table 16.1 differs significantly for Kennewick's third-grade reading growth pattern. Nationally, it appears that districts must produce annual growth as well as catch-up growth more consistently for more students in the lowest quintiles to mirror Kennewick's growth patterns. Between 30% and 48% of students in the two lowest quartiles are making less than annual growth. This observation is especially sobering when recalling that 8% of Kennewick students are still below the national 95% reading goal, that our district standard is set at the 37th percentile at third grade, while our state reading standard is set at the equivalent of the 53rd percentile. (See Figure 15.2.)

CHAPTER SEVENTEEN

SECONDARY SCHOOL SCHEDULING AND GROWTH REPORTS

"Elementary schools produce the same reading and math growth in two years that middle schools produce in three years."

— Dawn Adams, Director,
Kennewick School Board

No matter how well elementary schools do, middle and high schools across the country face a changed clientele. Kennewick has about 1,000 students at each grade level; and excluding transfers within the district, about 125 of them move in and about 125 move out of the district at each grade level in any given school year. Mobility among students is a deeper problem than poverty. Our stable students on free or reduced-priced lunches score nearly as well as those who are not.

For Kennewick, our most effective tools for change in the middle and high schools have been the Time and Focus Report in reading and math (Table 3.1), the Principals' Scheduling Report (Table 17.1), and the "Above/ Below the Line" Reports (Figure 17.2). The reports create tipping points—small, targeted pieces of data that cause rapid change by focusing on critical data points.

Our secondary schools, with master schedules and near-inflexible period lengths, have historically provided equal time in reading and math to those who are ahead as well as to those who are behind. The Principal Scheduling Report, in conjunction with the Time and Focus

Table 17.1
Summary of Middle School Principals' Scheduling Report, Fall 2002 and Fall 2003
Number of Students by Percentile and Grade in Two or More Math Classes

Fall 2002		Desert Hills			Highlands			Horse Heaven			Park			Percent of Students in Double Placement
Status	Grade	6	7	8	6	7	8	6	7	8	6	7	8	
Grade level	Students	221	242	177	119	161	116	199	191	176	199	191	94	
1 yr behind	Students	18	27	38	19	44	29	19	23	29	19	23	31	17%
	# in 2 classes	7	4	1	1	0	0	7	2	0	7	2	0	
1-2 yrs behind	Students	15	14	10	20	18	20	27	12	23	27	12	21	26%
	# in 2 classes	6	6	4	1	0	0	10	4	0	10	4	0	
2-3 yrs behind	Students	11	7	4	20	29	7	16	26	15	16	26	27	25%
	# in 2 classes	5	5	3	1	0	0	6	11	0	6	11	0	
3-4 yrs behind	Students	8	8	6	16	16	27	9	21	23	9	21	41	17%
	# in 2 classes	5	6	4	2	0	0	2	6	0	2	6	0	
Fall 2003		**Desert Hills**			**Highlands**			**Horse Heaven**			**Park**			
Status	Grade	6	7	8	6	7	8	6	7	8	6	7	8	
Grade level	Students	221	193	212	160	107	124	188	201	156	199	191	73	
1 yr behind	Students	26	32	49	28	21	63	34	31	50	19	23	33	45%
	# in 2 classes	15	21	0	19	8	10	5	24	27	7	2	20	
1-2 yrs behind	Students	19	11	28	22	15	26	22	15	17	27	12	23	81%
	# in 2 classes	15	7	0	19	8	2	17	15	17	10	4	21	
2-3 yrs behind	Students	13	10	8	17	10	14	4	16	16	16	26	8	75%
	# in 2 classes	3	4	0	15	6	5	4	14	15	6	11	6	
3-4 yrs behind	Students	8	10	6	18	10	16	11	18	16	9	21	26	54%
	# in 2 classes	1	1	0	9	3	4	11	15	16	2	6	14	

in 2 classes does not include after school remediation time and does not differentiate Resource Room time

Report and the Above-Below the Line Growth Reports, create the expectation that principals will double instructional time for those who are behind and that such interventionist scheduling should result in double annual growth. Certainly if instructional time were cut in half, we would expect growth to shrink to half as well.

Increasing the time spent in reading inevitably creates a series of staff and curriculum problems in secondary schools. Where does additional certified staff for reading or math come from and what about staff certified only in elective areas? What curricula can be used during the extra time for remediation?

Table 17.1 shows the change in Principal Scheduling Report data from fall 2002 to fall of 2003. The left column in the table shows students in categories at or above grade level, as well as one, two, three, and four years below grade level.[1] The percentages in the column on the far right indicate the students who were behind who received additional direct instructional time in math. In fall 2002, the percentages were:

> *"When placed in the same system, people, however different, tend to produce similar results."*
>
> — Peter M. Senge[2]

17% of students who were one year behind,
25-26% of students two-to-three years behind, and
17% of students more than three years behind.

The numbers dramatically increase by the second year as shown below. By the fall of 2003, the percentage of students receiving double instruction periods in math were:

45% of students who were one year behind,
75-81% of students two-to-three years behind, and
54% of students more than three years behind.

---

[1]For purposes of Table 17.1, students above the 50th percentile are at or above grade level; students between the 37th to 49th percentile are one year behind; 26th to 36th percentile are one to two years behind; 15th to 25th percentile are two to three years behind; and 0-14th percentile are three to four years behind.

[2]Peter M. Senge, *The Fifth Discipline: The Art and Practice of the Learning Organization* (New York: Doubleday Currency, 1990), 42.

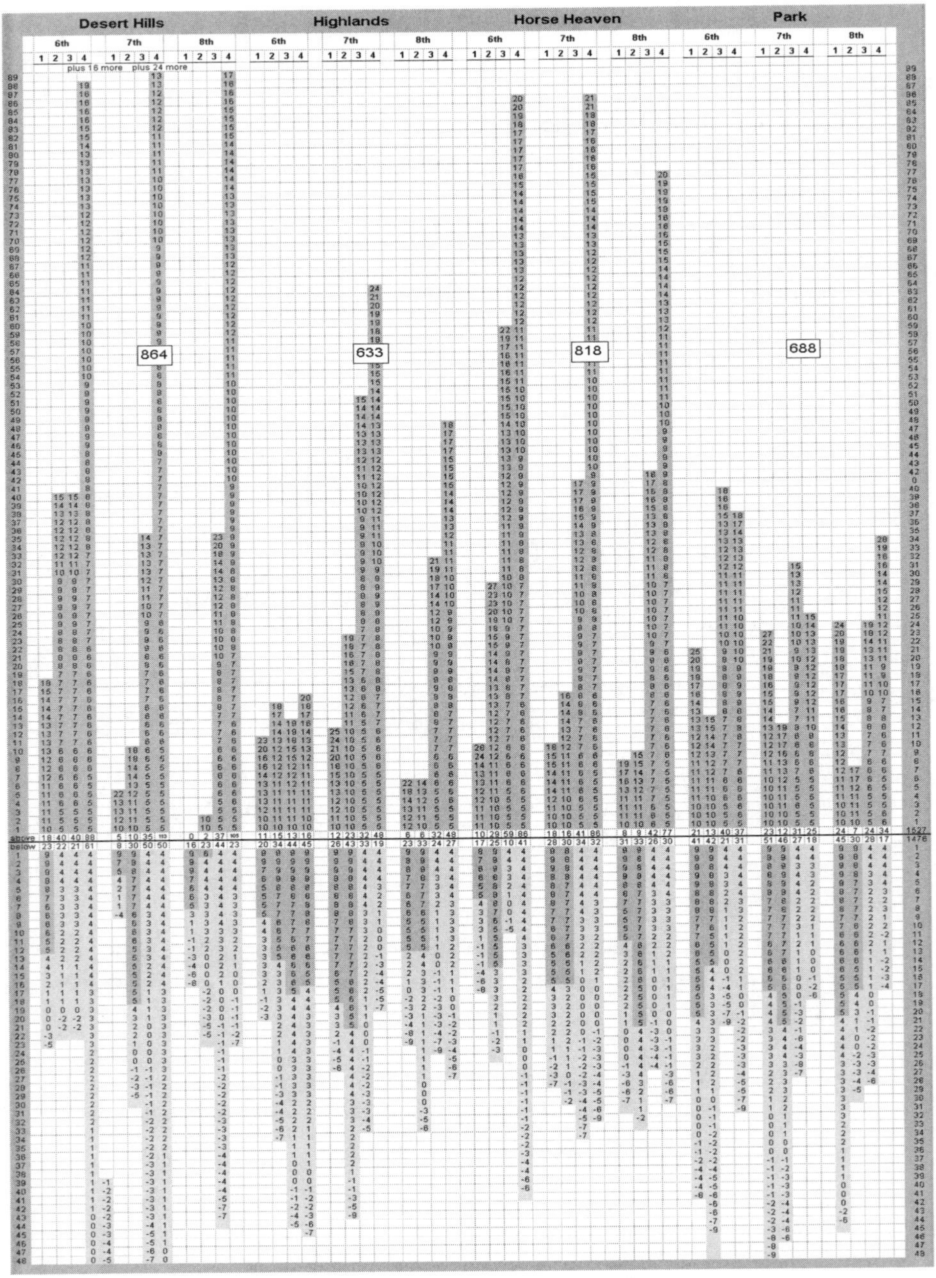

Figure 17.1. Above/Below the Line Math Growth Report for Four Middle Schools, 2003.

The report has focused attention on those below the 50th percentile resulting in more students receiving increased time in reading and math. The report is an extension of the basic concept of collecting the right data and keeping it in front of the right people. The report format clearly communicates policy intent that students who are behind in core subjects receive more direct instructional time in those subjects. It also highlights each school's decisions about the use of instructional time. Remedial time is highest and most consistent at Horse Heaven Hills. Phase-in at the eighth grade at Desert Hills is scheduled to occur in 2004-05.

The policy/report decision to increase direct instructional time creates program conflicts, especially for students in the 37th-50th percentile and just a few months to a year behind. Moving these students into remedial classes cuts into the established social studies curriculum. Administrators are trying to find ways to make additional growth in reading and math without cutting too deeply into other curricula at each of the middle schools. That is the good news. The bad news is that, without the additional time, the eighth-grade students advance into high school the following year where the catch-up growth required by our state standards will be even harder to achieve.

Achieving consistent annual and catch-up growth had not been a primary part of the job description of our middle and high school principals prior to 2001. The Time and Focus Reports, the Principal Scheduling Reports, and the Above/Below the Line Growth Reports create institutional changes within the system, raising the visibility of those responsibilities.

"The Above/Below the Line Report" in Figure 17.1 is like Figures 16.1 and 16.2 except that this figure sorts blocks of individual middle school students by fourths (quartiles) instead of fifths (quintiles) at the beginning of the year. The number inside the box shows math growth in RIT points during the school year.

After eliminating students for whom we had no beginning or ending scores, Figure 17.1 shows the 2,980 students who are left. Of that number, 52% are above the line and 48% are below the line. All students above the line have made annual growth or, if they were in the lowest two quartiles, double annual growth. Our education system is creating appropriate annual and catch-up growth for the students above the line.

However, 48% are below the line. Twelve percent of below-the-line students were in the lower first and second quartiles and achieved annual growth, but not double growth. They are shown below the line in dark gray. Of all students below the line, 36% did not make annual growth. Of additional concern are the 727 students (24%) in the upper third and fourth quartiles who did not make annual growth, including 260 students (9%) who made no growth at all.

One of the startling differences between our elementary and secondary schools is this: Many more students fail to make annual growth in middle school than in elementary school. Annual growth is not the norm in middle school. Annual growth and appropriate catch-up growth, as we began to apply the Targeted Accelerated Growth (TAG) loop in 2002-03 in Kennewick middle schools, occurs with only 52% of the students. Annual growth is no longer a given.

In addition, large numbers of students in all quartiles make less than annual growth. Students who have traditionally done better than most of their peers suddenly make less than half of normal growth. Rate of growth flattens nationwide at sixth, seventh, and eighth grades. Middle school students, on average, take three years to make the same amount of growth they would have made in two years in elementary school.[3]

The national decrease in rate of growth is visually displayed in Figures 14.1 and 14.2. The slopes of the lines showing rate of growth visibly flatten in both reading and math at sixth, seventh, and eighth grades. (See Chapter 14.)

Tables 17.2 and 17.3 show the amount of math growth by quartile in Kennewick and at a national level at sixth, seventh, and eight grades

[3]This is not a new finding. What appears to be a surge in the scores of students from other countries at middle school is actually a drop in the rate of growth in U.S. middle school students. "The mathematics and science performance of the United States relative to this group of [17] nations was lower for eighth-graders in 1999 than it was for fourth-graders four years earlier, in 1995." National Center for Education Statistics, U.S. Department of Education, *Pursuing Excellence: Comparisons of International Mathematics and Science Achievement from a U.S. Perspective, 1995 and 1999.* NCES 2001-028. (Washington, DC: U.S. Government Printing Office, 2000), Figures 18-19.

and reflect in tabular form what the Above/Below the Line report showed. The numbers are sobering. There is a huge range of growth within each quartile at each grade level. Large numbers of students are actually falling further below state standards and will continue to do so without significant intervention.

Table 17.2
Amount of Math Growth by Quartile by Grade in Kennewick Middle School Students, 2002-03

	Grade 6				Grade 7				Grade 8			
	Q1	Q2	Q3	Q4	Q1	Q2	Q3	Q4	Q1	Q2	Q3	Q4
Growth Measured in Yrs												
More than 2 years	37	30	31	28	31	29	17	32	25	17	22	35
Between 1-2 years	29	33	37	34	34	36	36	39	33	37	30	37
Zero to one year	18	23	22	26	19	22	23	20	24	29	24	18
No growth	16	14	10	14	16	13	24	9	18	17	24	10
Total	100%	100%	100%	100%	100%	100%	100%	100%	100%	100%	100%	100%

Table 17.3
Amount of Math Growth by Quartile by Grade in a National Sample of Middle School Students, 2002-03

	Grade 6				Grade 7				Grade 8			
	Q1	Q2	Q3	Q4	Q1	Q2	Q3	Q4	Q1	Q2	Q3	Q4
Growth Measured in Yrs												
More than 2 years	39	35	31	28	38	33	31	20	37	32	26	10
Between 1-2 years	24	25	26	27	24	26	27	30	24	26	28	24
Zero to one year	16	18	20	20	16	18	19	22	16	19	22	25
No growth	20	23	23	24	22	23	22	28	22	22	25	41
Total	100%	100%	100%	100%	100%	100%	100%	100%	100%	100%	100%	100%

Tables 17.2 and 17.3 were developed from Northwest Evaluation Association data. Used with permission.

A variety of factors influence middle school growth. Curriculum issues like the introduction of only 20-30% new math concepts a year and a reluctance to teach algebra account for some of the decline in math growth. The focus on literature instead of literacy may account for some of the decreased reading growth. The loss of student accountability as a student moves from one teacher to five teachers may account for part of this drop in achievement. However, the sheer number of middle school students making little or no growth clearly depresses the average quartile growth.

Perhaps as more national growth data become available from the NWEA, skilled researchers will be able to tease out the variables, which account for the decline of middle school growth. The next chapter explores district assessment systems and ways it can focus on growth data.

CHAPTER EIGHTEEN

Assessing Your Assessment System

"If I see farther than most men, it is because I stand on the shoulders of giants."

— Sir Isaac Newton

Kennewick's success is built on the invisible shoulders of the Northwest Evaluation Association. NWEA's precise assessments give us a huge advantage over most other districts by providing accurate data about our students who are most at risk. We get information fast, and the growth and achievement data allow us to build sophisticated reporting platforms to compare by students, classrooms, and schools. It is one of the most user-friendly assessment systems in the world.

An over-statement? We don't think so. Kennewick partners closely with the NWEA because it's the most powerful assessment system we've found. We're not saying you have to use it; but if your assessment system isn't telling you what NWEA is telling us, maybe you should start shopping.

The Northwest Evaluation Association has developed a bank of 20,000 test questions in language usage, reading, mathematics, and science. The questions are weighted according to difficulty from the beginning of second grade through high school, with each assigned a difficulty level along an equal interval growth scale. The scale has been developed using a theoretical model devised by Georg Rasch (1901-80), a Danish mathematician who devised a series of social science measures adaptable to education assessment.

Unlike percentile or rank order scales that compare fourth graders only to other fourth graders, the Rasch scale runs vertically across grades. In the Rasch model, the intervals are equal, so that each point of growth along the interval is substantially equal to every other point of growth. Each student's score is recorded as a *Rasch Unit* (RIT). Using the scale, a single student's growth can be measured over a decade, or this year's third graders in a single elementary school can be compared against the third-grade class's scores over the last four years. Percentile and rank order information is also available.

"The Rasch scale, now stable for over 20 years, not only allows you to measure achievement at each grade level and annual growth each year, it will allow you to compare Tony's achievement and his children's achievement and growth using the same scale."

— Susan Smoyer,
Executive Vice President, NWEA

NWEA administers its tests in two ways. The achievement level tests are paper-and-pencil, multiple-choice tests that are machine-graded in-district within three to seven days. Each student is given a pre-test (or his or her prior test results are consulted). Based on the score, the instructor gives him or her one of eight overlapping tests in which the 50 questions are targeted to the student's grade. Thus, the student's achievement, as well as the student's growth from the last time he or she took the test, is measured very carefully. The older achievement level tests are used primarily by districts who signed on with NWEA prior to its development of an Internet-enabled testing system in 1999.

"Assessment systems in over 90% of our nation's schools do not capture growth data or scores that are accurate for each child."

— Allan Olson,
Executive Director, NWEA

The newer-style tests are called Measures of Academic Progress (MAP) and are administered on the computer. The student is given an initial question based on prior scores or, if no score is available, given one of typical difficulty for the student's grade level. Depending on whether the student answers the question correctly, a mathematical algorithm selects a slightly easier or slightly more difficult question. The process continues as the program adaptively selects questions to determine with increasing precision the student's achievement level.

Both types of tests can be refreshed merely by exchanging a now-familiar question for another one of equal difficulty assigned from the same Rasch interval. Thus, teachers can "teach to the test"—the kind of instructional alignment to well-defined benchmarks we all want—but cannot "teach the test," a process that skews information about what students actually know.

How Good Are Your Assessments?

Thanks to ESEA, Kennewick's primary focus for the next decade is exactly the same as every school district's in the United States: achieving adequate annual growth for all students and catch-up growth for students below the state standard in core subjects. What do you know about where you stand? May we comparison-shop for a few minutes? Six questions may clarify the capability of your assessment system.

1. Does your current assessment system provide your board, superintendent, principals, and teachers with a clear way to determine the amount of student growth that has occurred this year in reading and math in grades 3-12?

Such growth, it goes without saying, is nearly essential to achieve compliance under NCLB legislation. It needs to identify three levels:

Which students failed to make annual growth?
Which students made annual growth?
Which students made double or triple annual growth?

> *"A lot of national voices deride frequent testing, but almost none of them have created or operate a high performance public school system."*
> — Linda Clark, Superintendent, Meridian, Idaho, District (serving 26,500 students)

Identifying a lack of annual growth is critical in a public school system whose primary historical function has been to create annual growth. Students who make no growth or less than annual growth fall behind. A 60th percentile fifth-grade mathematics student who makes no growth in the sixth and seventh grade will fall to the 35th percentile.[1] Lack of consistent annual growth in a K-12 education system is like pumping water through a rusty water pipe. Good growth from one year leaks out the next.[2]

Assuring annual growth must be the norm. If not, a student who is on grade level at second grade but experiences three years without annual growth will score three years behind on the college entrance SAT eight years later. A year without reasonable growth puts a youngster at risk. Multiple stagnant–growth years are devastating.

However, for students below grade level, catch-up growth is now essential. The only possible way for students who are three years below grade-level to catch up is for the sutdent to achieve annual growth plus three extra years of growth either in a single year—which is highly improbable—or spread the catch-up growth across several years. Either way, does your current assessment system capture this information?

Let us stress that we are not asking *can* your system provide the needed data or whether vendors *say* it will deliver these three kinds of growth data, but whether it currently *is* giving you these crucial data?

Here's another way to think about this first question. Do you as boards, superintendents, administrators, and teachers talk about how far individual students are behind in grade-level equivalents? How many did not achieve annual growth? How many achieved annual growth? How many are making annual plus catch-up growth? If you are not discussing compliance with your state's standards in these terms, the data from your assessment system probably don't let you. You should consider an upgrade.

---

[1] Students in the 60th percentile in math at the end of fifth grade have scored 221 on the RIT scale. Students scoring 221 at the end of sixth grade (one year later with no growth) are in the 46th percentile. Students scoring 221 at the end of seventh grade (two years with no growth) are now in the 35th percentile. See *RIT Scale Norms, for Use with Achievement Level Tests and Measures of Academic Progress*, August 2002, Appendix A-18, Spring Mathematics RIT Score to Percentile Rank Conversion Table.

[2] While averages are stable over time, actual individual student growth varies from year to year. It is not perfectly linear. As seen in Chapter 17, 19% of students grow less than half of a normal year in math at fourth grade, and 21% make between a half and a full year. Eliminating these individual valleys in favor of sustained, steady growth is what good instruction is about.

2. What is the turnaround time between administering the test and getting back the results?

With the NWEA computerized, adaptive MAP tests, the report to the student is instantaneous—about 10 seconds after completing the test. Twenty-four hours later, the teacher has the results, analyzed by class. The principal gets results for the school within two days. For spring and fall testing, Kennewick still uses NWEA's paper-pencil achievement level tests, which we score in-district. Results are currently available within three to five days. In Kennewick, teachers can see, believe, and own the fall-to-spring growth made by every student in their classroom. If your results aren't available at comparable speeds and available at the teacher's desk top, you should consider an upgrade.

States and district central offices run at a much slower pace. Many assessment procedures, including the national SAT tests, take 90–120 days to score and make the reports available. This lag makes them nearly worthless for classroom adjustments and individualized instruction, but they are still timely enough for use by states or by district central offices to determine overall growth by school and for annual accountability functions.

3. How relevant is your assessment?

We used to hear our teachers and principals lament, "The test doesn't test what we teach." We still hear it about some of the standardized state-mandated tests. Because the NWEA's tests are curriculum-based, we almost never hear it about the NWEA assessments. The indexing of NWEA items is currently being dramatically upgraded to improve the alignment of MAP tests with state standards. Do your teachers feel that your assessment system is giving them good information or just wasting their instruction time?

4. How accurate is your assessment system?

Most standardized tests have 50 questions, perhaps 70% of which are clustered at grade level plus or minus three fourths of a year. These 35 questions accurately measure students who fall within the 1.5-year span around grade level. In other words, about 11.6 questions are targeted toward determining each of the three half-year intervals making up this 1.5-year span. There is another 2.5-year range or five half-year intervals of student's skills *below* the focus of these tests. There is another two-year range of four half-year intervals *above* the focus of these tests. Only 15 questions are left to test within these nine half-year intervals. The difference between 11.6 questions and .5 questions per half-year grade interval is the ratio of the accuracy of most tests (except NWEA's)[3] inside and outside the focus area. Are your tests least accurate for the students who are furthest behind, the lowest 40%? Are you getting your poorest data for students for whom you need the most precision?

5. Does your assessment system accommodate sophisticated reporting platforms?

Can you identify a student's achievement this year and his or her achievement last year, calculate the intervening growth, and compare that growth to the aggregate growth in his or her class, school, and district? Can you compare his or her achievement to the state standard and calculate how long it will take to achieve the state standard, given his or her current rate of growth? Can you replicate those calculations in terms that parents, teachers, board members, superintendents, and even the student can understand? Are your data in a single database with the capability of easy retrieval of specialized views like growth per class, growth by quartile, or growth over time?

The prime, untapped users of growth data are students themselves. In Kennewick, an emerging feature in middle-school classes where students make extraordinary growth is their engagement with the data. They know their beginning scores. They know their growth target, and growth is incentivized. As a Kennewick priority, we are developing report formats so students can see their growth over their entire school career and chart exactly where they have been, where they are, and where they need to go. Does your testing system accommodate reporting platforms that are sophisticated enough to satisfy your broadening range of users?

---

[3] NWEA's instant online scoring and selection of the next test question based on the prior result targets most questions within the student's ability range.

6. Does everything work together?

When your car sits in your driveway because it doesn't work, the problem often lies in only a few—or maybe only one—of its systems. Perhaps the battery is low, so it doesn't start. Perhaps the battery is fine, but it's out of gas. Perhaps a clogged gas line means that it will die at critical times. While it sits, 90% of the other systems in the car are working just fine. You still don't use the car, because all these systems have to work together. The same is equally true of your data system. Do student data drive most of the decisions in the district? Or do most of your data just sit? If you don't see data surrounding most student decisions, look closely to see if critical parts of your data system just aren't working.[4]

To sum up, we hope that these questions clarify what a district assessment system should look like. Often there is no system at all—just a hodgepodge of different standard tests using different scales, different assumptions, and different testing times. They have limited utility for shaping instruction and virtually none at all for planning sustained, consistent growth.

---

[4]It is important to distinguish between a non-functional assessment system and a data-hostile or data-indifferent school culture. Data-hostile cultures tend to make their decisions based solely on "intuitive" and "feels good, feels bad" methods. Developing a culture that values data requires superintendents, boards, and principals who continually ask questions like, "So what data support your position?" or "How many students in your lowest two quartiles did not make annual growth last year?" or "What percentage of your below-grade-level students made enough catch-up growth to be at the standard within the next three years?" Data do not use themselves and can sit unused in a perfectly good assessment system in a data-indifferent or a data-hostile school culture.

PART THREE

Parent Accountability: Targeting the Source of the Achievement Gap

In Part One, we explored how schools, districts, and states can assure annual growth for all students and provide catch-up growth for those who are behind.

In Part Two, we examined how far students are behind, the national rationale and mandate for catching them up, and the various data systems and report formats that help Kennewick schools accomplish this purpose.

In Part Three, we identify how and when most students get behind in the first place. Most importantly, we explain a cost-effective alternative by which public schools can narrow the achievement gap before children enter kindergarten. Reacting to the problem after a child has started kindergarten is very expensive and much less effective.

At an average adult reading speed of about 300 words a minute, including sidebars, kickers, and footnotes, and spending 5 minutes on each figure or table, you can read Part Three in 1 hour and 4 minutes.

CHAPTER NINETEEN

A Low Stakes Assessment of the Achievement Gap

"It ain't what we don't know that hurts us.
It's what we know that ain't so."

— Josh Billings, American humorist

Public schools have taken a lot of blame for causing the achievement gap. Large numbers of students of every ethnic background read and have math skills that are two or three years or more behind the "average, 50th percentile, grade level" student. When did they get behind? How do we fix this problem? In keeping with the spirit of the times, this section begins with a short, five-question assessment.

Circle the Correct Answer

True or False 1. Most students enter kindergarten with virtually identical literacy and math skills.

True or False 2. To the extent that there may be academic differences at kindergarten, each ethnic group is proportionately represented at each level of readiness on the first day of kindergarten.

True or False 3. Public schools create the achievement gap in reading and math slowly and over time by failing to accomplish as much growth in some students as in other students.

True or False 4. Low SAT and ACT scores, especially among ethnic minorities, are caused by the failure of public schools to create equal growth over time.

True or False 5. National and state public school officials do not defend the public schools on this issue because there is no defense. Ineffective public schools cause the gap in achievement between quartiles and between ethnic groups.

1. False, 2. False, 3. False, 4. False, 5. False.

Our analysis of the data, set out in the following chapters, indicates that each of these statements is false. Instead, the data clearly establish that about 40% of students enter kindergarten with language and math skills typical of two, three, and four year olds. Or, to put it differently, almost half of incoming students are one to three years behind their "average" peers on the first day of school. Within this "below average" group, ethnic minorities are over-represented about three to one.

Even in kindergarten, some groups of students achieve at a higher level than "average." Some of these children enter school with the skills of first and second graders. In short, the children in today's average kindergarten classrooms possess a range of skills typical of children between ages two through eight.

Public schools create a year of growth during each year for most students. Thus, the incoming range of skills continues through middle and high school. The range is reflected on achievement tests at every grade level. It is surprising that the analysis of K-12 data didn't quantify the six-year gap in reading and the four-year gap in math and identify its source 50 years ago.

Yet the insights should not be ignored merely because they come late. The focus of the 21st century's educational reform is primarily to catch up the 40% of students who enter kindergarten behind, then stay behind year after year.

The achievement gap has its origins in a child's early years. The home really is a child's first classroom. Between birth and age five is the most leveraged opportunity for schools and parents, especially ethnic minority parents, to prevent children from falling behind. It will not take care of no-growth years especially in middle school. However, when parents become skillful in preparing their children to enter kindergarten with age appropriate pre-literacy and pre-math skills, the achievement gap that haunts public schools will be greatly diminished.

Merely equalizing the difference between achievement levels at each quartile between Caucasians and ethnic minorities—the focus of considerable discussion—is an empty success, when all of the lower quartile and most of the second quartile of students are still below most states' minimum standards.[1]

On a more practical note, the No Child Left Behind legislation gives the public schools until 2014 to gradually catch students up at every level. After 2014, we will no longer have until 10th grade to catch up those who come to us already lagging. Ninety-five percent of students must be at grade level three or four years after kindergarten—by third or fourth grade. School districts can either choose to enlist the help of parents and family members to achieve normal growth during a child's early years or to accept full responsibility for the child's academic outcomes and the necessary catch-up growth if they choose to "go it alone."

[1]The term "achievement gap" is often used to refer to the racial gap in achievement (i.e. the disproportionate number of ethnic minorities scoring below Caucasians in most achievement tests). More frequently, the term now refers to the number of students of all ethnicities scoring below state standards, a numerically larger problem.

CHAPTER TWENTY

THE SOURCE OF THE ACHIEVEMENT GAP

"The data suggest that about 40% of students enter kindergarten with language and math skills typical of two, three, and four year olds. They are already two to three years behind 'average' kindergarten children on the first day of school."

— Lynn Fielding

Students enter kindergarten with a range of academic skills that predetermine their likely success or failure in school. Students show a four-year range in math skills and a six-year range in reading skills by the beginning of second grade. When and where did these differences occur? Could they have developed in kindergarten and first grade? Four factors indicate that they did not.

Characteristics of Entering Kindergartners' Academic Abilities

1. The wide range of incoming scores. Four measures of abilities most accurately predict whether an entering kindergarten student will read at or above grade level by the end of third grade: alphabet letter recognition, alphabet letter sound recognition, phonemic awareness, and the ability to print his or her first name.[1]

When Kennewick began testing its incoming kindergarten students in fall of 1999 using these four measures, we found a startlingly

[1]Catherine E. Snow, Susan M. Burns, and Peg Griffin, eds., *Preventing Reading Difficulties in Young Children* (Washington, DC: National Academy Press, 1998), 108-33. See especially Table 4, p. 108.

broad range of skills among our incoming kindergartners. (Figure 20.1) In the fall of 2000, when we had worked most of the bugs out of the testing, 23% of our 1,000 incoming kindergarten students scored 9 or fewer points out of 98, and 50% of our students scored under 30 out of 98 points. Our district norm for typical kindergartners would be scores in the 30-35% range, right where 50% of our kindergartners were. In other words, 23% of our very low scorers and 50% of our under-30 scorers, who comprise the first and second quartiles of the assessment, are below the standard on the first week of kindergarten. Our data mirror those of other districts that also assess entering kindergartners.

A new student who can identify a lower case "a" and upper case "A" and knows that they make an "aaah" as in "apple" sound scores three points on Kennewick's assessment.

On the other end of this incoming kindergarten spectrum, we have students who know all the alphabet letters and their sounds and who can isolate most of the individual sounds within words. Several of them are reading. Why are these students better prepared?

When a child is young, phonological awareness is generally more predictive than I.Q of a student's success in learning to read.[2] On entering kindergarten, students who have high phonological awareness will be able to hear ending sounds of words (rhymes), hear beginning sounds in words (alliteration), and tap out breaks in words (syllables).

The shaded areas within each bar in Figure 20.1 show achievement by ethnicity. There is a nearly equal distribution between Caucasians and other ethnic groups in the lowest 50% of students. However, when we look at just the ethnic minority populations, about 76-80% of these students start kindergarten scoring less than 30. Incoming kindergarten data from Maryland, Florida, and Idaho show similar ranges in scores with correspondingly similar breakdown by ethnicity.[3]

[2]See J. K. Torgesen et al., "Preventing Reading Failure in Young Children with Phonological Processing Disabilities: Group and Individual Responses to Instruction," *Journal of Educational Psychology* 91 (1999): 579-93.

[3]School Readiness Baseline Information, February 2002, Maryland State Department of Education 2002, Appendix B (http://www.marylandpublicschools.org); Florida Department of Education, Florida School Readiness Uniform Screening System: State Report of District Results, Fall 2003; Idaho State Department of Education, IRI Proficiency Levels, Winter 2002, State Report (http://www.sde.state.id.us).

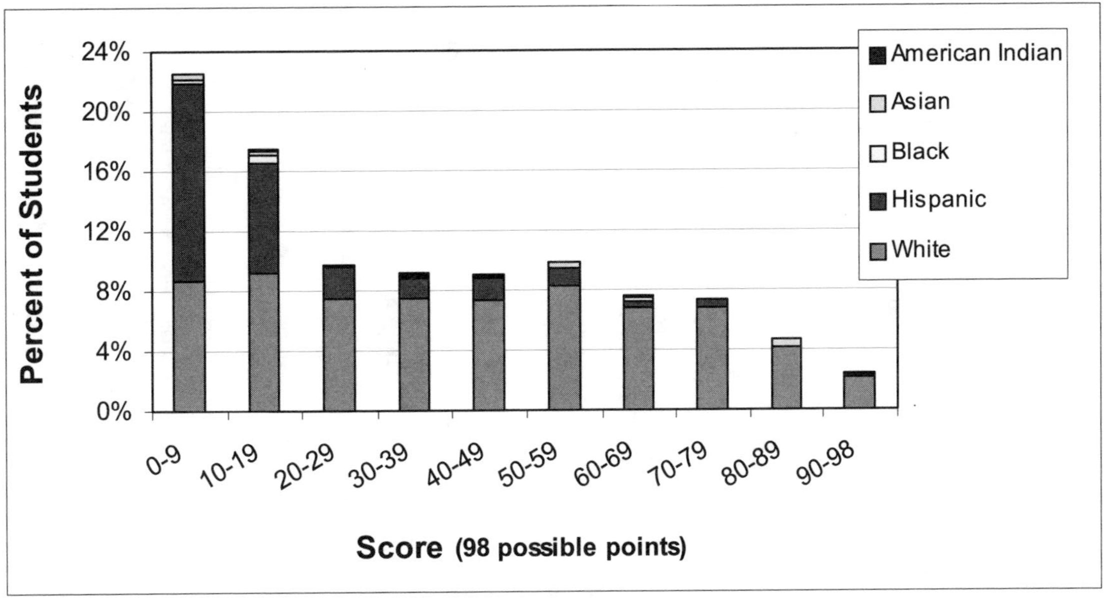

Figure 20.1. Kennewick Entering Kindergarten Scores, Fall 2000.
This figure shows the scores of 1,000 entering kindergarten students in Kennewick's 13 elementary schools in September of 2000. The assessment measures a student's skill in naming upper and lower case alphabet letters (52 points), identifying their sounds (26 points), identifying rhyme or ending word sounds (10 points), and identifying alliteration or beginning word sounds (10 points). The scores within each bar or point range are broken down by ethnicity. A score of 30-35 is considered an age-appropriate level for entering kindergarten students. Half (50%) of Kennewick's students scored fewer than 30 points.

In summary, there is a wide range of skill levels the first week of kindergarten, and perhaps three-quarters of ethnic minorities enter kindergarten with skills in the 1st-40th percentiles.

These data show a wide range of incoming skill levels as well as a disproportional representation of low-skill levels in ethnic minorities. Do these data clearly establish a four-to-six year gap before kindergarten? Probably not. However, there are other clear indications in the data for the four-to-six-year gap in reading and math prior to kindergarten.

2. Rank Order. When we compare the rank order of kindergarten students in the fall of 2000 with their rank order as third graders, we find that students who scored low, middle, or high in kindergarten are likely to maintain those same low, middle, or high rankings at first, second, and third grade. While socio-economic status is often cited as a strong correlation to reading difficulties, the correlation of incoming kindergarten scores to third grade reading, when measured on an individual student basis, (.58) is more than twice as strong as the correlation with socio-economic status as measured by free and reduced-price lunch counts (.22-.25).[4]

3. Skill Scales. Skill scales offer a non-statistical way to look at the same issue. We can compare the skills of actual incoming kindergarten children with literacy and math abilities typical of children from age two through third grade. Skills of incoming kindergartners form a continuum starting at a level typical of two year olds and continuing on up. (See Chapter 23 for age-specific examples.) While

[4] When the rank order of Kennewick students entering kindergarten in the fall 1999 assessment is compared to rank order of third graders according to their scores on NWEA functional level tests in the fall of 2003, the correlation was .58, a correlation which holds over most other three-year ranges, i.e., when rank order of entering third graders scores are compared with their rank order as entering sixth graders. (See Appendix H.) For less statistically inclined readers, if the pre-literacy achievement scores of 100 entering kindergarten students were sorted from high to low, and their reading scores as entering third graders were again sorted from high to low, the correlation would be 1.0 if the order of the students between kindergarten and third grade was identical. Such a correlation is nonexistent in education. A .58 correlation is a very high correlation. By comparison, the much talked about correlation of free or reduced price lunch count of schools and their achievement scores is about .68 when the *school* is used as the unit of analysis (i.e., the average SES of a school or district is compared against the average achievement of the school or district). However, when the unit of measurement is the *student* (i.e., the student's SES is compared to the student's achievement), the correlation is much weaker: .22-.25. Snow, Burns, and Griffin, *Preventing Reading Difficulties in Young Children,* 126. That is, the correlation of incoming kindergarten scores to third-grade reading is more than twice as strong as socio-economic status.

we have not done skill-scale studies of low-scoring incoming kindergarten children, our teachers' anecdotal observations are that students who score from 0 to 30 on the kindergarten tests have language and math skills described in the skill continuum in Chapter 21 as typical of two, three, and four year olds.

4. Input Factors. The input factors that create growth in grades two through five are present in kindergarten to first grade as well. These inputs include virtually identical structure,[5] similar curriculum, teachers, and supervision. K-1 resources are typically reallocated toward the lower quartiles in the form of extended day kindergarten for those who are behind, preferential morning scheduling, smaller class size where students are need-grouped, and over-allocation of instructor and aide time. The input factors at K-1 provide no rationale to suppose that the six-year gap occurs during K-1.

So what we know is that there is a four-year achievement gap in math skills and a six-year gap in reading by the beginning of second grade. All available data[6] indicate a similar range in measurable incoming kindergarten reading skills, a rank order that is quite stable during kindergarten and first grade, and a similar or higher reallocation of resources to the lowest quartiles. These indicators taken together provide *no evidence that the kindergarten and first-grade years cause or increase the gap,* and provide some argument that these years may actually decrease the gap, at least in literacy, and probably in math as well.

---

[5]Classrooms, class size, length of instruction periods, and even recess are similar.

[6]"Settling in" research by Jeni Riley, professor of education at London University, is one of the few pieces of research showing differential rates of learning during kindergarten and first grade. Her research shows that students' ability to "settle in" to kindergarten strongly affects their ability to learn to read. However, the same research acknowledges large differences in starting points among students and identifies "settling in" as an independent variable that cuts across all quartiles regardless of starting points. "Those children who did not adjust positively and quickly to school after the first half term as judged by their teachers, were four times less likely to be reading by the end of the year—whatever their skills on entry." Jeni Riley, *The Teaching of Reading: The Development of Literacy in the Early Years of School* (London: Paul Chapman Publishing, 1996), 5. As important as the "settling in" research is, it is does not provide evidence that the six-year gap is caused or increased by students failing to settle in.

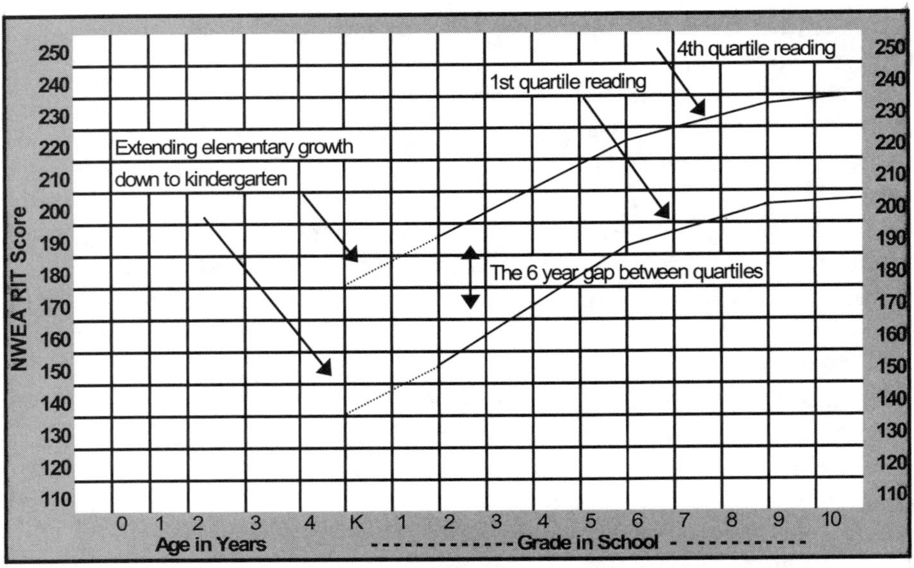

Figure 20.2. Extending Grades Two to Five Growth and Achievement Data to Kindergarten. The solid black lines from second through tenth grade capture the growth and achievement of the first and fourth quartiles, and the dotted line projects the rate of elementary growth downward for first grade and to the beginning of kindergarten. The solid lines are based on the NWEA database of over a million students. The dotted lines are projections.

Extending the Growth Curves to Kindergarten

If you can conclude, as we have, that

- A six-year gap in literacy and a four-year gap in math exist at the beginning of second grade,
- These gaps are not created in kindergarten or first grade, and
- The growth rates during this period are similar to the growth rates in grades two through five,

then the kindergarten and first grade growth rates can be graphically illustrated on the NWEA scale. Using the national first and fourth quartile information already presented in Figure 13.1, we can extend the growth curves from fifth to second grade, and then back to the beginning of kindergarten (Figure 20.2).

"Children who acquire basic skills during their early years have a big advantage when they start school. They start ahead and stay ahead year after year."

— Nancy Kerr

Extending the growth and achievement curves, with their four- and six-year spans to kindergarten, parallels the findings of Jeni Riley, head of Primary Education at the Institute of Education, University of London, who observes:

> It is common to find within a kindergarten classroom a five-year range in children's literacy-related skills and functioning. What this means is that some kindergartners may have skills characteristic of the typical three-year-old, while others might be functioning at the level of the typical eight-year-old.[7]

So where did this difference in achievement occur? When high-performing five year olds enter kindergarten with language and math skills typical of eight-year-olds, they have made eight years of progress during their five preschool years at home. On the average, this is 1.6 years of growth per year.[8]

Figure 20.3 captures most of the essential and known elements of student growth from birth to age 16. Growth in the top quartile is nearly three times that of the lowest quartile in language and math during the first five years of life, resulting in a six-year span in emergent literacy and math skills by kindergarten. Thereafter, despite superior skills in the upper quartiles, annual growth in all quartiles is the norm. Somewhere between 70-80% of ethnic minorities are in the lowest two quartiles at kindergarten.

When students enter kindergarten with language and math skills of typical three year olds, they have made only three years of progress

[7]Dr. Jeni Riley, as quoted in a joint position statement of the International Reading Association and the National Association for the Education of Young Children: *Learning to Read and Write: Developmentally Appropriate Practices for Young Children* (1998) retrieved on October 15, 2003 from International Reading Association at http://www.reading.orgpositions/devel young.html.
[8]Eight years' growth divided by five chronological years equals 1.6 years of growth per year.

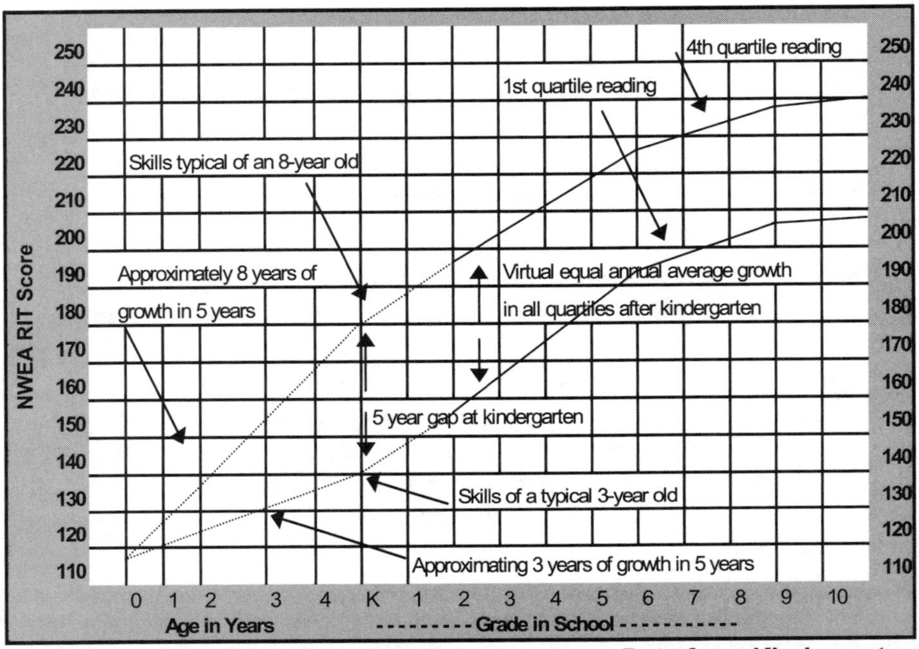

Figure 20.3. Extending Growth and Achievement Data from Kindergarten to Birth.

in five years or an average of .6 years of progress per year.[9] Using the NWEA elementary average of 8 RIT points of growth per year, we can now graphically approximate quartile growth from birth to five by providing for 24 points of growth (three years) for the lowest quartile and 64 points of growth (eight years) for the top quartile over the five years from birth to entering kindergarten[10] for emergent literacy skills.[11]

---

[9]Three years of growth divided by five chronological years equals .6 years of growth per year.

[10]The difference between the midpoints of the first and fourth quartile at the beginning of second grade is the difference between 156 and 196 on the RIT scale or 40 RIT points. See *RIT Scale Norms: For Use with Achievement Level Tests and Measures of Academic Progress, 2002,* Appendix A-2 and A-3. If we extend the curves downward to the beginning of kindergarten, they encompass the difference of 140 and 180 or the same 40 points of growth. Assuming that the 40-point span represents the same five-year spread that it does starting at second grade, growth each year is 8 points. Three years' growth in five years will be represented by 24 points, and eight years' growth will be represented by 64 points. The starting point five years earlier is 116.

[11] Perhaps we should clarify what we are *not* saying as well. There are dozens of other skills that a young child could learn from birth to five including heightened taste, smell, reflex speed, and mobility. Many of these skills have great survival value in other cultures and even in our own culture. There is no evidence that the learning rate of the top quartile would be three times the rate of the bottom if we were measuring skills other than emergent literacy and math. We focus on emergent reading and math skills because of their importance in how our society is currently organized.

What we are trying to do in Kennewick is to shift the quartiles upward. We are working to assure that less than 15% of students enter kindergarten below grade level, that only 10% of students are below the 38th percentile by third grade, and that 5% are below the historical 50th percentile by fifth grade. This is a dramatic shift in the historical curves described in Figures 14.1 and 14.2.

Figure 20.3 invites some less obvious observations as well.

First, the rate of growth of the highest quartile is about three times that of the lowest quartile during the first five years of life.[12]

Second, ages zero to five is the only place where the rate of growth is significantly different between the first and fourth quartiles, until students begin dropping out in high school.

Third, by 2013 when the phase-in period for NCLB is finished, elementary schools will be faced with making up the difference between low quartile growth during the preschool years and state standards in reading and math in K-3 or K-4.

Perhaps we should conclude this chapter where we started. *Public schools do not create the achievement gap.* Public schools merely maintain the gap. They add to its already large range in math at the lowest quartile. Figure 20.2 is a graphic representation consistent with the best-known data of where the four-to-six-year achievement gap occurs, and how it persists from birth through tenth grade. For most children, the gap in measurable skills in pre-reading and pre-math occurs prior to kindergarten. It occurs in their homes.

The next chapters share how and why we measure the gap at kindergarten.

---

[12] The two growth rates can be compared by dividing the average years of growth of the top quintile by the average years of growth of the lowest quintile: 1.6 years of growth divided by .6 years of growth equals 2.66 which we have rounded up to 3.

CHAPTER TWENTY-ONE

KINDERGARTEN TARGETS: SKILLS TYPICAL OF FIVE-YEAR OLDS

"What should average incoming kindergarten students know? If you have no idea, you are not alone—neither do most parents, board members, central office administrators, and legislators."

— Steve Halliday, Marketing Director
READY! For Kindergarten

What are the pre-emergent literacy and math skills of typical five-year olds? And how can these skills be measured?

This chapter provides the National Children's Reading Foundation's incoming targets by skill area. The incoming kindergarten targets and an incoming kindergarten test are a quick way to get you up to speed in this area.

Incoming kindergarten targets are not exclusion criteria. Students are not denied or delayed their legal right to an appropriate education at public expense based on their incoming literacy and math skills, or lack thereof.

These are basic skills, and achieving the targets is natural for most children. Almost any parent, with simple tools and training, can ensure that his or her child will acquire these skills with very little time or effort by starting at birth. Pre-schools or federal child-care programs, at an average of 10 times the cost, can replicate this effort but don't do a better job.

Incoming Kindergarten Targets

A five year old with these skills
is ready to succeed in school.

READY! for Kindergarten

1. Letters and Sounds: enjoys being read to and can retell a story; recognizes and names 10-15 alphabet letters and their sounds; repeats beginning and ending sounds in words; speaks in complete sentences; prints his or her first name; and understands 4,000 to 5,000 spoken words.

2. Math: counts in order from 1 to 20; recognizes numbers and quantities to 10; names and sorts items by color, shape and size; understands concepts such as more, less, same, above, below, big and small.

3. Social: settles into new groups or situations; can concentrate on a task for 5 minutes; follows simple directions; shows kindness and concern for others.

4. Bi-lingual: comes to school speaking English, if other languages are spoken at home.

Reading aloud 20 minutes a day helps your child master these skills.

Our targets indicate skills in the 50th percentile.[1]

[1] Other lists in contrast are: "At age 5, most kindergartners are able to sound as if they are reading when they pretend to read, enjoy being read to, retell simple stories, use descriptive language to explain or to ask questions, recognize letters and letter-sound matches, show familiarity with rhyming and beginning sounds, understand that print is read left-to-right and top-to-bottom, begin to match spoken words with written ones, begin to write letters of the alphabet and some words they use and hear often, and begin to write stories with some readable parts." U.S. Department of Education, *Helping Your Child Become a Reader* (2002 edition). Idaho, Maryland, Florida, and Virginia test most of the same concepts but typically set their expectations in different places. Some of the material in Sally Shaywitz, *Overcoming Dyslexia: A New and Complete Science-Based Program for Reading Problems at Any Level* (New York: Alfred A. Knopf, 2003), 98, 108-9, suggests that children should come to school knowing most of the alphabet letters and their sounds.

In the last three decades, without really being explicit about it, many early childhood experts defined age-appropriate targets somewhere around the fifth to 10th percentile. At this level, most children could achieve them, and most parents would feel good about it. However, reaching a target such as knowing only two to three alphabet letters and their sounds virtually guaranteed starting two years behind.[2]

Many early childhood philosophies also focused on "developmentally appropriate practices" and the "whole child." These approaches have obvious strengths. However, preschool curriculum based on these approaches allocates so little instructional time to language and math development that these skills are effectively ignored. The older "developmental" or "whole child" models do not prioritize, align, or focus on the activities that most highly correlate with K-3 academic success, with the exception of socialization skills.

Measuring Kindergarten Skills

A modified version of Kennewick's kindergarten test appears on the next two pages. Scanning the test allows those who are not kindergarten teachers to get a feel for the basic skills we are discussing.

---

[2]For example, in 1987, the National Association for the Education of Young Children (NAEYC) declared, "Activities designed solely to teach the alphabet, phonics, and penmanship are much less appropriate for [three, four, and five year olds] than providing a print-rich environment that stimulates the development of language and literacy skills in a meaningful context." Sue Bredekamp, ed., *Developmentally Appropriate Practices in Early Childhood Programs Serving Children from Birth through Age Eight,* expanded ed. (Washington, DC: National Association for the Education of Young Children, 1987), 6. About 13 years later, NAEYC published the third edition of its Position Statement, in conjunction with the International Reading Association (IRA), which corrected the acknowledged flaws of the earlier editions (1987, 1997). This work addressed the previously "ongoing concerns about misrepresentations of developmentally appropriate practice as meaning no teaching about literacy to young children." The revision of the document was spearheaded by IRA President John J. Pikulski whose own "work with kindergarten teachers led to his concern that many opportunities for learning are missed in the name of developmentally appropriate practice." Susan B. Neuman, Carol Copple, and Sue Bredekamp, eds., *Learning to Read and Write: Developmentally Appropriate Practices for Young Children* (Washington, DC: National Association for the Education of Young Children, 2000), 1.

SAMPLE KINDERGARTEN LITERACY ASSESSMENT
KENNEWICK SCHOOL DISTRICT (100 points possible)

1. Letter Recognition (26 points possible). Using letter cards, student identifies upper case letters. If student doesn't know a letter, skip it, and go on to the next letter. Teacher records correct response by circling letter on answer sheet.

D F C B A P S Q T Z R E J G M U X H W I K N V O Y L

2. Letter Recognition (26 points possible). Using letter cards, student identifies lower case letters. If student doesn't know a letter, skip it, and go on to the next letter. Teacher records correct response by circling letter on answer sheet.

d f c b a p s q t z r e j g m u x h w i k n v o y l

3. Letter Sound Recognition (26 points possible). Using the lower case letter cards, student identifies consonant sounds and short vowel sounds. If student gives long vowel sound or soft sound for g/c, teacher redirects. Teacher records correct response by circling letter on answer sheet.

d f c b a p s q t z r e j g m u x h w i k n v o y l

4. Rhyming Recognition (5 points possible). Begin by explaining that two words rhyme when they sound the same at the end of the word. Give example: cat/hat. Give an example of one that doesn't rhyme: bed/rug. Ask student to tell you "yes" if the words below rhyme and "no" if they don't rhyme. Circle correct answers.

lip / sip   tell / sell   boy / duck   sick / desk   can / van

5. Rhyming Production (5 points possible). Remind student that words that rhyme sound the same at the end of the word. Give example: cat/mat. Ask them to think of another word that rhymes with cat. Ask them to make up some rhyming words to go with the words below. Nonsense words count. Write their responses on the lines.

cat________ run________ fill________ let ________ mop________

6. Initial Sound Recognition (5 points possible). The teacher names the object in the target picture (bed) and then four objects shown in pictures. Student then points to the picture row that starts with the same beginning sound as the target picture. Process is repeated five times.

bed/bird   top/turtle   sun/sock   moon/monkey   fish/fork

7. Initial Sound Production (5 points possible). Using the second set of pictures, teacher names each picture. Student writes word for each picture. Response is correct if initial sound is represented correctly. Child is shown four pictures for each letter choice.

p   s   b   d   m

8. Printing (2 points possible). Child is asked to print his or her first name.

SAMPLE KINDERGARTEN MATH ASSESSMENT
KENNEWICK SCHOOL DISTRICT (100 points possible)

1. **Counting Aloud to 30** (30 points possible). Student counts to 30 in order. If the student makes an error before reaching 30, give credit for the numbers said correctly before the error.

2. **Numeral Recognition 1 to 20** (20 points possible). Using the numeral cards, student names each numeral. If student doesn't know a numeral, skip it, and go on to next numeral.

5	3	8	6	1	7	2	4	10	9
16	15	11	18	20	12	19	13	17	14

3. **Two-Step Pattern Recognition and Extension** (12 points possible, 6 for naming the pattern and 6 for reproducing and extending the pattern). Using a pattern card and colored cubes or colored squares, student names the Blue Yellow (BY) pattern then extends it by placing colored cubes that would continue the pattern.

B	Y	B	Y				

4. **Three-Step Pattern Recognition and Extension** (12 points possible, 6 for naming the pattern and 6 for reproducing the pattern). Using a pattern card and colored cubes or colored squares, student names the Red Blue Yellow (RBY) pattern, then reproduces and extends it by placing colored cubes or colored squares that would continue the pattern.

R	B	Y	R	B	Y			

5. **Count Objects 1-to-1 Correspondence** (20 points possible). Using a card with 20 of the same shapes on it, student points to and counts the shapes. If the student makes an error before reaching 20, give credit for the shapes counted before the error.

6. **Recognize numerical value of amounts to 5** (6 points possible). Using the numerical value picture cards or a die cube, student identifies the number of dots on the card or die face, without counting. Teacher records correct response by circling the numbers on the answer sheet.

The scope of Kennewick's pre-emergent literacy assessment is fairly narrow. It is given one-on-one during the school day and takes about 25 minutes. It is weighted heavily toward letter recognition and phonemic awareness, because these skills have the highest measurable correlation to successful third grade reading.[3] While a subsequent chapter deals with how these skills are acquired, it must be emphasized here that there are several foundational concepts children understand first. Through interesting and real-life experience children should learn that (1) print is speech written down, (2) the black squiggles symbolically represent sounds in words, (3) that print has rules and conventions, and (4) individual alphabet letters generally track to individual sounds. This general awareness gives children a context to learn the specific skills.[4]

Items Assessed	Possible Points
Recognizing each lower case letter	26
Recognizing each upper case letter	26
Recognizing letter sounds	26
Recognizing ending sounds (rhymes)	5
Producing ending sounds (making rhymes)	5
Repeating beginning word sound	5
Reproducing beginning word sounds	5
Printing his or her first name	2
Total	**100**

The math portion of the assessment follows a similar pattern of shape recognition, quantity association, and pattern and sequence ability. The math section was piloted in the spring of 2003 and given in the fall of 2003. We had anticipated that the average score would be similar to

[3]After a child has this foundation, the "three literacy-related skills (concepts about print, ability to write his or her own name, and the ability to identify and label the letters of the alphabet) assessed by the researchers in September were all shown to be positively related to the ability to read the following July. Jeni Riley, *The Teaching of Reading: The Development of Literacy in the Early Years of School* (London: Paul Chapman Publishing, 1996), 5, agrees: "But by far the most powerful predictor of later success in reading was the child's knowledge of the alphabet, acquired incidentally and informally [before] school. . . . A recognition of individual letters and an ability to hear the sounds in words are the first steps in the development of the orthographic and phonological processing capability essential in literacy." See also 11, 26, 108-18.

[4]"Concepts of Print" in Chapter 23, "Age Level Targets."

the literacy test–somewhere in the mid-thirties. Surprisingly, the average entering fall math score was 65, which now seems to be a good indication of median skill.

The assessment is fairly simple, because more extensive information is not particularly helpful in the classroom for instruction. A Kennewick student will typically learn to read at or above grade level with minimal intervention, if he or she scores 30-35 on the literacy part of our September kindergarten assessment.

Table 21.1
Fall and Spring Kindergarten Scores for 13 Elementary Schools in Kennewick, 1999-2003

School	Amistad		Canyon View		Cascade		Eastgate		Edison		Hawthorne		Lincoln	
Year	Fall	Spring	Fall	Spring	Fall	Spring	Fall	Spring	Fall	Spring	Fall	Spring	Fall	Spring
99-00	21	68	49	91	40	84	24	86	33	84	44	85	43	90
00-01	14	81	41	96	42	90	23	84	22	77	43	87	35	90
01-02	16	92	34	94	40	94	22	90	23	86	43	92	38	91
02-03	22	94	48	95	49	93	25	89	30	88	36	89	41	96
03-04	33	92	46	88	42	89	25	91	27	85	44	88	54	95

School	Ridgeview		Southgate		Sunset View		Vista		Washington		Westgate	
Year	Fall	Spring	Fall	Spring	Fall	Spring	Fall	Spring	Fall	Spring	Fall	Spring
99-00	49	86	49	88	49	93	42	99	40	92	30	96
00-01	46	90	49	93	55	91	38	98	26	90	27	84
01-02	46	93	49	95	54	91	44	96	37	94	23	91
02-03	54	93	51	95	50	94	43	92	37	94	28	90
03-04	49	88	56	96	62	95	37	94	36	97	45	92

Incoming kindergarten scores have been remarkably stable at each of the schools over the five tested years. Incoming scores have *generally* inched upwards, in part due to the Reading Foundation message and more recently because of READY!, combating the previous trend suggested by most of our kindergarten teachers—that every year kindergarten students entered with slightly lower skill levels. The stability of incoming scores indicates that public schools do not create the gap in achievement. The achievement during kindergarten also shows that skilled instruction works for nearly all students and suggests that, if parents were similarly skilled, this learning could have occurred earlier for children in the lower quartiles.

The test itself measures markers, or the most easily accessed indicators of more complex and interrelated skills.[5] Students can learn these skills separately and during kindergarten, but on deep levels, they are not "caught up." Vocabulary provides a good illustration. Students who come to kindergarten with vocabularies of 1,000-2,000 words rarely learn the 1,000 plus words to make normal growth plus the 1,500 new words necessary to catch up in a year or two.[6] Even if they do, the process of neurally connecting linking word sounds to word meanings and then to hundreds of other known words cannot be anywhere as rich as being continually exposed to language from birth.

> *"When children score low on entering assessments, it's more a reflection of their opportunities to learn than their intelligence. Kindergarten targets and parent training are designed to close the 'opportunity gap' for kids."*
>
> — Nancy Kerr

Reading in kindergarten, first, and second grade is about first decoding and then rapidly (fluently) and accurately saying some 300 words. Increased vocabulary of 4,000-5,000 words relates to comprehension which does not become evident until fourth grade.

The third section of the targets defines social skills. Some kindergarten children have grade-level language and math skills but not the social skills typical of five-year-olds. Students lacking basic social skills have an additional and independent limit to ordinary learning.

---

[5]The concept of markers is best illustrated by looking at these critical skills in isolation. "When Gibson and Levin (1975) and Ehri (1983) set out to teach children the letters of the alphabet directly, prior to school entry, there was no positive link with successful later reading." Riley, *The Teaching of Reading,* 12. Likewise, despite the strong correlation between exposure to quantities of words at ages 12-36 months and the size of vocabulary in grade three, there was no similar correlation with reading and math tests scores at grade three. Betty Hart and Todd R. Risley *Meaningful Differences in the Everyday Experience of Young American Children* (Baltimore, MD: Paul H. Brookes Publishing, 1995), 65.

[6]The average root word vocabulary of an entering kindergartener is approximately 3,500 words. "Prior to grade three, children [gain] an average of 860 words a year. . . . Little is done in primary classrooms to address this vocabulary 'gap.' While some words are taught. . . the low vocabulary children are starting kindergarten with smaller vocabularies, and continue to acquire fewer words during the primary grades so that by the end of grade two, they have 2,000 fewer words. [...] Thus by the end of grade two, children in the lowest quartile had vocabularies of about the same size as average children had in kindergarten." Andrew Biemiller, Institute of Child Study, University of Toronto, *Addressing Developmental Patterns in Vocabulary: Implications for Choosing Words for Primary Grade Vocabulary Instruction,* (In press 2004), 4.

They have difficulty asking for information. They have difficulty concentrating. They often are not relaxed and happy in the classroom. When a child is uneasy in his or her environment, the blood which normally flows to the outer levels of the brain (cerebral cortex), where most higher level thinking and learning occurs, is often pulled to the central brain stem areas where fight-or-flight responses are controlled. Each time the flight-or-fight stimulus directs blood flow to the brain stem region, it takes 45 minutes before normal levels are restored in the cerebral cortex.

These are our kindergarten targets, based on skills typical of five year olds. Most parents, with simple tools and training provided by the school district, can ensure that their children acquire these basic skills.

CHAPTER TWENTY-TWO

Seven Reasons to Adopt and Assess Incoming Kindergarten Targets

---

"The first five years matter! During this stage of a child's life, parents have a key role in nurturing their child's language and math skills so that he or she will start kindergarten ready to learn."

— Bev Abersfeller, Program Coordinator
READY! for Kindergarten

It is a pity that more districts don't test in kindergarten. Where large numbers of students read below grade level in a district, the initial and logical policy response by superintendents and boards should be to implement uniform district-wide assessment at kindergarten.[1] It requires minimal funding, because most kindergarten teachers do it already. All districts need to do is standardize what is already being assessed and collect the results.

Incoming kindergarten assessments tell which students are coming to school ready to learn and which ones are already far behind. Identifying these students gives your district early notice to begin the catch-up process.

---

[1] Actually it should be the first policy response by state legislators as well. To date, only North Carolina (http://www.ncpublicschools.org), Maryland (http://www.marylandpublicschools.org), Virginia (http://pals.virginia.edu/), Idaho (http://www.sde.state.id.us), and Florida (http://info.fldoe.org) assess incoming kindergarten students in September. North Carolina assesses and uses these results on its statewide report card to determine whether parents are sending their children to school ready to learn. Virginia implemented Phonological Awareness Literacy Screening (PALS-K) in 2002-03. Maryland began baselining incoming kindergarten performance in the fall of 2001, using the Maryland Model for School Readiness and the Work Sampling System. Idaho also uses an assessment it developed.

Incoming kindergarten assessments indicate whether parents are doing simple school readiness activities with their children. The data provide opportunities for inexpensive intervention. Earlier we suggested that educators would be consumed during the next decade by:

- catching students up from kindergarten through high school, and/or
- assuring that they did not fall behind in the first place during the preschool years from birth to kindergarten.

Kindergarten assessment provides the data to begin working on the latter strategy: identifying the sub-skills of reading and math readiness and a means to measure them.

Why should school districts set reasonable kindergarten targets and clearly, consistently communicate them to parents? Why should school districts assess to determine starting skill levels of their youngest students?

1. The targets and assessments strike at the root of the achievement gap. No matter what we do in public schools to catch up K-12 students, a new wave of kindergarten students will enter our schools each September with the same four-to-six-year academic gap. Devising catch-up programs starting in kindergarten and continuing through 12th grade is a reactive strategy. The pro-active response is to establish reasonable targets and provide parents with basic tools and training to assure their child's normal growth in the first five years.

2. The targets and assessments create uniform accountability. NCLB is holding all of our public schools and teachers accountable for minimum standards. The targets extend this accountability to the home where the achievement gap originates. The current need for uniform expectations is great.

3. The targets and assessments create clear expectations. Most parents have little knowledge of the skills a typical five year old should have when entering kindergarten. Their common response to public schools–"We raised them, you teach them"–is not unreasonable, if public schools have made little or no attempt to share information with parents about basic cognitive development during the prior five years.

4. The targets are research based. The simple targets capture the skills that most accurately predict subsequent reading and math success. Letter and sound recognition skills at kindergarten are most predictive of third-grade reading, as are first-grade phonetic awareness skills. Reading and math are the two languages essential for school success. With few exceptions, seniors graduating with high achievements are those students who were reading proficiently and mastering grade-level math concepts nine to twelve years earlier.

5. The targets are scaleable. The targets can be sequenced with activities that are appropriate for each earlier age level. Parents can engage their child beginning at birth in activities that gradually ramp up to mastering these skills by age five. For example, knowing 10 to 15 alphabet letters at kindergarten could sequence in this order: doing simple eye tracking exercises with newborns, displaying eye-tracking cards on the crib at six months, repetitious viewing of letters and feeling their shapes at ages one to two, learning the first letter of his or her first name at age two to three, learning all the letters of his or her first name at age three to four, and learning five or six other letters and their sounds as a four to five year old.

> *"Children are born learning, and they love to learn. When parents enjoy just a few minutes a day exploring and interacting with their child, they are building strong minds and relationships."*
>
> — Nancy Kerr

6. The targets are "opportunity to learn" statements instead of "socio-economic statements." It is language and math activities that teach language and math skills. The targets can be achieved with simple tools, easy and pleasant activities, and a small investment of time by every parent, without changing the economic status of parents.

7. The targets are a cost-effective alternative to catch-up growth. School districts spend an additional $4,000 or more for each student in the lowest two quartiles every year. The number of students needing this level of intervention could be dramatically reduced. Adopting targets and advertising them costs about 50 cents per year for each full-time equivalent (FTE) student. Operating a local Reading Foundation to encourage parents to read aloud to their child 20 minutes a day costs about $2 per student per year. Marketing the age-level targets, and offering parent three 90-minute classes a year, with skilled instructors where age-appropriate tools and activities relating to the targets can be provided for parents, costs $300 per child per year.[2]

[2]Kennewick delivers its program using the National Children's Reading Foundation's targets, tools, and training curriculum. More information about READY! for Kindergarten is available at www.readingfoundation.org.

CHAPTER TWENTY-THREE

AGE-LEVEL TARGETS FROM BIRTH TO FIVE

"Now accountable, schools choose to accept that responsibility alone or to involve and invest in families. If schools choose to invest in parents, it's essential they make smart decisions so that measurable results come from the investment."

— Kathy Daily, Director,
Kennewick School Board

What can school districts do about incoming kindergarten skill levels? Kennewick believes that it is far less expensive to encourage skillful parenting and provide parents with basic tools and training during the pre-school years than to pay the bill for catch-up growth for students in K-12. The financial costs of remediation don't attempt to calculate the emotional toll on students who lag behind their peers for years.

This chapter shares age-sequenced skills developed by the National Children's Reading Foundation's READY! for Kindergarten program. This program supports parents as they enjoy learning at home with their child. The skills transition smoothly in complexity from a newborn to a five year old ready for kindergarten. Parents are trained in age-appropriate materials and activities to do with their child. READY! organizes the training by four skill areas: visual, auditory, thinking skills/vocabulary concepts, and social skills. Each of the four major skill areas has five to eight sub-skills, starting with the most basic skills at birth to twelve months and ramping up each year with increasing sophistication.

Program Description

READY! for Kindergarten classes provide targets, tools, and training to Kennewick parents of children ages newborn to five. Parents attend three sessions a year (fall, winter, and spring), separated into one of five classes depending on their child's age. The classes are 90-minute, interactive, age-appropriate lessons. About 65% of the time is allocated to hands-on training and activities, 30% explains research and child development, and 5% ties the tools and activities to the targets. A trained instructor, using the latest in presentation technology and information, leads each class. READY! for Kindergarten's sequence of learning activities creates a predictable, consistent, and reproducible outcome.

Program Specifications

A. Parents receive:

1. Targets (course objectives)—The research-based curriculum is built on a series of about two dozen measurable skills used to evaluate the child's progress at each age level.
2. Training—Instructor-led classes in a support-group setting.
3. Learning tools—Each parent is given about $50 worth of learning aids to use while playing with his or her child at home. These include music tapes, floor puzzles, colorful wooden shapes, blocks, magnetic letter sets, number sets, and age-appropriate books.

B. READY! provides a "turnkey" lesson presentation:

1. The 15 age-sequenced READY! for Kindergarten lessons training parents to develop learning skills in their children ages birth to five.
2. Training for the site coordinator.
3. Equipment, including a multimedia computer, a projector, and a wireless mouse for each classroom.
4. The parent "tools and activities" described above.
5. Instructor teaching aids including a PowerPoint presentation with music, activities, videos, outlines, handouts, and animations.
6. On-line registration—a customized self-registration program with reports linked to the district's home page.
7. Masters for printed parent materials in English and Spanish.

C. The district provides:

1. Personnel—Program coordinator, registrar, and instructors for age-group classes.
2. Facilities—Classrooms with projection screens, tables or desks, chairs, parking, and restrooms.
3. Site coordinator, part- or full-time, office phone, and computer.
4. Advertising—READY! supplies sample advertising materials.
5. Child care—Encourages attendance at READY! classes.

The targets give parents something to aim for. Not every child will hit every goal. The same range of skills that exist in kindergarten and second grade exists in varying degrees from birth to five. Many children will exceed these "average," "grade level," 50th percentile standards. Accelerated children will reach many of these targets one or two years earlier, especially as parents get into a rhythm, spending more time than the recommended "20 minutes a day reading plus five minutes doing activities," and discovering that this time with their child is more fun and beneficial than other activities they were doing. The same K-3 learning factors of time-on-task, teacher's skill, and level of student ability and engagement advance a child's early development as well.

Having the undivided attention of a responsive adult is something every child loves. When children are exploring and interacting with their parents, they are not "working" or "getting ready for school." They are just spending happy, quality time with their favorite people.

We think you will agree, as you peruse this chapter, that 80-90% of parents can easily provide this training to their children once they are trained themselves. This training is not intended to increase the child's IQ, but it does give each child a head start on pre-basic literacy, math, and social skills.[1]

---

[1] READY! focuses on achievement, not IQ. Research supports gains of only 3-4 IQ points from early intervention, but such gains, while statistically significant, are invisible in the classroom. Exotic claims from early childhood interventions of 8-20 IQ points gains, returns of $4.37 for every dollar invested prior to age five from "sleeper" effects, social benefits accruing after age 16, and taking advantage of "developmental windows" before they "close" often miscite four studies in their support. In the 1966 *Milwaukee Project* (35 black children deemed at risk based on impoverished economic circumstances and mothers' initial IQ below 70), initially reported gains of 25 IQ points; but these gains had dropped to 10 points by age 12. Achievement in reading and math for both control and intervention groups was inexplicably similar for both groups and, even more strikingly, showed the intervention group as one to two years behind by the fourth grade. In the early 1970s *Abecedarian Project* (107 impoverished black children, whose mothers had IQs lower than 70), the IQ in the intervention group increased 18 points over the control group in the first six months, but thereafter declined to an increase of 8 points by age five despite interventions conducted six hours a day, five days a week, 50 weeks a year. IQ further declined to three-point gains by age 8. *The Infant Health and Development Program* (1985-88) focused on low birth-weight babies and found that little sustained IQ effect resulted from the early intervention. *The Perry Preschool Project* (123 impoverished black children with IQ scores of 70-85) showed an IQ increase of 11 points between the intervention and control group by kindergarten; but by second grade, the difference was slight and, by fourth grade, was virtually nonexistent. These studies are reviewed in a variety of places including John T. Bruner, *The Myth of the First Three Years* (New York: Free Press, 1999), 144-80.

READY! Age Level Targets	Infants, Ages Birth -1 year
Visual	
Eye Movements	My eyes smoothly follow an object tracing an "H" and a "cross."
Colors	I hear my parents say the names of colors. I may point to yellow or blue things.
Matching Letter Shapes and Naming Sight Words	I see interesting shapes around my crib and room. I recognize the faces of my family.
Naming Letter Shapes	
Matching Number Shapes	
Copying and Tracing	By 12 months, I am able to hold a thick crayon and scribble.
Printing First Name	
Auditory	
Listening Experiences	I hear recorded music and gentle speaking.
Singing, Chanting, and Nursery Rhymes	I am sung to daily. I hear simple nursery rhymes, the ABC and number songs
Phonemic Awareness	
Verbal Development	I hear loving words in "parentese" about 30 times an hour.
Verbal Skills	
Reading Engagement	I hear a story being read to me for 20 minutes a day, perhaps in five-minute segments.
Concepts of Print	I point to a book during story time.
Thinking Skills - Vocabulary - Concepts	
Counting	I hear my parents count various items each day.
Sorting	
Patterns and Sequences	My parents play predictable games like clapping or peek-a-boo with me using patterns of twos and threes.
Spatial Relationships	I hear the vocabulary of spatial relationships: up, down, around, on, in, out, etc.
Geometric Shapes	
Add/Subtract	
Social Skills	
Relating to Others	I feel secure and connect with my family by eye contact and gentle touching.
Increasing Attention Span	I am an observer, contented to be entertained and pampered. I listen to books read each day which builds my attention span.
Following Instructions	
Taking Responsibility	I am very dependent on my family.
Developing Calmly and Competently, with Emotional Security	I feel secure because my needs for food, comfort, love, and care are being met.

From Birth to One Year

I am your child,[2] and I am born learning. Within a few hours of birth I work purposefully to imitate your simple face, tongue, and lip movements.[3] My vision is limited to distinguishing between bright and dark with my range for focusing initially restricted to 8-10 inches. This is the distance from the crook of my mother's arm to her face.

During my first six weeks of my life, my eyes and head move together. The six muscles in each of my eyes practice working together when my parents use a brightly colored object to make a slow, wide "H" movement. I start to follow moving objects at 8-12 weeks, watch your face when you talk to me at 10-12 weeks, notice and watch my hands at 12-16 weeks, and start looking for the toys I drop by 32-38 weeks.

My hearing is well developed at birth. Listening to singing or music daily, hearing simple nursery rhymes, being read to, and being talked to regularly in "parentese" (when parents intuitively speak softly and sweetly, emphasizing the vowels which are the hardest sounds for me to hear) all help me develop my ability to hear words, enjoy rhymes, and build vocabulary.

I easily slip into an exclusive "bubble" with you. Attachment theory suggests this is an ideal time for us to establish a deep emotional bond. Hold and cuddle me all you want. You can't spoil me with too much love!

The real news is what is going on inside my brain. During my first year, it nearly triples in size–to about 70% of adult size. Waves of electrical energy pulse through my brain every second, creating new connections between my neurons. Today I cannot distinguish a single alphabet letter. Yet with your help, using a series of simple tools and activities, I will soon be processing signals from my eyes, sending signals to my lungs to draw a breath, and commanding my tongue to form certain shapes–the skills necessary to read aloud when I am older.

---

[2]This chapter is drawn from the READY! for Kindergarten curriculum and is used by permission. "I am your child, and I am born learning" is the beginning sentence of the excellent series of videotapes available from the I Am Your Child Foundation at http://iamyourchild.org.
[3]Alison Gopnik, Andrew N. Meltzoff, and Patricia K. Kuhl, *The Scientist in the Crib: What Early Learning Tells Us about the Mind* (New York: HarperCollins, 1999), 29.

READY! Age Level Targets	Babies, Ages 1-2 years
Visual	
Eye Movements	My eyes smoothly follow an object tracing an "H" or a "cross." I can focus near, then far.
Colors	I hear the names of colored objects and can point to three colors: red, blue, and yellow.
Matching Letter Shapes and Naming Sight Words	I identify horizontal, vertical, and angled lines, arcs, and v's.
Naming Letter Shapes	I repeatedly see my first initial displayed around my house.
Matching Number Shapes	I match number shapes to 3.
Copying and Tracing	I scribble up and down (14 mo.) then in circles (24 mo.).
Printing First Name	
Auditory	
Listening Experiences	I listen to tapes of music, sounds and stories, including the ABC and 1-2-3 songs.
Singing, Chanting, and Nursery Rhymes	I sing parts of the ABC and number songs with others and frequently hear nursery rhymes.
Phonemic Awareness	
Verbal Development	I hear my parents use "scaffolding" and speak in "parentese" about 30 times an hour.
Verbal Skills	I use one word to represent many. After I start talking, I will learn 2-4 new words a day. I can imitate several animal sounds.
Reading Engagement	I hear a story read to me for 20 minutes a day. I can answer "Where is..." questions by pointing.
Concepts of Print	I point to 3 parts of a book: i.e., the book, a page, and a picture.
Thinking Skills - Vocabulary - Concepts	
Counting	I hear my parents count things like my toes, bites of food, and toys. My parents use numbers to describe my things: "You have two shoes."
Sorting	I am beginning to sort blocks and clothing by color.
Patterns and Sequences	I play the "Wherever a Butterfly Goes" game with my parents and recognize simple spatial words like up, down, above, and below.
Spatial Relationships	I enjoy filling and emptying containers of water and sand.
Geometric Shapes	
Add/Subtract	
Social Skills	
Relating to Others	I feel loved and safe because my parents praise me and cuddle me.
Increasing Attention Span	I focus for a short time when others interact with me.
Following Instructions	I am beginning to obey a simple instruction.
Taking Responsibility	I often cooperate during daily routines.
Developing Calmly and Competently, with Emotional Security	I follow my parents' example and say "please" and "thank you."

Ages One to Two

I am leaving the emotional cocoon of my first year. Until a few months ago, it encompassed you and me. Now I am into "things"—things I can clearly see, things I can grasp and hold, things I can crawl or toddle to, things I can put in my mouth.

My parents do the simple "H" and "cross" tracking game with me. They check my ability to focus near and far. They point out visual details in the things around me, especially items that are red, blue, and yellow. I am becoming a little "copy cat," and I learn best by imitation. I learn to imitate from thousands of gentle repetitions of activities in a safe, supportive environment.

My hands can feel the three simple shapes that make up our 26 lower case alphabet letters: the line, arc, and "v." I can even match number shapes to 3. I don't know their names, or even their quantity, but matching their shapes helps train my eyes to see subtle differences. The first letter of my first name is taped up throughout my house using four- inch high cards, and my parents repeatedly point it out to me.

My first words may include "mama" and "dada" (around 12 months). In the next six weeks after I produce my first word, I usually say 25 more.

My parents recite to me lots of simple nursery rhymes, a vital step in phonemic awareness. They talk to me 30 times an hour when I am awake, modeling the new research.[4] While I barely speak, I understand a lot—the first step to learning the 5,000 or so words I will know on entering kinergarten. Every day my parents read to me 20 minutes, asking me "Where is . .?" questions that I gleefully answer by pointing.

I hear my parents count everything—like my toes, bites of food, and socks. I sort my blocks and clothing and play a simple game of spatial relationships when the butterfly goes *above, below, around,* and *behind* me. When it's not fun, my parents stop. When it's too hard, they adjust. But all the time, they continue the endless, interactive dance with me—responding to me, leading me, following me.

[4]Betty Hart and Todd R. Risley, *Meaningful Differences in the Everyday Experience of Young American Children* (Baltimore, MD: Paul H. Brookes Publishing, 1995).

READY! Age Level Targets	Toddlers, Ages 2-3
Visual	
Eye Movements	My eyes follow an object tracing an "H" and "cross", focusing near then far, and on the field of vision.
Colors	I know six colors: red, blue, green, yellow, black, and white.
Matching Letter Shapes and Naming Sight Words	I match the shape of different letters including 'a-d-m-s-t' when the letters are 2-3 inches tall.
Naming Letter Shapes	I identify and match the shape of the first letter of my name.
Matching Number Shapes	I match number shapes to 6.
Copying and Tracing	I begin to trace shapes with my finger, crayon, in sand and with food.
Printing First Name	Near age 3, I may draw the first letter of my name.
Auditory	
Listening Experiences	I recognize the sound of the first letter of my name.
Singing, Chanting, and Nursery Rhymes	I sing more of the ABC and number songs. I am familiar with several nursery rhymes and can say parts of them.
Phonemic Awareness	I play "Odd Word Out" with ending sounds of words and clap the syllables in familiar names.
Verbal Development	I hear my parents speak to me about 30 times an hour.
Verbal Skills	I am putting 2-4 words together. I recognize about 500 words. I can imitate several animal sounds, words, and expressions accurately.
Reading Engagement	During story time, I supply words and discuss characters. I respond to "why" questions and play "Extend My Sentence" and "I Spy with My Little Eye."
Concepts of Print	I identify 10 print concepts; the previous 3, plus front/back covers, top/bottom, print, words, letters.
Thinking Skills - Vocabulary - Concepts	
Counting	I count a little and show my age with my fingers.
Sorting	I sort by color and shape with assistance.
Patterns and sequences	I do two-step color sequences.
Spatial Relationships	I know 10 prepositions.
Geometric Shapes	I identify circles, squares, rectangles, and triangles.
Add/Subtract	I recognize groups of objects to 3. I know bigger and smaller.
Social Skills	
Relating to Others	I occasionally attend group activities with my extended family and children my same age.
Increasing Attention Span	I play independently for short periods of time or focus on an engaging activity with an adult.
Following Instructions	I remember and follow a two-step instruction.
Taking Responsibility	I like praise when I "help" with appropriate tasks. I am beginning to develop self-help skills.
Developing Calmly and Competently, with Emotional Security	I show kindness to others, but mostly I am concerned with my needs. I respond well to being redirected.

Ages Two to Three

I'm at the exciting and stimulating age often called the "terrible twos." I am young, newly mobile, and ready to go. Think of me as a 16 year old with my first driver's license, new wheels, and a whole world calling. I can walk, run, and even jump. I have fully functioning vision and reasonable hand-eye coordination. I am intent on becoming a grown-up human being.

Using simple "toys," I have learned to identify and name things that are red, blue, green, yellow, black, and white. I can consistently name and identify the first letter of my name. I have been hearing such designations for two years now, so naming them is only a tiny step for me. A bigger step is learning to match (but not yet name) different looking letters like a-d-m-i-s-t and numbers 1, 2, 3, 4, 5, and 6. Tracing the shapes with my finger helps me learn.

I wash my hands for as long as it takes to sing the ABC song. During my 20 minute story time, I supply words, discuss characters, and answer "why" questions. During the extra five minutes we spend on activities, Dad plays "Odd Word Out" with me: "cat, fat, dog" and "ball, cow, tall." I am getting better and better at hearing the ending sounds in the rhymes, a second step in phonemic awareness.

None of this is work for me. It's play! I count a few numbers, sort by color and by shape, and know that "a pattern is not a pattern unless it repeats itself." I see two-step patterns in shirts and socks and recognize two-step sound patterns. I have learned names for things that are round, square, and have three angles. I have mastered the difficult mathematical concepts of "more than," "less than," and "equal to," and I practice my skill with these concepts every time we have dessert. ☺

I am also learning to follow two-step instructions. "Wash your hands and then dry them." "Put on your shirt and then get your shoes." I can remember two things, but remembering three things is tougher. Occasionally I enjoy activities with other children my age that help me get comfortable with my peers. We play independently for short periods of time, and I like praise when I "help" with appropriate tasks. With the help of my parents, some tools, and activities, I am having fun doing the things that will prepare me for school.

READY! Age Level Targets	Roamers, Ages 3-4
Visual	
Eye Movements	I appropriately respond to the "H," "Cross," "Near-Far," "Field of Vision," and "Distant Detail" Tests.
Colors	I know nine colors: red, blue, green, yellow, black, white, orange, purple, and brown.
Matching Letter Shapes and Naming Sight Words	I match similar letter family shapes including a-e-o-c, m-n-r-h-u-v-w, and b-p-d-q-g.
Naming Letter Shapes	I identify and match the shapes of the letters in my first name.
Matching Number Shapes	I match number shapes to 9.
Copying and Tracing	I copy and trace letters and numbers. I draw and name circles and squares.
Printing First Name	I am beginning to print the letters in my first name.
Auditory	
Listening Experiences	I name and say the sounds of all the letters of my first name .
Singing, Chanting, and Nursery Rhymes	I sing the ABC and number songs independently, and watch my parents point to printed letter or number strips. I can recite 4-5 rhymes.
Phonemic Awareness	I match sounds that are the same, tell which sounds are different, and play with nonsense rhyming. I play Odd Word Out with beginning sounds and clap the syllables in familiar names and words.
Verbal Development	I hear my parents speak to me about 30 times an hour.
Verbal Skills	I use 3-5 word "sentences" and recognize about 2,000 to 3,000 words. I accurately reproduce any phonetic sound I hear and want to say.
Reading Engagement	During the 20 minute reading time, I supply increasingly more information from memory about familiar books and give 3-4 word responses to "what" and "how" questions. I respond to techniques of "comment and wait," "ask and wait," and "respond and wait."
Concepts of Print	I know the 10 earlier concepts, plus commas, periods, and spaces. I also know that printing represents spoken sounds, and that meaning comes from words, helped by pictures.
Thinking Skills - Vocabulary - Concepts	
Counting	I count by rote to 10. I show my age with my fingers.
Sorting	I sort quickly by color and shape.
Patterns and sequences	I begin to copy patterns and create two-step color patterns and three-step sound sequences.
Spatial Relationships	I know 20 prepositions and do simple puzzles.
Geometric Shapes	I match and name circles, squares, rectangles, stars, and diamond, triangle, parallelogram, cross, oval, and heart.
Add/Subtract	I recognize groups of objects to 6. I know more than, less than, greater than, smaller than, equal to.
Social Skills	
Relating to Others	I regularly attend peer group activities and play alongside but independently of other children.
Increasing Attention Span	I focus on play activities, and with the help of an adult I can accomplish simple tasks through sustained effort.
Following Instructions	I easily remember and follow two-step instructions.
Taking Responsibility	I am able to dress myself, pick up toys, help with simple chores, and take more responsibility for my bathroom needs.
Developing Calmly and Competently, with Emotional Security	I enjoy being with others, but I would rather play by myself and I do not share easily. I can show empathy for others. I understand basic safety rules and am learning not to bite or hit others.

Ages Three to Four

I am curious and full of energy. I'm very much my own little person, and I often work at pleasing you. I share with my little playmates, and I regularly imitate my older siblings, cousins, and friends.

I like it when you read to me, especially when you stop to talk about what has already happened and ask what I think might happen next. This activity develops my comprehension and helps me to remember the beginning, middle, and end of stories. It's helpful when you comment, add, or respond to what I say and then wait six to eight seconds for me to produce a response.[5] I know that eight seconds is a really long time for an adult to wait, but it is great exercise for my growing brain. Your constant talking to me and encountering uncommon words in books has helped me learn 2,000-3,000 words.

You are teaching me the letters in the rest of my name by using letters that are 1-2½ inches high. I can now distinguish between and match similar looking letters like a-e-o-c and m-n-r-h-u-v-w. Two years ago, I learned to match numbers 1, 2, and 3. Last year I learned to match numbers 1-6, and this year I can match numbers 1-9. It's easy with the Velcro-backed game pieces my parents got from READY!

I have heard the ABC and number song thousands of times, can sing them by myself, count by rote to 10, and identify groups of objects to six. I know 10 or more prepositions ("under," "on top of," "beside," etc.), as well as the names of some common shapes (rectangles, triangles, and stars). I can copy two-step patterns and create three-step sound sequences. I speak in sentence fragments that have at least as many words as the years I am old — now 3-4 words. I can hear the beginning sounds of words, another step in my phonemic awareness development.

My parents encourage me to regularly participate in activities with my peers. I play next to but usually independently of them. I am encouraged to dress myself and take responsibility for my bathroom needs. I am learning to be kind to other people and pets and not hurt them. I like myself.

[5]The "Comment, Add, Respond" formulation is based on work by the Washington Research Institute in its excellent series "Begin with Language," 150 Nickerson Street, Seattle, WA 98109, (206) 285-9317. This work utilizes the research of Grover Whitehurst, while professor of education at State University of New York at Stonybrook.

READY! Age Level Targets	Pre-Schoolers, Ages 4-5
Visual	
Eye Movements	I respond to the H, Cross, Near-Far, Field of Vision, Distant Detail, and Close up Detail Tests
Colors	I know 12 colors: red, blue, green, yellow, black, white, orange, gray, brown, purple, pink, and tan.
Matching Letter Shapes and Naming Sight Words	I match and distinguish among the shape families of a-e-o-c, m-n-u-r-h-v-w, b-p-d-q-g, and j-f-i-l-k-x-y-s-z. I recognize the printed words for five common objects labeled in my room.
Naming Letter Shapes	I match and name 12-15 lower case letters including my first name.
Matching Number Shapes	I match number shapes to 12.
Copying and Tracing	I copy and trace. I draw numbers to 5. I name and draw circles, squares, triangles, and rectangles.
Printing First Name	I print or "draw" my first name.
Auditory	
Listening Experiences	I name and reproduce the sounds of 12-15 letters including those in my first name.
Singing, Chanting, and Nursery Rhymes	I sing and chant the ABC and number songs independently while pointing to the letters and numbers. I recite 5-10 nursery rhymes and match words that rhyme.
Phonemic Awareness	I hear and repeat beginning, middle, and ending sounds in words. I say the first sound of most words, say the individual sounds in words, and tap out the syllables in common words like familiar names.
Verbal Development	I hear my parents speak to me about 30 times an hour.
Verbal Skills	I speak using complete sentences and know about 5,000 words. I speak with few inaccuracies. I am able to listen to someone say a word and then repeat it without distortion.
Reading Engagement	During the 20 minute reading time of familiar stories, I know what's coming and can offer alternative plot suggestions. I respond to questions and can retell the entire story.
Concepts of Print	I know the previous 15 concepts, plus title, author, letter groups make words, reading moves from left to right, top to bottom, and the left page followed by the right, from front to back of the book.
Thinking Skills - Vocabulary - Concepts	
Counting	I count in order to 20.
Sorting	I name and sort items by color, shape, and size.
Patterns and sequences	I create and repeat two-to-three-step color patterns, copy three-to-four-step sound sequences, and play increasingly complex memory games.
Spatial Relationships	I know 30 prepositions and do more complex puzzles.
Geometric Shapes	I name and draw 16 basic geometric shapes.
Add/Subtract	I recognize numbers and quantities to 10 and accurately use "more than," "less than," "greater than," "smaller than," and "equal to."
Social Skills	
Relating to Others	I "settle in" to new groups or situations with minimal stress.
Increasing Attention Span	I focus on a task for at least five minutes.
Following Instructions	I remember and follow a three-step instruction.
Taking Responsibility	I take care of all my dressing and bathroom needs and sometimes I try to help others.
Developing Calmly and Competently, with Emotional Security	I play cooperatively and can share. I am able to show kindness and empathy for others, but I may go from smiles to bossiness in seconds.

Ages Four to Five

In less than a year, I will be holding your hand and reassuring you that I will be okay as we walk into kindergarten. Doesn't it seem like yesterday that you brought me home from the hospital, a helpless little peanut wrapped in a soft blanket?

You may have noticed that my hand-eye coordination is approaching a pre-Nintendo level. I can place small objects in small openings and talk about places, objects, and people I've seen elsewhere. I can even roll my eyes in a pre-teenage sort of way.

But after all is said and done, this year is important for me. If I start kindergarten ahead, chances are I'll stay ahead. However, if I start one or two years behind, it will be really hard for me to catch up. So I'm working to master the big ones:

I can identify 12-15 alphabet letters and their sounds.
I can talk fluently, print my first name, and know 5,000 words.
I can identify numbers to 20 and count quantities to 10.
I can settle in to new groups.

These learning activities are just an extension of what we have been doing together each day since I was born. My eyes are getting better at recognizing tiny differences in letters and numbers. My ears are getting so they can distinguish the tiny sounds in the middle of words.

My vocabulary is exploding, and I use my pre-wired neurons to retain the sound, meaning, relationship, and connections to all of my other words. When you help me reason through alternatives, put together puzzles, and practice my skills, you reinforce critical brain pathways, making them faster and more robust. Do you wonder why I want to hear my favorite book for the thousandth time? I am endlessly practicing–like a high-performance athlete perfecting my jump shot, so to speak.

The READY! program generally costs $300 per parent per year and $120 per session for child-care providers. About 30% of Kennewick parents with children ages birth to five attended each session in 2003-04.

Organizations interested using these targets, tools, and training materials for parents or child-care providers of children from ages newborn to five can contact READY! at (509) 222-5035, visit www.readyforkindergarten.org and www.readingfoundation.org, or direct questions to:

Lynn Fielding at lynnfielding@hotmail.com,
Nancy Kerr at nkerr@readingfoundation.org,
READY! at info@readyforkindergarten.org.

CHAPTER TWENTY-FOUR

THE FACE OF A READER IN THE 21ST CENTURY

"Early success in school depends on how children are prepared to go to school, and that happens mostly at home."

— Dr. Sara Zirkle, pediatrician,
Mid-Columbia Reading Foundation Board

In this chapter, you will meet Rusty and Sara. They are the children of the Mindy and Tony whom you met in Chapter 12. Their lives reflect the two new dominant educational focuses of 21st century education: preventing the gap before kindergarten for most children and creating immediate catch-up growth in K-3 for those who start behind.

Preventing the Gap

Rusty is three years old. The YMCA provides childcare services at the local elementary school while his mother, Mindy and his father Bob, attend 90-minute parent training sessions provided by their school district three times a year.

It's the 21st century. Public schools reach out to parents with information and support during the preschool years. "Parents are a child's earliest and most effective teacher," Mindy remembers the superintendent of schools saying. "Every child is homeschooled for the first five years. You provide the smallest class size your child will ever have during that critical time for developing visual, auditory, and social skills. We offer free training and tools to help you become more skillful parents. Working together your child can come to school ready to learn."

Other reasons for the training and tools were broadcast on TV. Researchers showed that 20% of students entered kindergarten with literacy and math skills of only three year olds. Board members explained how schools were spending nearly twice as much money each year on these students to catch them up, often unsuccessfully. The superintendent explained that it is far more cost effective to comply with the "adequate yearly progress" provisions of the federal law by starting with parents at birth than it is to pay for pre-kindergarten school-based programs or remediation in kindergarten.

So Mindy and Bob attend district classes to learn how Rusty's young eyes and brain recognize alphabet and number shapes, at first haltingly and then rapidly. Last year, the district provided Mindy and Bob with four-inch high red-letter "R's" for Rusty. As a two year old, Rusty had a whole year to learn the first letter of his name. He now can instantly recognize an "R," finding and pointing out "Rs" on license plates, the "R" in Burger Ranch and on the Rice Krispies box. He can recognize the "s" and "t" as well, although he doesn't know their names or sounds. He learned as a two year old to recognize and match different looking letters as a, d, m, s, and t.

This year, as a three year old, Rusty will learn the shapes and sounds of the rest of his name. Using fun and easy games, he will learn to match more similar looking letters like the "a-e-o-c" family and the "m-n-u-r-h-v-w" family of letters. READY! will also give his parents many ideas for helping him learn simple geometric shapes, pattern recognition, and social skills.

Next year, as a four to five year old, Rusty will learn four or five other letters. When he comes to kindergarten, he will know the shapes and sounds of 10-15 alphabet letters.

The district classes also taught Mindy and Bob how Rusty's ears and brain recognize sounds. They try to talk to him 30 times an hour. They have sung nursery rhymes, the ABC song, and "Ten Little Puppies" to him almost every day since he was born. As a two year old, he loved the rhyme in Dr. Seuss's *How the Grinch Stole Christmas.* Mindy plays Odd Word Out[1] with him using ending (rhyming) sounds. This year he will play the same Odd Word Out game using the beginning sounds and begin learning to tap out the syllables in his name (/Rus/ /ty/ -

two taps). By the time he is four or five, he will be able to hear each distinct sound (phoneme) in most words and tap them out as well.

At first, Mindy and Bob were concerned about how much time it would take to teach these sounds, shapes, and basic concepts. It turns out that it takes almost no additional time at all. The READY! activities fit easily into daily routines. "You have one, two, three, four, five toes on this foot," Bob and Mindy would say as they lightly tickled his foot and put on his sock. "And you have one, two, three, four, five toes on this foot! Five? Were there five toes yesterday? Five toes? Not four toes?" Rusty delightedly tells them, "Fife toe!" He laughs as they hug him, and they continue, "So how many eyes do you have today?"

They have been reading 20 minutes a day with Rusty since birth. Many of the learning activities occur right during the reading time and progressively engage Rusty as his mind develops. "Where Questions and Point to Answers" progressed to "where" and "what" questions and then to "how" and "why" questions.

"So where is the Grinch?" Mindy asked when Rusty was eighteen months.[2]

"What color is the Grinch's hat?" Mindy asked when he was two.[3]

"Why do you think the Grinch stole the toys?" she asks now he is three.[4]

"I think they should put the Grinch in jail," she will comment when he is four, waiting six to eight seconds for Rusty to respond as she reads the book for 100th time.[5]

Bob was not inclined to spend much time talking with the infant Rusty until he learned about a ground-breaking study of 41 families who monitored the talking patterns to their young child for 30 months between ages one and three.[6] Now he tries to talk to him all the time, because he knows that the vocabulary, reasoning, the rules of the

---

[1]Odd Word Out can be used to first teach ending sounds (c<u>at</u>, h<u>at</u>, bird) then beginning sounds (<u>b</u>e, <u>b</u>at, cow).

[2]This is an example of an "ask and point" question appropriate for one to two year olds.

[3]This is an example of "what and where" questions appropriate for two to three year olds.

[4]This is an example of "why and how" questions appropriate for three to four year olds.

[5]Mindy models the CAR technique: comment and wait, ask and wait, respond and wait. See Washington Research Institute's excellent series *Begin with Language*, footnote 5 in Chapter 23.

language, and social interaction imbedded in the soft clay of Rusty's mind before three will be reproduced in the form of vocabulary by third grade. Mindy makes time in her professional day for these activities as the same research convinced her that child-care and preschool simply cannot replace the kind of intergenerational transition of skills that occurs in families. Some children will come to kindergarten having heard 3 million words during their lifetime. Not Rusty. He will have heard 14 million.

Bob also likes the district classes, because he has learned new ways to bond with Rusty. He did not grow up around little children. Bob is intrigued that tiny children learn by gentle repetition. He is delighted by the folders where he helps Rusty match increasingly complicated shapes, dots, and numbers. The puzzles are fun too, and Bob is finding ways to play with Rusty while teaching two- and three-step patterns using colors and then sounds. Hundreds of repetitions of these simple activities create electrically wired patterns in Rusty's brain that were not there before. The recognition patterns grow faster and faster until they are almost instantaneous.

> *"Tuition at some of New York's top private kindergartens in September [2003] will exceed $26,000 for the first time, almost as much as the cost of attending Princeton University and twice the price of state universities . . . . 'To us, this is a great investment,' [said a marketing executive planning to enroll his son in one such school.]"*
>
> — Liz Willen, "Private Kindergarten Tuition in N.Y. More Than $26,000," *Seattle Times*, Nation & World, February 16, 2004; www.seattletimes.com

Rusty is learning more than shapes, sounds, and vocabulary. At two and three, he learned to follow two-step instructions, such as "Get your cup and put it on the table." By four, he concentrates long enough to complete activities. He works things out for himself, seeking help only as a last resort. By five, he follows three- to four-step instructions. His parents provide him opportunities to play regularly with other children, sometimes at their houses. He even enjoys occasional sleep-overs at his cousins' house. Mindy believes that helping Rusty learn to play well with other children is part of her role as a parent.[7]

[6]Betty Hart and Todd R. Risley, *Meaningful Differences in the Everyday Experience of Young American Children* (Baltimore, MD: Paul H. Brookes Publishing, 1995). This research provides some of our best clues about why effective families work better than most government programs.

These are simple practices with simple tools; but when Rusty comes to kindergarten, he will have the literacy, math, and social skills typical of five year olds.[8] In fact, he will have skills more typical of seven to eight year olds.

Beginning Kindergarten

Summer finally draws to a close. School begins. Kindergarteners are usually five by September. They weigh 25-35 pounds. They come in a vast array of colors, sizes, and shapes. Some of them have the language, math, and social skills of five- to eight-year olds. They are ready for kindergarten and love it. Rusty is one of them.

Other children like Sara have skills typical of three and four year olds and are not ready. They come anyway. Sara does not like kindergarten, and she is having a hard time.

Sara will attempt very little without guidance or reassurance from her teacher. She seldom concentrates for very long on anything. Often her teacher must repeat instructions several times before she understands or asks for help. She clings to her teacher, is fretful, and watches the door.

She is beginning to take her coat off and put it on by herself and can deal with most of her toilet needs but frequently asks for help. She plays pretty much by herself and rarely initiates contact with other children. She does not know how to share materials or to take turns. Able to speak only in simple three-to-four-word fragments, she has a limited vocabulary to describe her thoughts and needs. "The girl has got to learn to get along with other kids," her father Tony often says, and of course, he's right.[9]

---

[7]"Parents of socially competent toddlers and preschoolers believe that helping their children learn to play well is part of their role as parents. . . [and generally] attribute their social gaffes to transitory, fixable factors like 'She's tired. We let them play too long. The group is too large.' " J. J. Goodnow, R. Knight, and J. Cashmore, 1985, as quoted in Jack P. Shonkoff, ed., *From Neurons to Neighborhoods* (Washington, DC: National Academy Press, 2000), 170.

[8]Entering kindergarten students in the 40th to 60th percentile (the third quintile) typically know 10-15 lower case letters and their sounds, can hear the beginning, ending, and syllable breaks in words, can speak fluently in full sentences, have a 5,000 word vocabulary, and are able to print or "draw" their first name.

While Sara has great difficulty drawing even the first letter of her name with a crayon, she knows the "S" shape, its name, that it makes the "sssss" sound, and she is proud of it. She likes chanting "S—Snake" and tries to make up rhymes herself. She cannot recognize beginning sounds or tap out the two syllables in her name.

While a para-pro conducts a class activity, their kindergarten teacher spends 20 minutes giving Rusty the district's kindergarten assessment test. Rusty identifies lower and uppercase letters, plays Odd Word Out with beginning and ending sounds of words, and prints his first name. It is a game for Rusty, and he scores 85 out of 100.

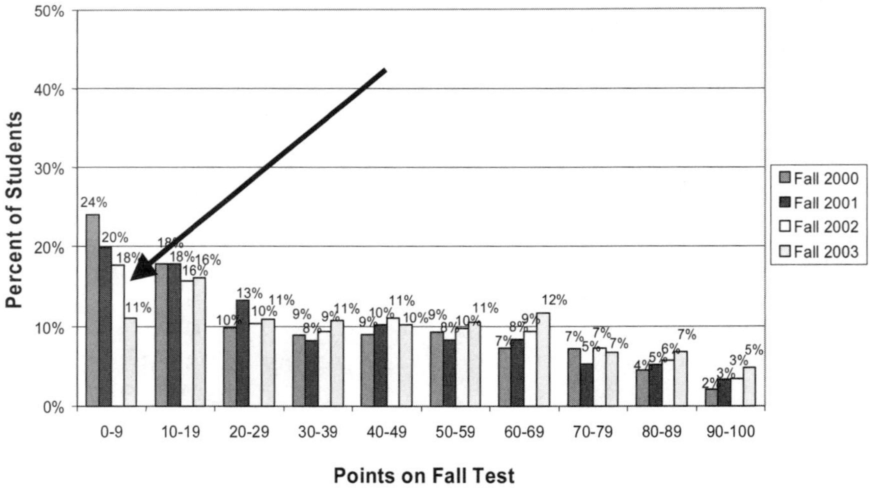

Figure 24.1. Four Years of Incoming Kindergarten Scores in Kennewick, 2000-03. The arrow indicates a significant drop in the number of students with the lowest scores after the first year of READY! classes. A score of 35 is considered "grade level."

[9]"Parents of socially maladroit children see social competence or its lack as more inherent (i.e., aggressive children are born that way), devalue the importance of social skills, and argue that teaching social skills is the job of the schools or others with formal training." K. H. Rubin, R. S. L. Mills, and L. Rose-Krasnor, 1989, quoted in Shonoff, *From Neurons to Neighborhoods*, 170.

When it is Sara's turn, she can barely draw her "S", and knows only two other alphabet letters. She guesses right on some ending sounds and gets one beginning sound right. The teacher stops the questions in a section when Sara misses three consecutive ones, and she finishes in less than 7 minutes. It was not a fun game for Sara, and her score was 8. Sara is a lot like her dad was 20 years before, but there is a big difference. Sara will read at grade level by the end of third grade.

It's Data Time: Catch-Up Begins

The kindergarten assessment is a magical moment for Sara that never occurred for her dad, Tony. The assessment provided information about her academic skills in a modern school district that responds to data. Like feeble vital signs in a hospital, Sara's weak emergent literacy skills cry for immediate attention. The lack of critical language and literacy experiences necessary for normal growth for Sara during her preschool years has been identified. The burden of catch-up, in large part, is now shifted to the schools. The schools will begin assuring annual growth and, because of early identification, begin to compensate for the two years of missing growth. It is rare to catch up in a single year, but Sara is beginning a successful journey.

There will always be children entering kindergarten with less than full and normal development, but thanks to the relatively inexpensive early-learning school programs that engage most parents, the number is steadily dwindling.

Even though her social skills serve as a major hindrance to her academic progress, by the end of kindergarten, Sara will learn all of the alphabet letters and sounds. Extensive exercises focusing on the sounds of words (first ending sounds and then beginning sounds) will start to wire a critical area in her brain. Teacher-parent conferences will share information fairly directly, and

"Just because a program works across town, or just because it worked last year with last year's students isn't good enough any longer. It must work this year, with this year's students, in this school. Parachutists may debate styles of chutes and different ways to pack them, but there is one thing they do not debate. No matter what the brand name or how it is packaged, their parachute, when they jump, had better open. Parachutists, like our students, take no comfort in something that worked at a different time and place with a different person, but doesn't work for them."

The 90% Reading Goal, 153

invited to a parent academy to learn more ways to support and share in Sara's education.

By the end of the year, Sara will print her name just like Rusty, even though her letters will still be shaky and less clear, and her ability to write will still lag behind.

During first grade, the normal reading block of time is 120 minutes for both Rusty and Sara. Sara has an additional 45 minutes with the district reading specialist, 30 minutes with a Title I instructor, and 20 minutes with a Team Read volunteer tutor reading aloud, for a total of 215 minutes a day. The time is eyeball-to-eyeball teaching, not working alone or with a pile of dittos. After lunchtime, recess, and library, there is not much time left for other subjects. Sara's elementary school made some obvious but fairly gut-wrenching decisions to cut Sara's (but not Rusty's) curriculum in social studies to free up that time. Slowly Sara is making up the two- to three-year deficiency with which she entered kindergarten. Does she mind? No. She desperately wants to learn to read.

During second grade, Sara again gets 180-220 minutes a day of direct reading instruction. Her small reading group is need based. The NWEA MAP testing allows a quick on-line assessment in the fall and spring and at three additional times. All in all, she is tested three or four times more than the district or the state requires. Most of her additional direct instructional time is targeted to the sub-skills where she needs the most help. None of the "pull-out" time occurs during regular reading instruction time.

By third grade, her dad has finally started reading aloud regularly with her. Twenty minutes a night is tough. Tony has never seen it done, and he has reading problems of his own. But his confidence is growing and Sara loves it, because it's time she would not otherwise be spending with him. The K-3 period is critical, because up to third grade, Sara and her friends learn to read. After third grade, they read to learn.

Sara is now in the fourth grade. Sara is staring at her science book. It's from a national publisher, carefully written on a fourth-grade level.

So scientists believe that there never was any water on the moon. The moon is a dry, airless and very barren place.

This is what the sentence looks like to adults like you and me with high school diplomas. It's what the sentence looks like to Sara, too.

And So It's "Now" Again

Sara has graduated from high school. Her experience in the public schools was different than Rusty's. Needed glasses were slow in coming. She had less money for co-curricular activities. She never had a taxi-cab mom to shuttle her around. She had to work harder for an increased vocabulary that Rusty just absorbed from his parents. She does not have the connections for a summer job, nor parents like Bob and Mindy who are alumni of the college she wants to attend.

All of these differences remain. But the differences between Sara and Rusty are a fraction of those between their parents. Sara learned to read at grade level by third grade and remained at or above grade level through high school. She graduated, and has the reading skills necessary for most entry-level jobs and for college.

Her teachers tell her that she missed some art, science, and social studies in first, second, and third grade, but for the life of her, she has no idea what it was. She can read, and now working harder will make an incremental difference in the result. Third-grade reading does not guarantee that Sara will have a successful life, but it does guarantee her a world of options that were never available for her dad.

And equally, if not most important, Sara's children will have a mom who reads.

PART FOUR

THE FACES AND FORCES OF CHANGE

Change often comes from outside an industry.

A young Dutch janitor and dry goods salesman, Anton van Leeuwenhoek (1632-1723), began grinding better magnifying lenses. He started with a lens that would magnify a dime to the size of a quarter; and by the time he was finished, his microscopes magnified objects with clarity up to 270 times. With his innovation, he single-handedly created modern microbiology and probably modern astronomy.

Centuries later, a Swiss watchmaker developed a digital watch and showcased it at an international trade fair. The Swiss were unimpressed with the device that had no cogs, wheels, or hands. No one even bothered to patent it. United States and Japanese companies adopted the technology and transformed the watch industry in a decade.

More recently, Michael Jordan has been a spectacular performer who added many nuances to the game of basketball. But the unknown individuals who added the 3-point line and the 24-second shot clock, faceless and nameless as they may be, made far deeper and more fundamental changes to the game.

Public education is changing and Part Four provides short sketches of four faces and forces of that change. Allan Olson and Bill Sanders are developing the new growth assessment technology. America's legislators have irrevocably changed the rules of the game. The Bill and Melinda Gates Foundation have focused on the toughest problem in education. The book then concludes with 99 maxims which summarize the book's major points.

At an average adult reading speed of about 300 words a minute, reading Part Four, including sidebars, kickers, and footnotes, will take 52 minutes.

CHAPTER TWENTY-FIVE

Allan Olson and the Northwest Evaluation Association

"Always introduce the least amount of energy into an education system necessary to change it. The more energy that is introduced, the more likely the system will become unstable."

— Allan Olson, Executive Director,
Northwest Evaluation Association

Allan Olson is the executive director of the fastest growing educational assessment group in the world. For the last 11 years, the non-profit Northwest Evaluation Association (NWEA), based in Portland, Oregon, has increased in size by 50% each year. In 2003-04, NWEA served over 1,400 school districts, administering six million tests.

Allan would rather spend an evening meditating than watching an NFL football game. He prefers to ski alone, backpack alone, and trim his bonsai trees alone. Still, he is anything but a recluse. He spends most of his waking hours traversing the U. S., meeting with educators and policy makers, and presenting at conferences. He is intolerant of incompetence, low quality, and consumption at the cost of future generations.

Born in Minnesota to second-generation Swedish parents and educated in Minnesota public schools and at the University of Minnesota, Allan connected to his life work in his early thirties.

In the midst of a project for school districts in Seattle, Washington, and Portland, Oregon in 1978, Allan began to see how assessments could be the primary lever for change in the public schools—but only if they were fundamentally different from any current version.

He found like-minded collaborators. From those intense conversations and absorbed tinkerings that consumed every waking moment for the next two years, the vision of a new assessment emerged. In this vision, assessments would:

- Be accurate and fair for each child, especially those who are well behind and well ahead.
- Measure growth during the school year and across school years in each core subject.
- Be fully scaled across grade levels from grades two to twelve.
- Allow teachers in the school district setting to see what changes were needed and follow up with data to determine the effect of those changes.

The result of this vision can be seen in NWEA's assessment system which communicates growth and achievement to every user at every level, from the student and parent to state-level policy makers. The achievement level tests, and Measures of Academic Progress (MAP) tests are supported by NWEA's 20,000 item bank of scaled questions. The impact of this system on the districts that use it may be indirectly seen in the renorming in 2002. While there is little evidence that scores in reading and mathematics significantly improved nationwide, in the 1980s and 1990s, achievement at third grade level in the cohort of school districts served by NWEA moved up more than half a year when measured against the fixed RIT scale. (See Chapter 18.)

As powerful as the data produced by the assessment are, Allan may well be remembered 50 years from now for two other NWEA technologies.

The backbone of the NWEA testing system is the Rasch Equal Interval (RIT) Scale. It is the first and oldest yardstick in education to measure both student growth and student achievement over time. Educators have long lacked a common measurement scale for academic achievement and academic growth. Letter grades are universal but classroom specific. An "A" from different ninth-grade math classes within the same school tells us almost nothing about comparative achievement and absolutely nothing about growth of the two students. The "A" is even less meaningful when one from Louisiana is compared to another from Iowa or New York. Major test publishers' calibrations often offer little more, relying on three-to-five-year norms developed from small sample groups.

Chapter 15 presents an example of the power of a national scale in comparing where states have set their NCLB standards. The RIT scale reporting platform was elegant, fully comparable across states and across grade levels. One other major study, performed by the *Princeton Review* staff, used the more cumbersome and less accurate NAEP as a common yardstick.

Obvious uses of a national scale include:

- A clear way to compare state standards to each other.
- A common way to evaluate district and school growth.
- A common way to evaluate individual student growth.
- A common vocabulary to describe expected growth and catch-up growth.
- A common criterion for college entrance.

Allan's crowning technology may be the creation of the NWEA Growth research database. Developed in conjunction with the University of Indianapolis, the NWEA has used warehoused data from several hundred districts. These thousands of datasets include unique student scores over multiple test seasons correlated by ethnicity, SES, instructional programs, federal census tracts, and class size.

It is a researcher's dream. The test scores for students are the most accurate available in the United States. Because of the characteristics of each record, a researcher can construct a nationwide "control group," perfectly matching for ethnicity, gender, SES, geography, and initial achievement.

Similarly, school districts can compare their schools and districts to similarly situated student populations with greater precision and speed than is possible in any field study.

"Our success stems from our employees commitment to making a difference in children's lives and carrying that mission in their hearts."

—Susan Smoyer

Obviously, Allan has had help with the development of these technologies and is the first to point to his long-time collaborator, Susan Smoyer, and his capable department leaders and staff. Susan started as NWEA's first employee, and as Executive Vice President, has focused relentlessly on ensuring that the highest possible quality of service is provided during the organization's rapid expansion. Allan is also quick to say that NWEA is not done. "We have barely scratched the surface of what we can and will do to help teachers, schools, districts, and states improve learning. For instance, we will soon provide educators with the tools to access appropriate instructional resources to address the needs of each child; do real-time analysis of achievement data for a student, class, school, or district; and use technology-based analysis to diagnose anomalies in student learning as well as school-wide system effects. The information tools of the very near future will provide educators with the opportunity and impetus to transform our schools into constantly improving systems for learning."

CHAPTER TWENTY-SIX

The Legislators

"If you cannot measure it, you cannot change it."

— Edwards Deming

These are the people who changed the rules. From those members of House and Senate education committees at the state and federal level has come the mandate that those students who are furthest behind catch up.

Have you ever wondered how 49 states passed very similar educational reform legislation in an eight-year period—legislation that sets minimum academic standards, benchmarks the current number of students at or above the standards, and expects increasing numbers of students to reach the standard each subsequent year?

Among the faces and forces of educational change, we have included the legislators on the education committee. In lieu of their five hundred to one thousand collective faces, we have included a symbol of where they do their work.[1]

[1] Photo courtesy of http://free-stock-photos.com/.

This educational reform could have been propelled by a variety of entities such as the universities or the K-12 professional educational associations—the National School Board Association, the American Association of School Administrators, or the National Education Association, etc. It was not. Legislators have controlled the shape of this reform. And while the educational groups have reacted to and reshaped many legislative proposals, the primary guidance for this reform has come from the business community.

In the late 1970s and early 1980s, our U.S. business and labor advantage, which had been slowly eroding in relationship to international competitors for some time, began to slip and then rapidly slide. Asian firms were trouncing General Motors in the car business, Xerox in the office automation business, and a multitude of other businesses in between.

A Nation at Risk was published in 1983.[2] For educators, it was a lightning rod. For business, it was a tipping point. Educators directed every conceivable criticism at the study. Business leaders, fairly inarticulate about specific shortcomings in their workforce, began elaborating on their own industry experience around the study. During the mid-1980s, they began to slowly identify the specific academic skills missing in its workforce. But the economic pressures, especially from Asia, continued to grow.

> [By 1986], Japan first surpassed the United States as an international creditor. A year later, Japan's per capita income surpassed America's. A year after that, the Dai-Ichi Kangyo bank overtook Citibank and the Bank of America to become the largest bank in the world. A year after that, the eleven largest banks in the world were all Japanese, the shares listed on the Tokyo Stock Exchange were worth twice as much as all the shares on the New York Stock Exchange . . . .[In 1986], the real-estate value of Japan's land was higher than the value of all the land in America . . . [despite its being] only 4% of the size of the United States . . . [and with] none of the oil wells, gold fields, fertile Midwestern cropland or other natural assets. In 1989 . . . the land in metropolitan Tokyo alone was worth more than all the land in America.[3]

[2]National Commission of Excellence in Education, *A Nation at Risk: The Imperative for Educational Reform* (Washington, DC: U.S. Department of Education, 1983).

By 1989, President Bush and state governors identified and endorsed six National Educational Goals.[4] In 1990, the National Center on Education and the Economy (NCEE), a nonprofit association with strong Democratic party ties, published *High Skills or Low Wages*,[5] the results of the study conducted by the Commission on the Skills of the American Workforce that effectively linked minimum student skills with themes of international industrial and economic competition.

By the early 1990s, the Business Roundtable and the National Alliance of Business, supported by six or seven other national business coalitions and with the help of the National Center on Education and the Economy, developed a framework of nine criteria for identifying "Essential Components of a Successful Education System" and began analyzing the "gap" between the criteria and K-12 systems, state by state. These gap analyses served as the basis for making specific legislative policy recommendations, which were then included in state education reform legislation.[6]

Meanwhile, public educators continued to propose a rich and wide range of initiatives focusing on inclusion, process, and developmental models. To them, core skills sounded like "back-to-the-basics." "Basic job skills" was reminiscent of technical or trade schools. Twenty years of social promotion defied any practical way to implement academic accountability as well.

The first sign that the public educators' approach was in trouble was when Connecticut's ambitious educational plan, developed over 18 months by its Commission on Educational Excellence, died in legislative committee without hearing or debate.

---

[3]James Fallow, *More Like Us: Putting America's Native Strengths and Traditional Values to Work to Overcome the Asian Challenge* (Boston: Houghton Mifflin Company, 1989), vii-viii.

[4]The six national educational goals were (1) that by the year 2000, all children will start school ready to learn; (2) that 90 percent of high school students will graduate; (3) that students will be competent in basic subjects and exhibit responsible citizenship; (4) that U.S. students will lead the world in mathematics and science; (5) that every American adult will be literate; and (6) that schools will be drug-free and safe.

[5]Commission on the Skills of the American Workforce (CSAW), *America's Choice: High Skills or Low Wages* (Rochester, NY: National Center on Education and the Economy, 1990).

[6]The nine points include standards, performance and assessment, school accountability, professional development learning, readiness, technology, school autonomy, parent involvement, and safety and discipline. James L. Meadow, "Business Coalition Education Agendas" (Ph.D. diss., University of Washington, 2003).

Public Agenda[7] was commissioned to find out what happened. Its national findings, *First Things First*,[8] and the companion study for Connecticut[9] established deep public support for tougher and more challenging courses in the basics (75-96%), safe campuses and disciplined classrooms (54-72%), elimination of social promotion, and achieving minimum standards as a condition of high school graduation (81%).

The first foray of the U.S. Congress into educational standards was a complicated structural reorganization of funding from the federal government to states to classrooms in *Goals 2000: Educate America Act*, in March 1994. Met with high levels of public educator criticism, the legislation was substantially repealed. Some states continued progressive reforms but most adopted a "wait and see" approach, unwilling to reinvent a wheel that the federal government had started working on. State standards-based education began to drift.

It was in 1995 that Lou Gerstner, then CEO of IBM, threw down a gauntlet. As the guest speaker at the National Governors' Conference, Gerstner emphasized that K-12 public education had always been the responsibility of individual states and it was time that states stopped waiting for the federal government and got back to work. If the governors would attend a major educational summit, Gerstner would guarantee that a CEO from a major business from each state would attend as well.

The 1996 National Educational Summit was organized and held in IBM headquarters in Palisades, New York. Hosted by then Governor Tommy Thompson of Wisconsin, all fifty governors signed a "Commitment to Action" statement endorsing standards-based education. At the time, 14 states had standards-based systems in place.

Within six months, with a board of three Republicans, three Democrats, and three business CEOs, Achieve, Inc.,[10] was organized as

[7]Public Agenda is a national, nonpartisan, nonprofit public opinion research organization, located in New York City and well respected for its influential public opinion polls. Founded in 1975 by Cyrus R. Vance, the former U.S. Secretary of State, and Daniel Yankelovich, a social scientist and author, its mission is to inform leaders about the public's views and to inform citizens about government policy.

[8]Jean Johnson and John Immerwahr, *First Things First* (New York: Public Agenda, 1994).

[9]John Immerwahr, *The Broken Contract: Connecticut Citizens Look at Public Education* (New York: Public Agenda, 1994).

[10]Acheive, Inc. may be contacted at http://www.achieve.org.

an independent, bipartisan, non-profit organization to help states raise academic standards, improve assessments and strengthen accountability. Aided by special task forces, blue ribbon commissions, the National Conference of State Legislators, and more than 1,500 state business groups, [11] the creation of high academic standards, aligned assessments, and accountability became state law in 35 more states within four years. (See Appendix I, State Content Standards). By 2002-04, Achieve had become a primary resource to states to try to get the reform pieces right. Business and state legislatures began expanding their attention to educational capacity issues like the quality and effectiveness of teachers.

No Child Left Behind, Congress's second major foray into education, became law in January 2002. Like Goals 2000, it has been heavily criticized as well but for different reasons. Our own suggested changes to the legislation are offered in Appendix F.

Educational policy, controlled by select groups of professional educators in the 1970s and 1980s has moved into the hands of some 500-1,000 legislators on state and federal committees. There is no reason to believe that we have seen the end of their influence, nor the sway of the business community through them, on the structure of education.

---

[11]James L. Meadow, ibid.

CHAPTER TWENTY-SEVEN

BILL SANDERS AND VALUE-ADDED

"When the unit of measurement is individual student growth, the proportion of ethnic minorities in the school will provide little help in predicting student growth."

— Bill Sanders

Imagine a wizened man, slightly stooped, gray hair, 140 pounds, with four or five pens in his shirt pocket. Then you stop noticing anything but the brightness of his eyes and smile as he talks about his data. You have Dr. William L. Sanders. With a Ph.D. from the University of Tennessee at Knoxville, Dr. Sanders is a Senior Research Fellow with the University of North Carolina and is currently employed by SAS Institute in Cary, North Carolina.[1]

[1] Dr. Sanders was professor of statistics and director of the University of Tennessee's Value-Added Research and Assessment Center for 34 years.

Dr. Sanders provides a very different paradigm of educational growth and achievement. He developed the educational concept of value-added assessment. His model remains the most rigorous and robust measure of student progress available, having withstood both the test of time and the scrutiny of intensive review by the statistical community.

It happened almost by accident. In the early 1980s, Tennessee's Governor Lamar Alexander was considering merit pay for teachers, but testing experts contended that student growth data could never be accurately linked to teacher evaluation. Sanders suggested to a graduate class that this problem could be solved with a methodology that had been available in the statistical literature for decades. By following individual students' academic progress over time, and linking each student's scores from grade to grade over subjects, a base could be established in which each student serves as his or her own control.

With such a base, the effects of extraneous factors could be separated out [2] and unequal starting points identified. Then the effects of individual educational influences–the district, school, and teacher–on the rate of student growth could be objectively measured.

This graduate class example evolved into the Tennessee Value-Added Assessment System (TVAAS) in 1992 and spread beyond Tennessee to more than 300 districts nationwide. What has Dr. Sanders learned?

- If the variability in student academic progress is partitioned into three "buckets"—among districts, among schools within districts, and among teachers within schools within districts—what is the relative amount of the variability that will go into each bucket?

  About 5% among districts,
  About 15% among the schools with the districts, and
  About 65% among teachers within schools within districts.

[2] The methodology allows exogenous factors to be separated out, if not completely, then nearly so.

- Differences in teacher effectiveness are the dominant factors affecting student academic growth in all subjects, especially in math.[3]

- One third of teachers create consistent gain in all their students. Two-thirds of teachers fail to create gain in either their top, middle, or low performing students, i.e., in about one-third of their students.

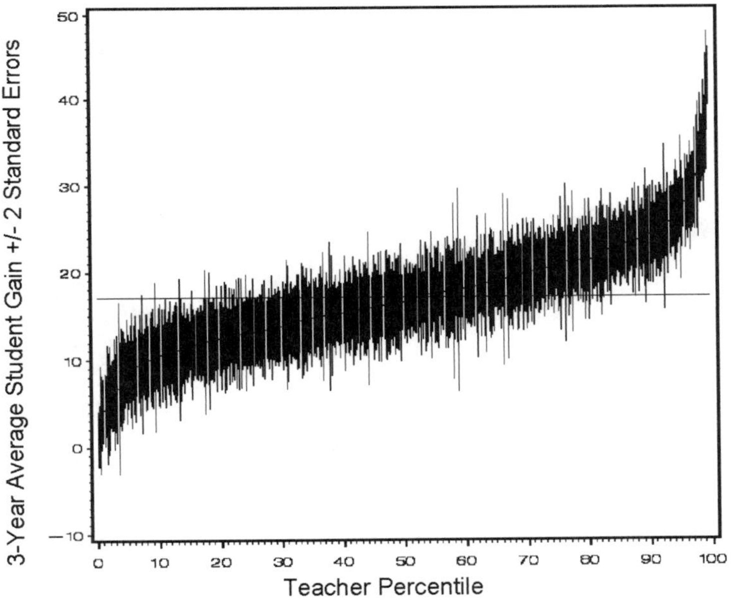

Figure 27.1. Variability in Effectiveness among Math Teachers, Tennessee, 1996-97. The horizontal line represents the average gain of students by individual math teachers during eighth grade. Each vertical line shows the three-year average growth of the students for one teacher.

- The average beginning teacher is much less effective than the average 10-15 year experienced teacher. While 10-15 year veterans profile at about the 55th percentile in a growth distribution, beginning teachers profile at about the 35th percentile.

[3]Dr. Sander's studies do not include length of direct instruction time as a variable.

- Teacher effects are cumulative and additive. The sequence of math teachers during a three- or four-year period can have a profound effect on each student's ultimate achievement in math.

- Teachers who leave after one year of experience on average were generally less effective than those who stayed. The teachers who leave after one year of experience and who began teaching in schools with more than 75 percent minority students profile at about the 22nd percentile relative to all teachers.

- Inner city schools have a disproportionate number of beginning teachers and have higher turnover rate of teachers than suburban schools.

- A high percentage of middle school math teachers are teaching with emergency certification without math endorsements.

- Retardation of math gain rates for high achieving inner city middle school students is more pronounced than for lower achieving inner city students.

- Some rural districts that have very effective elementary schools have high schools that are not extending academic growth opportunities to average and above-average achieving students. In some cases this disparity is so severe that advanced students, if admitted to a four-year university, would most likely be required to take remedial courses.

- The effectiveness of a school in helping students make gains cannot be predicted based on its racial makeup.

Insights from Dr. Sanders and his collaborator and wife, June Rivers, will continue to influence educational policy for the foreseeable future. SAS is a privately held software company located in Cary, North Carolina and markets Dr. Sanders's approach to value-added assessment under the banner of SAS EVAAS for K-12. Their website can be accessed at www.sas.com under *government and education.*

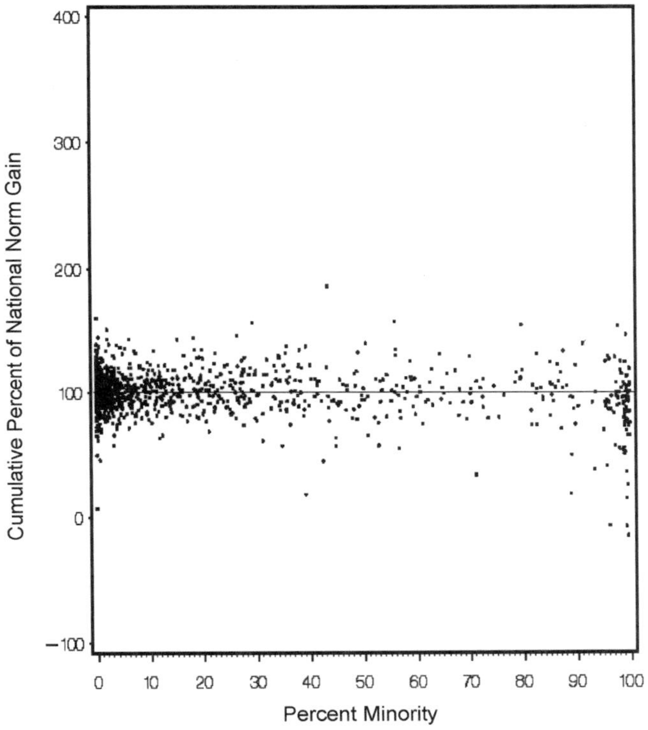

Figure 27.2. Cumulative Gain of Tennessee Schools in Reading Compared with the Percent of Minority Students in the School. This scatter gram represents the amount of reading growth in schools with differing proportions of minorities. Each dot represents one school in Tennessee. The horizontal line at 100% represents gain equal to national norm gain. When a dot is at the 100% line (y-axis) it means that school is making 100% of average growth in reading. If the dot is at 150%, that school is making 150% (or a year and half of normal growth) each year. A dot near the y-axis means it has a low percentage of minorities whereas if the dot is at the far right, the school has a high degree of minorities. Although schools with high populations of minority students sometimes show lower average raw scores, the gains their students make are comparable to those of schools with a small population of minority students. When a school's influence on student scores is estimated longitudinally looking at multiple subjects simultaneously, the proportion of ethnic minorities in the school provides little help in predicting student growth. This is contrary to observations about schools when the results of a single achievement test are reported. In the reporting of single achievement test results, the relationship between the schools' average scores and average student SES at the schools is quite strong.

CHAPTER TWENTY-EIGHT

THE BILL & MELINDA GATES FOUNDATION

"A few years ago, Bill and Melinda asked themselves how they could dramatically help the most people per dollar spent—and then set out to spend more dollars on the ideas they came up with than have ever before been devoted to any philanthropic effort."

— Warren E. Buffett
Time, 2004

Bill Gates was 45 in 2000 when he and his wife, Melinda, gave $24 billion to their foundation. Since then, the foundation has given $2.1 billion to public education. Yet America's 50 states spend about 324 billion dollars a year on education.[1] In 2003, Bill and Melinda Gates spent $233,882,844— about seven-tenths of 1% a year. So what is the big deal?

The big deal is that all of the Gates money is used outside existing contract and program commitments. It is water committed to prime the pump of change. Just a little bit can make a huge difference.

[1] Frank Johnson, "Revenues and Expenditures for Public Elementary and Secondary Education: School Year 1999-2000," U.S. Department of Education, National Center for Education Statistics, May 16, 2002. Retrieved on June 8, 2004, from http://www.policyalmanac.org/education/archive/doe_education_spending.shtml.

In a public school budget, approximately:

80% goes to wages, payroll taxes, and benefits;
10% to supplies and materials;
7% to heat, light, power, insurance, travel, and outside services;
2% to equipment and technology.

There is rarely more than 1-3% of uncommitted funds. Prudent business managers hold most of that in reserve until spring, so that some unexpected expenditure doesn't leave them, their superintendent, and the board short. Although the percentages may shift a little from district to district, the tiny sliver that is left to fund change rarely does. Gates money is all change money. The Gates Foundation is the most significant benefactor to K-12 public education since the Carnegie Foundation.[2]

The other part of the big deal is that the Gates Foundation has taken on the most intractable problem in public education—low-performing high schools. "High school is the culmination of all that comes before," notes Melinda French Gates.[3]

High school is where all the preceding student deficits in reading and math come home to roost. One in five entering ninth graders have reading skills typical of fifth or sixth graders, and another one of the five reads at seventh or eighth grade level. In math, the story is a little worse. The lowest 20% have math skills of fifth graders, having come into kindergarten one to two years behind, falling behind a year in elementary school and falling an additional year behind in middle school. Entering ninth graders in the 20th-40th percentile will have math skills of sixth to seventh graders.[4]

It is of little surprise that of 100 entering high school students, 30 will drop out. "And the prognosis is even worse for African American

[2] Over the course of his life (1835-1919), Andrew Carnegie contributed over $350 million to support numerous educational, cultural, and peace-making causes. "Carnegie, Andrew," *Microsoft® Encarta® Online Encyclopedia 2004.* http://encarta.msn.com © 1997-2004 Microsoft Corporation. All Rights Reserved. By summer of 2004, the Bill & Melinda Gates Foundation contributed $7.2 billion in grants, of which $2.2 billion have been to public education.

[3] Remarks by Melinda French Gates in address to the National School Boards Association, Orlando, Florida, on March 22, 2003. Retrieved from www.gatesfoundation.org on June 1, 2004.

[4] See Figures 14.1 and 14.2 in Chapter 14.

and Hispanic students—nearly half of them will never see their graduation day."[5] Overall, out of the four million incoming ninth graders this year, about a million will be gone by their senior year.

Of the 70% who do graduate four years later (see Appendix J), the foundation estimates that a third of them graduate "totally unprepared for college, for work, and for citizenship in this country." Two in every three students entering community college will take one or more remedial classes (for which they do not get credit) to compensate for skill deficiencies in core subject areas.

Melinda French Gates

Graduation rate is one of the slipperiest and most embarrassing statistics in public education. Some states have used the number of enrolling seniors in the fall as their denominator and the number who graduate in the spring as the numerator to calculate their graduation rate, knowing that most students drop out during their freshman and sophomore years.

One way to get past denial in your community is to divide the number of graduating seniors by the number of incoming high school students in that class three or four years earlier. If this is done for a period of five to ten years, a remarkably stable completion rate should emerge. By calculating completion rates at the end of the freshman, sophomore and junior years, the patterns of when most students drop out should emerge as well.

The current strategy of the Bill & Melinda Gates Foundation is to encourage the development of new, small high schools and to transform large, impersonal high school to smaller, focused, rigorous schools or learning communities.

"Large comprehensive high schools have two fatal flaws," say

[5] Remarks by Melinda French Gates, to the National Conference of State Legislatures, "Educating All Children Well: Do We Want to Do It Badly Enough?" San Francisco, CA, June 25, 2003. Retrieved

Tom Vander Ark, executive director of education for the foundation. "They are large and comprehensive."[6]

It is too early to tell if the Gates strategy of reducing school size will consistently result in annual reading and math growth for all students and the necessary two to four years of additional catch-up growth during the high school years for those who are behind .

However, as more students come to kindergarten with skills typical of five-year olds, and as more elementary and middle school staffs learn how to make annual growth for all students and catch-up growth for those who are behind, the seemingly insurmountable challenge to assure students have reading and math skills at state standards will shrink. The sharing of successful new techniques and organizational structures developed in the more than 1,000 Gates schools will diminish the size of the problem as well.

The Gates process has clearly worked in Kennewick. In 2000, Kennewick applied for and won a $7.3 competitive Gates grant for district-wide school reform for 2000-05. Within the provisions of the grant, we have been able to send teams to some of the most progressive districts in Texas to look at new approaches for English language learners, to San Diego School District to see the Alvarado and Fink techniques, to the Harvard Institute for School Leadership, as well as to visit and learn from high performing schools within our own state. The grant has accelerated our instructional framework described in Chapter Six, provided outside consultants to accelerate change of the district and school building cultures, and also initially funded peer literacy and math coaches at our middle and high schools.

In turn, we offer what we have learned to you. We hope that it will help accelerate student achievement in your district as well.

---

[6]Remarks by Tom Vander Ark, to the House Appropriations Committee, "Testimony for the House Appropriations Committee," May 22, 2001. Retrieved from www.gatesfoundation.org on June 1, 2004.

CHAPTER TWENTY-NINE

MAXIMS OF ACHIEVEMENT AND GROWTH

"Throughout the centuries there were men [and women] who took first steps down new roads armed with nothing but their own vision."

— Ayn Rand

Birth to Kindergarten

Maxim 1. Babies are born learning. Within hours of birth, they begin to imitate the lip and tongue positions of their parents.

Maxim 2. Babies, toddlers, and preschoolers learn best by imitation and gentle repetition. Hundreds of repetitions in a safe, supportive environment develop and strengthen networks of neurons which wire the young brain.

Maxim 3. About 20% of children make only three years of language and math growth their first five years of life. They enter kindergarten with the skills of three year olds.

Maxim 4. Another 20% of children make four years of language and math growth in their first five years. They enter kindergarten with skills typical of four year olds.

Maxim 5. Other children make five to eight years of growth in language and math in their first five years. They enter kindergarten with skills typical of five, six, seven, and eight year olds.

Maxim 6. On the first day of kindergarten, the range between students in the bottom and top quartile midpoints is six years in reading skills and four years in math.

READY! for Kindergarten ®

Maxim 7. Public schools do not create the achievement gap.

Maxim 8. 100% of the achievement gap in reading and 67% of the gap in math originates in the home before a student's first day of kindergarten.

Maxim 9. Most parents want their children to have a good start in kindergarten. They are receptive to targets, tools, and training provided by their local schools.

Maxim 10. For approximately $300 per year per child, districts can use the READY! curriculum to provide training and materials to support parents in preparing their children to be successful in kindergarten.

Maxim 11. Creating widespread awareness of kindergarten and age-level targets among parents and child-care providers significantly increases the number of students entering kindergarten with grade-level skills.

Maxim 12. Incoming kindergarten targets include recognizing 12 to 15 alphabet letters and their sounds, identifying beginning and ending sounds in words, counting to 20, knowing quantities to 10, mastering simple social skills like "settling in" to new groups, focusing on a task for five minutes, following three-part instructions, and coming to school bilingual if from a non-English-speaking home.

Maxim 13. These targets can be achieved when parents read with their child 20 minutes a day from birth and spend five minutes a day on simple age-appropriate activities.

Maxim 14. Parent training consists of three 90-minute sessions for each age level. Instructors share specific tools and activities related to the age-level targets.

Maxim 15. Quality tools and activities draw parents to the classes. Parents leave with about $50 worth of learning tools and activities from each session.

Maxim 16. Our data show that providing targets, tools, and training to parents decreases the number of students coming to kindergarten with skills below grade level by 14% in a single year. READY! ® creates growth achievement.

Maxim 17. Most school districts spend $1,800-$3,400 per child per year on students who need remediation. Catch-up growth in public schools is very expensive and historically unsuccessful. Fostering "annual" academic growth in emergent reading and math skills is five to ten times less expensive from birth to age five than in grades K-5.

Maxim 18. Devising catch-up programs starting in kindergarten and continuing through 12th grade is a reactive strategy.

Annual Growth and Catch-Up Growth in Elementary School

Maxim 19. All students need to make "annual growth." Annual growth is a year's worth of progress in core subjects each year.

Maxim 20. Excellent teaching creates annual growth.

Maxim 21. Annual growth is fairly uniform during elementary school.

Maxim 22. Annual growth is less uniform in middle and high school. Only 62% of students make annual growth in math in grades 6-8.

Maxim 23. A substantial portion of the flattened growth curves in middle school can be attributed to reduced numbers of students making annual growth.

Maxim 24. Annual growth perpetuates the initial four-to-six-year range in incoming kindergarten abilities. Students who are in the first quartile of math are the exception to this maxim. First-quartile students fall a little further behind every year.

Maxim 25. Students who are behind need to make catch-up growth. Catch-up growth is annual growth plus some additional part of a year's growth.

Maxim 26. The primary burden of catching up the student shifts from the parent to the public school system when the student enters kindergarten.

Maxim 27. When students leave kindergarten three years behind in reading, they must make two full years' growth plus annual growth in the first, second, and third grades to be at grade level by the end of third grade.

Maxim 28. Trying to show system growth by making significant catch-up growth just before the high-profile assessments works only for the first year. Equal efforts the second year merely maintain the prior year's level of achievement but without any increase in system growth.

Maxim 29. Student growth in a single year is often mistaken for system growth. System growth is measured by the difference between ending achievement at the same grade level between different years.

Maxim 30. Catch-up growth is easiest to make early. It is easiest from birth to kindergarten. It is more difficult from kindergarten to third grade. It is more challenging still in middle school. It is hardest of all in high school.

Clear Goals

Maxim 31. The 90% reading goal creates a clear line of sight between where each student and each elementary building is and where they need to go. It requires educators to catch up students who are in the back of the academic pack.

Maxim 32. The power of a 90% reading goal at third grade is that it focuses the elementary systems on delivering the single most crucial academic skill—reading—which is the foundation to lifelong learning.

Maxim 33. Districts that do not or cannot teach 90% of their students to read at or above grade level by third grade will rarely achieve 95% reading and math goals at subsequent years.

Maxim 34. No Child Left Behind legislation uses goals to drive nationwide, systemic change. NCLB has institutionalized minimum competency goals in reading and math and requires 95% of all students to reach them by 2014.

Maxim 35. The 95% federal goals will have the same result that the 90% reading goal had in Kennewick if the district supports them.

Targeted Accelerated Growth

Maxim 36. What works: instructional leadership, superb teaching, and excellent testing which assures annual growth and the four-phase TAG loop which assures catch-upgrowth: (1) diagnostic testing to identify sub-skill deficiencies, (2) proportional increases in direct instructional time, (3) teaching to the deficient sub-skill, and (4) retesting to be sure the skill has been learned.

Excellent Data Systems

Maxim 37. An excellent data system is predicated upon an excellent assessment system.

Maxim 38. An excellent assessment system measures growth and achievement by student, classroom, building, and district. The reporting is as accurate in low and high quartiles as it is near grade level. Data should be intelligible to students and parents. Scoring and reporting time should occur within a week.

Maxim 39. Most tests are least accurate for the students who are furthest behind. Thus, educators may have the poorest data for the students for whom they need the most precision.

Maxim 40. A school district must assess at every grade level and in every subject for which it is unwilling to be data-blind.

Maxim 41. Measuring annual and catch-up growth requires district-wide assessment in core subject areas in the spring of each year and often in the fall as well. An excellent assessment system can determine whether each student has made annual growth and/or the amount of targeted catch-up growth.

Maxim 42. There is no point in testing if you don't look at the data, don't understand it, and don't change.

Maxim 43. "Caterpillar" charts visually show the four to six year range in student achievement at each grade level.

Maxim 44. Growth reports are the "new" kids on the block. The "Above and Below the Line" Reports highlight annual growth and catch-up growth.

Maxim 45. In the next decade, the primary users of data will be instructors, students, and parents.

Maxim 46. Data do not use themselves and can sit unused in a perfectly good assessment system in a data-indifferent or a data-hostile school culture.

Maxim 47. The numbers are what they are.

Excellent Initial Instruction

Maxim 48. School structure affects instruction. Elementary teachers have a primary responsibility to 25 students and 50 parents. Middle and high school teachers share responsibility for 150 students and, if they switch at the semester, for 300 students and 600 parents.

Maxim 49. Rigor, engagement, lesson purpose, and results are hallmarks of excellent instruction. High rigor, engagement, and purpose occur during only 17% of instructional time in most classrooms.

Maxim 50. Students learn more quickly with direct instruction than they do with seatwork, entry tasks, homework, and other teaching techniques involving non-eyeball-to-eyeball teaching or practice time.

Maxim 51. Excellent instruction is increased when it is honored. Learning walks, instructional conferences, and split-screen videotaping of lessons celebrate the best practices.

Maxim 52. Few districts can currently quantify the amount of growth that occurs annually in each classroom. Few districts can quantify at which quintile or quartile most growth occurs in a given classroom.

Maxim 53. Elementary school teachers generally feel responsible to create growth in students. Middle and high school teachers are more likely to provide students with the opportunity to learn.

Maxim 54. Students who move frequently and English language learners are two groups that have the greatest difficulty meeting high standards. Highly mobile students spend substantially less time on task. English language learners must subtract the time it takes to learn English from time on task.

Diagnostic Testing

Maxim 55. Diagnostic testing initially involves analyzing the sub-skill deficiencies of individual students from the district or state assessment data.

Maxim 56. Sub-skills for reading include phonemic awareness, phonics, accuracy, fluency, and comprehension. Each sub-skill has sub-categories.

Maxim 57. Sub-skills for math include addition, subtraction, and multiplication facts, one to one correspondence, counting, and sequencing.

Maxim 58. Diagnostic testing is typically done more often and more effectively at the elementary than at the secondary level.

Maxim 59. High performance schools embrace assessment, especially diagnostic testing. High performance schools test more frequently and more precisely than districts or states require.

Maxim 60. Principals who deride assessment as a valid measure of growth to high standards typically support a building culture that continues practices that are not working.

Proportional Increases in Direct Instructional Time

Maxim 61. Most elementary reading blocks are 60-80 minutes long with 20-27 minutes of direct instruction per student.[1] Most middle and high school periods are 45-55 minutes long.

Maxim 62. Standard amounts of instructional time usually generate standard amounts of growth or "annual growth" across all quartiles.

[1] Most math classes in elementary school are 45-55 minutes long and most language arts and math periods in middle and high school are the same 45-55 minutes. Most Title I programs provide only an additional 30 minutes a day of reading instruction when the time is averaged over a week.

Maxim 63. When students start their educational marathon in kindergarten with a "six mile" difference between initial starting points and when each student runs a mile during the year, they will still be six miles apart at the end of the year. Kindergarten children who began the year with the entry skills of three-year-olds will have the skills of four-year-olds at the year's end. Kindergarten children with the entry skills of five-year-olds will have skills of six-year-olds. They all make a year of growth but the six-year achievement gap will remain.

Maxim 64. Catch-up growth is rarely achieved by pressuring students who are behind to "run faster" in the same amount of time. Catch-up growth is typically achieved by allowing them to "run longer" and "run smarter," i.e., dramatically increasing direct instructional time and using it wisely.

Maxim 65. The primary driver of catch-up growth is increased instructional time. This is true in math as well as reading.

Maxim 66. Increases in instructional time should be proportional to the level of deficiency. Students who are three years behind need more minutes of direct instruction than students who are one year behind.

Maxim 67. It is fairly simple to calculate how many additional semesters a student needs to catch up when administrators know the current percentile rank of the student and the percentile rank equivalent of the target the student needs to achieve.

Maxim 68. On a national level, in elementary reading each 13 percentile points represents approximately one year of growth.

Maxim 69. Students who are three years behind at the end of kindergarten may require 160 to 220 minutes of direct reading instructional time each day during first, second, and third grades to catch up by third grade.

Maxim 70. Calculations of direct instructional time should not include practice time, silent sustained reading, or time spent reading in the content area.

Maxim 71. The research shows that silent sustained reading improves the abilities of students who already read well but results in very little improvement for those who don't read at grade level.

Maxim 72. Parents who read 20 minutes a day with their child provide significant support to the direct instruction he or she receives at school.

Maxim 73. By focusing on scheduling, building principals can double or triple the amount of direct instructional time for students who need targeted instruction in a single semester.

Maxim 74. Doubling instructional effectiveness generally requires several years of staff training and experience.

Maxim 75. Elementary and secondary principals are primarily responsible for scheduling proportional increases in instruction time for students who are behind.

Maxim 76. Elementary schools are typically more flexible than middle schools. Elementary schools generally develop five or six tailored programs to increase catch-up minutes for students. Elementary schools are smaller and nimbler and usually function well as teams.

Maxim 77. Middle and high schools are run from equal time-based master schedules. Middle and high school administrators understand increased instructional time in terms of additional classes.

Maxim 78. The implicit assumption of most master schedules is that students who are the furthest behind learn faster than students who are ahead. That is, students who are three years behind in reading or math will catch up to other students with the same amount of time on task.

Maxim 79. The implicit assumption of uniform master schedules is wrong. Students who are behind do not learn at faster rates than students who are ahead. They require additional time and direct instruction tailored to their deficient sub-skills.

Maxim 80. Low-performing schools seem more resistant to increasing instructional time. It seems to require more encouragement from the board and superintendent to increase instructional time at low-performing schools than at high-performing schools. This resistance could stem from leadership, entrenched refusal to change, disregard of the data, or apathy.

Maxim 81. Monitoring whether principals actually schedule lagging (low quartile) students for additional classes or time is the first step in assuring proportional increases in instruction.

Maxim 82. Superintendents and boards can use principal scheduling reports to create accountability for scheduling proportional catch-up time and classes.

Teaching to the Deficit Sub-skill and Retesting

Maxim 83. Merely allocating additional time does not mean that it will be spent on the deficient sub-skill.

Maxim 84. Just because diagnostic testing occurs does not mean that instruction will be directed to the deficient sub-skill.

Maxim 85. Directing instruction to the deficient sub-skill is fundamentally different than reteaching the morning's lesson.

Maxim 86. Teaching to the deficient sub-skill requires nimbleness, flexibility, and a high level of ability to adapt material (or create it, if necessary) for the targeted student.

Maxim 87. The catch-up process that we learned working with K-3 in reading and math will work at middle and high school as well.

Good to Great

Maxim 88. Deciding to teach 90 to 95% of students to read at grade level by third grade is "like a single, clear, perfectly struck note hanging in the air in the hushed silence." It is the perfect "hedgehog" strategy for U.S. elementary schools and absolutely essential in every great district.[2]

Maxim 89. We like to think we follow our beliefs. In reality, our beliefs follow our experience. Until you change your behavior, you cannot really change deep, embedded beliefs.

Maxim 90. "You must never confuse faith that you will prevail in the end–which you can never afford to lose–with the discipline to confront the most brutal facts of your current reality."[3]

Maxim 91. We had thought it was a matter of doing more of what we were already doing. We simply didn't know how to teach 90% of our students to read to standard by third grade.

Maxim 92. It may take a decade for your district to learn how to teach 95% of students to read and do math at grade-level.

Maxim 93. "We will find a way or we will make a way."[4]

Here to Stay

Maxim 94. We are in the middle of the third educational reform in a century.

Maxim 95. The social, economic, and political forces that passed minimum standard reform legislation in 50 states, and at the federal level thereafter, not only will persist but will grow stronger.

---

[2]Jim Collins, *Good to Great* (New York: Harper Business, 2001), 116.
[3]Ibid., 85, quoting Admiral Jim Stockdale, the highest ranking U.S. officer captured and tortured in Vietnam.
[4]Attributed to the military leader Hannibal on his decision to cross the Alps.

Maxim 96. Every piece of major legislation gets tweaked and improved. No Child Left Behind will be no different.

Maxim 97. Efforts expended to defeat the standards may ease the burden on adult educators but increase the economic and social burden of students who do not reach reasonable minimum competency levels.

Maxim 98. When public services like police protection and public education fail, the burden is disproportionately borne by the poor who cannot compensate with gated communities and private academies. The only hope for the poor is that we in public education deliver on our promise.

Maxim 99. Every student entrusted to our care, every citizen who financially supports public education, is depending on us to **deliver on our promise**. We can do it.

ACKNOWLEDGMENTS

We wish to acknowledge the contributions of those, without whose efforts, this book would not have been possible.

This book is a partial biography of the last decade of the Kennewick School District, the National Children's Reading Foundation, and READY! for Kindergarten. Many of their staff agreed to very candid discussions including Jan Fraley, Greg Wishkowski, Stephanie Walton, Angie Clark, Deborah Peterson, and Claudia Glover. A group of our principals provided insightful perspectives including Dave Montague spotlighted with Washington Elementary, as well as other equally hard-working and deserving principals and their schools: Dorothy Fanning, Judy Long, Ted Mansfield, Rob Phillips, and Chuck Watson.

The READY! for Kindergarten material has been the result of the long-term efforts of many including Beverly Abersfeller, Jeni Abersfeller, Steve Halliday, Janie Easton, Meloni Kerr, Hilda Brown, and Sonnet Fielding.

Early drafts of the book were reviewed by Bob Butts, Mary Delagardelle, Greg Fancher, Jan Fraley, Carl VanHoff (who we thank for his invaluable personal coaching), James Hager, Connie Hoffman, Jim Huge, Marlis Lindbloom, Anne Loring, Chuck Namit, and Jeni Riley as well as by the Kennewick School Board directors: Dawn Adams, Kathy Daily, Ed Frost, and Dan Mildon. Certain other sections were reviewed by staff at NWEA, Dave Montague, Dr. Joe Montgomery, Stephanie Watson, June Rivers, and Tom Vander Ark. Our family members offered a variety of improvements to the text and tone as well. These reviewers generously offered advice about an evolving product, while continuing to express faith in the final outcome.

We express special thanks to Amy Smith (our chief "minion") and Rose Thompson for the countless details they cheerfully and competently managed, to our editor, Lavina Fielding Anderson, and our designer/typesetter A Melody, who all met amazing deadlines throughout the whole process with exemplary grace and refreshing wit.

APPENDIX A

ORDER FORM

For additional copies of

Delivering on the Promise

Please mail this form to:
The New Foundation Press, Inc
114 Vista Way
Kennewick, WA 99336

Or FAX your order to: (509) 783-5237

Quantity			**Price**		**Total**
1-10	______	**x**	**$17.95**	**=**	__________
11-50	______	**x**	**$14.95**	**=**	__________
50-100	______	**x**	**$10.95**	**=**	__________

WA residents: Add 8.7% for sales tax __________
Shipping: Add $1.00 per book __________
TOTAL $ __________

Price includes shipping and handling.
Please print clearly.

Name [ ] Mr. [ ] Mrs. [ ] Ms. [ ] Dr.______________________________
Organization______________________________
Address______________________________
City______________________State________Zip______________
Telephone____________________E-mail____________________

[ ] Check or Money Order Enclosed (payable to the New Foundation Press, Inc.)
[ ] Charge my Visa/MC (circle one) Account #____________________
Expiration date______________
Signature ______________________________
[ ] School District purchase order attached: P.O. #______________

You may also order copies of *The 90% Reading Goal* by the same authors at the same quantity discounts at the above address.

APPENDIX B

KENNEWICK'S DECEMBER 1995 READING WHITE PAPER

As boards and superintendents invite schools to make the changes necessary to reach a seemingly impossible goal, we should ease the restrictions, real or perceived, under which principals and their staff must function. One of the clearest ways of expanding those parameters is in a position paper or, to use the British parliamentary term, a "White Paper." Unlike a board policy or regulation, a white paper allows broader input from educators and the community. It expresses a philosophy, articulates values, and defines expectations but in a flexible format that allows for developing competing ideas, dealing with problems, and updating.

1. THE BUILDING-BY-BUILDING APPROACH: Primary planning and program change are to be on a building-by-building basis.

a. Accountability programs should be distinguished from instructional programs. The overall accountability system should be uniform across the district. It makes sense to have common district benchmarks, assessments, reporting, and sharing of strategies. But it is not equally reasonable to have district-wide instructional programs.

b. The logical extension of selecting a single instructional approach is to keep bumping the decision higher until finally each state's Department of Education prescribes the instructional program. We all know that doesn't work. Most boards and superintendents are very emphatic that the state has the right and responsibility to define goals and standards, but they want to be free to determine how to reach these goals in a way that is compatible with local conditions and demands. It is only fair to give individual principals the same flexibility that we superintendents and boards ask from our states. We should tell elementary schools what we want and then give them the freedom to determine how best to do it.

c. When central administration (or the state) selects a single instructional program, the building's job is to implement that program and provide paperwork demonstrating its thorough compliance. This replaces the goal of actually teaching the children. The principal's job is clear: to implement the process as flawlessly as possible. But the responsibility for getting 90% of children to the goal has shifted to central administration (or to the state). Central administration models and state-wide models have not worked in the past.

2. PLANNED, INCREMENTAL, AND CONTINUOUS IMPROVEMENT: Each school is starting from a different place with different levels of incoming students, different parent support, different expertise, and different effectiveness. The district expectation is for significant continuous progress at each grade level. It expects that each building will develop a plan, based on its population and reading levels, for immediate implementation within existing resources. Some schools will reach and maintain the goal more quickly than other schools. Some schools will have immense difficulty reaching the goal within three years. The district expectation is that significant, measurable progress will be evident each spring on the functional-level reading tests.

3. PRIMARY ACCOUNTABILITY: Primary accountability is with building principals. Elementary principals will be expected to provide significant leadership to achieve this goal, including reprioritizing existing activities. Because building principals do not teach reading, they should view their role as supporting those who do. An increasing portion of elementary principals' annual evaluations will result from the district's professional appraisal of effective leadership in this area.

4. INCREASED RESOURCES: Decade-old paradigms have limited the resources spent on reading. Each building should identify and alter old and limiting assumptions. Paradigm shifts redirecting more resources to reading which have been suggested within the district to date include:

a. More time. An extremely effective method of reading improvement is simply to spend more time on it. This common-sense notion is supported by research and also allows immediate action within existing budget constraints. Each K-3 teacher will be asked to evaluate the amount of time spent on reading. Elementary teachers have permission to expand the time spent on reading and cut the time spent on other areas immediately.

b. More people. Ways to increase the people involved in reading at the school site include the use of student peers, the use of fourth and fifth graders with K-3 graders, the use of high school students at the elementary schools, and the expanded involvement of parents and community volunteers.

c. More effective programs: K-3 teachers will be asked to identify and evaluate their current instructional techniques. Effective commercial programs should be evaluated. How effectively are we using reading specialists, Title 1 reading teachers, and special education staff?

d. More effective structural organization. Schools have permission to restructure the K-3 program.

e. More money: We plan to request as much as a half million dollars of increased funding in the levy in 2/1996 (not available until April 1997).

5. CHANGES K-3: The summative evaluation at the end of the third grade is designed primarily for feedback for the K-3 process and not for remediation commencing in the fourth grade. Changes in the K-2 processes should include specific kindergarten expectations and increased reading activities in grades 1-2 and some kind of K, 1, and 2 testing so that teachers and principals can monitor the process early.

6. RESULTS, ORIENTATION, AND DISTRICT SUPPORT: The district is not adopting a model or theory. District-wide adoptions in the past have resulted in our current reading levels and will likely only maintain them in the future. The district's primary effort will be to support building programs and actions, which appear reasonably calculated to achieve the third-grade summative reading goal.

7. EXPECTATIONS FOR STUDENT PERFORMANCE: We get what we expect. Effective programs with low socioeconomic children are characterized by overt structure and high expectations. Our instructional strategies should focus on structural approaches that match a school's student body.

AUTHORS' COMMENT, JUNE 2004: *The Reading White Paper was an invitation for elementary schools to alter the rules and create more security for change. Boards and administration encourage more dramatic action when they decrease the perceived disadvantages and reduce the risks involved. Decreasing the downside does not insure that faculty and administrators will, in fact, willingly take risks. But when those who must do the work—teachers and support staff—are debating alternatives in faculty meeting, those who do not want to change the curriculum have one less argument with which to oppose those who do.*

APPENDIX C

Appendix C
Kennewick's "Look Fors" for Purpose, Rigor, Engagement, and Results

Teacher Indicators	Guiding Questions	Student Indicators
Purpose = teacher intentionally plans and instructs for student achievement of essential learnings.		
Clearly sets and reinforces outcome throughout the lesson; links activities to the outcome.	How does the identified outcome guide the learning?	Can explain what he or she is learning and why.
Supports students in making connections to prior learning and life situations.	How is the learning made relevant to students?	Applies learning in different settings and situations.
Prioritizes instructional strategies according to student needs.	How are learning activities appropriately matched to student needs?	Demonstrates understanding of concepts and mastery of skills.
Has and communicates a clear plan for assessing student work.	How does assessment help frame the learning?	Understands how his or her work will be assessed.
Rigor = Each learner is appropriately challenged as the teacher moves students to higher levels of thinking.		
Varies question type, uses wait time, and asks higher level questions.	How do questions support student learning?	Gives thoughtful responses, asks meaningful questions.
Builds to more complex concepts, anticipates likely confusions, reteaches and provides enrichment as appropriate.	How does the content of the lesson provide the correct level of difficulty?	Challenged by new concepts, builds on prior learning, and learns from mistakes.
Intentionally builds conceptual knowledge, chooses to cover less breadth for more depth.	What is the evidence of deeper understanding?	Synthesize, analyzes, generalize thinking.
Stresses student responsibility and accountability, accepts only quality work, consistently encourages all students.	How are high expectations an influence on learning?	Produces quality work, demonstrated willingness to "rewrite/redo."

Appendix C (Continued)

Engagement = Teacher and students actively participate in the learning and are focused on the lesson.		
Facilitates discussion, monitors learning activities, and stimulates interest in learning.	How is participation demonstrated?	Asks and responds to questions, completes assignments, contributes to discussions.
Shows joy and passion for learning.	What is the evidence of motivation?	Shows persistence and enthusiasm for learning.
Seeks feedback, analyzes his or her work, and uses reflection to inform next steps.	In what ways is reflection part of the classroom routine?	Seeks feedback, evaluates his/her work uses reflection to deepen understanding.
Tries new instructional strategies, demonstrates being a learner.	How is risk-taking modeled?	Shares his/her thinking and work, participates in new learning experiences.
Results = The intended learning is achieved.		
Creates opportunities for students to demonstrate learning, gives timely feedback.	How is student understanding monitored?	Completes learning tasks, uses vocabulary, and demonstrates mastery of skills.
Use multiple measures over time to gather data.	How are assessments used to evaluate learning?	Completes a variety of assessments.
Evaluates results and adjusts instruction both for groups and individual students.	How is data used to improve performance?	Sets personal learning goals.

APPENDIX D

WASHINGTON ELEMENTARY'S REPORT TO THE BOARD OF EDUCATION, 2003-04

Note: DRA stands for Developmental Reading Assessment. WASL stands for Washington Assessment of Student Learning. The WASL is Washington's statewide assessment given at the fourth, eighth, and 10th grades.

Kindergarten Test Results
Fall and Spring at Washington Elementary
Average Percentage Correct

School Year	Upper Case Letter Recognition		Lower Case Letter Recognition		Letter Sound Recognition		Rhyming Recognition		Rhyming Production		Initial Sound Recognition		Initial Sound Production		Write First Name		Total	
	Fall	Spring	Fall	Spring	Fall	Spring	Fall	Spring	Fall	Spring	Fall	Spring	Fall	Spring	Fall	Spring	Fall	Spring
99 - 00	**59%**	**96%**	**43%**	**94%**	**14%**	**85%**	**72%**	**98%**	**48%**	**92%**	**44%**	**94%**	**22%**	**94%**			**40%**	**92%**
00 - 01	**41%**	**94%**	**29%**	**91%**	**6%**	**88%**	**46%**	**92%**	**29%**	**84%**	**31%**	**87%**	**10%**	**92%**			**26%**	**90%**
01 - 02	**54%**	**97%**	**43%**	**96%**	**14%**	**91%**	**51%**	**95%**	**38%**	**96%**	**33%**	**95%**	**15%**	**93%**			**37%**	**94%**
02 - 03	**55%**	**97%**	**40%**	**95%**	**20%**	**92%**	**44%**	**91%**	**33%**	**90%**	**32%**	**90%**	**20%**	**92%**			**37%**	**94%**
03 - 04	**50%**		**37%**		**10%**		**69%**		**56%**		**50%**		**25%**		**63%**		**36%**	

Percentage of Washington Elementary's First Grade Students Passing the DRA in February and after Retesting in May

School Year	Number of Students	Meets Standard		Borderline		Substantially Below	
		February	May	February	May	February	May
1999 - 2000	79	47%	**61%**	9%	**18%**	44%	**21%**
2000 - 2001	76	50%	**75%**	22%	**17%**	28%	**8%**
2001 - 2002	74	57%	**78%**	16%	**11%**	27%	**11%**
2002 - 2003	90	64%	**94%**	23%	**6%**	12%	**0%**
2003 - 2004	89	74%		10%		16%	

First Grade DRA Test History for Washington Elementary

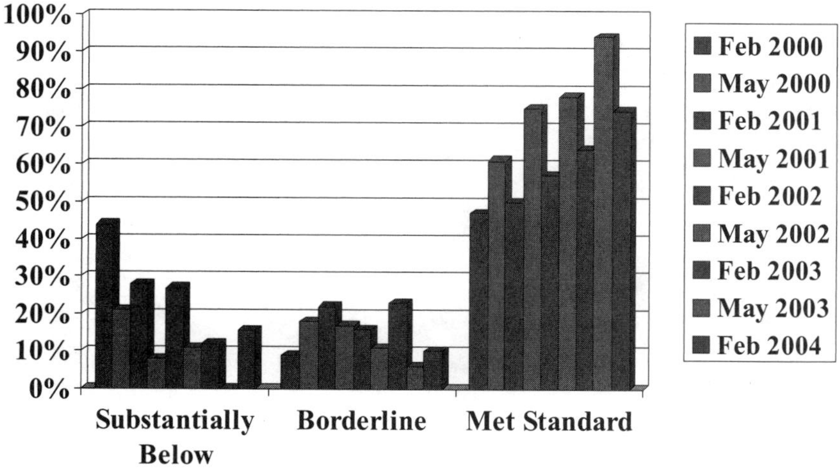

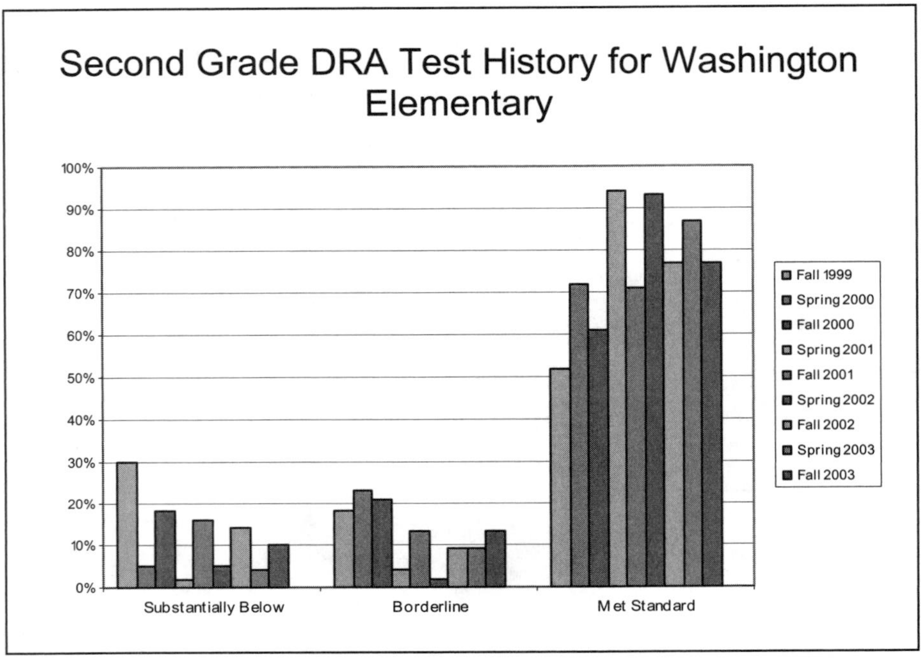

Percentage of Washington Elementary Second Grade Students Passing the DRA in the Fall and after Retesting in the Spring

School Year	Number of Students	Meets Standard		Borderline		Substantially Below	
		Fall	Spring	Fall	Spring	Fall	Spring
1999-2000	71	52%	**72%**	18%	**23%**	30%	**5%**
2000-2001	85	61%	**94%**	21%	**4%**	18%	**2%**
2001-2002	84	71%	**93%**	13%	**2%**	16%	**5%**
2002-2003	77	77%	**87%**	9%	**9%**	14%	**4%**
2003-2004	90	77%		13%		10%	

Percentage of Third Graders Reaching a Fall RIT of 188 and a Spring RIT of 194 on Functional Level Reading Tests

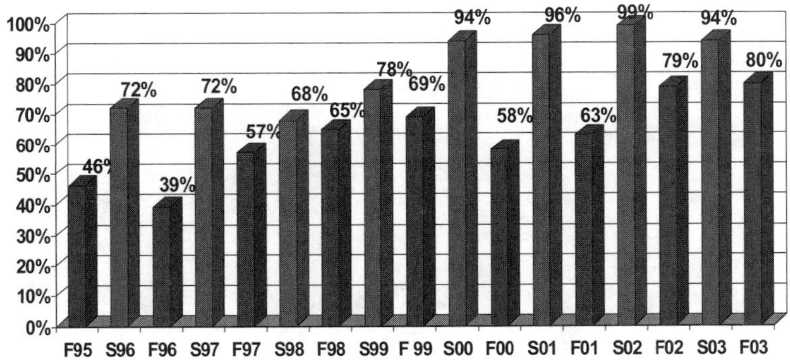

Percentages are based on total enrollment.

Mean RIT Growth by Third Graders on Functional Level Reading Tests

	95 - 96	96 - 97	97 - 98	98 - 99	99 - 00	00 - 01	01 - 02	02 - 03	NWEA
Fall RIT	183	182	187	193	195	192	191	193	188
Spring RIT	198	200	200	202	205	210	209	208	198
Growth	**15**	**18**	**13**	**9**	**10**	**18**	**18**	**15**	**10**

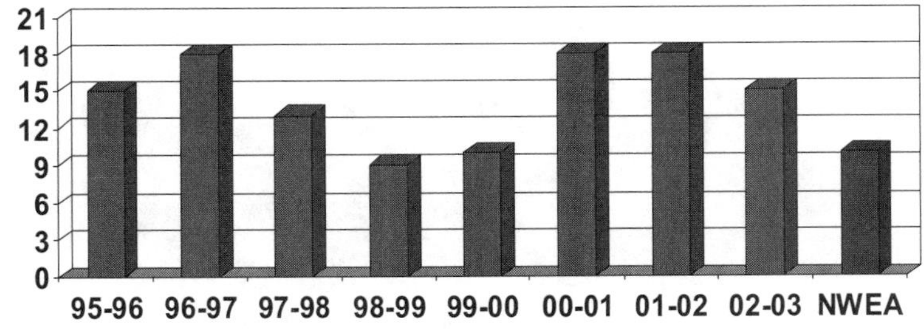

Percentage of Fourth Graders Reaching a Spring RIT of 199 on Functional Level Reading Tests

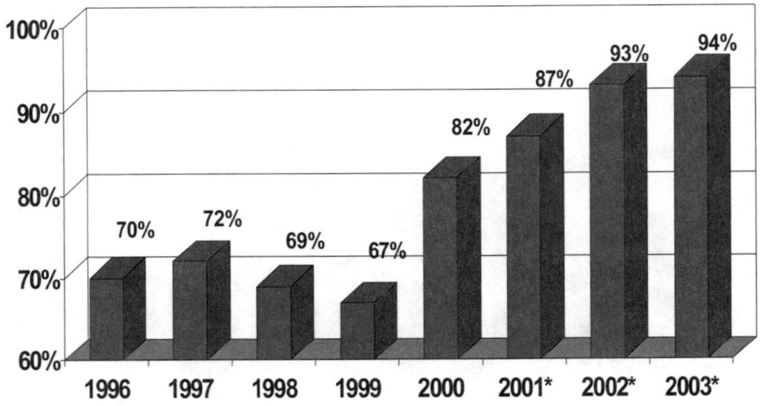

Percentages are based on total enrollment.

Percentage of Fifth Graders Reaching a Spring RIT of 207 on Functional Level Reading Tests

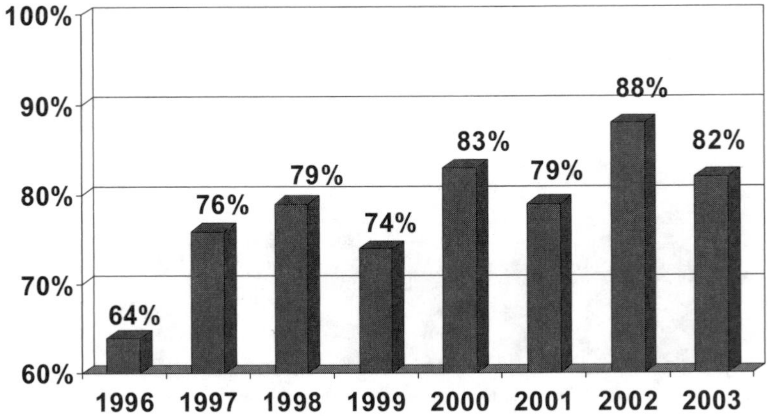

Percentages are based on total enrollment.

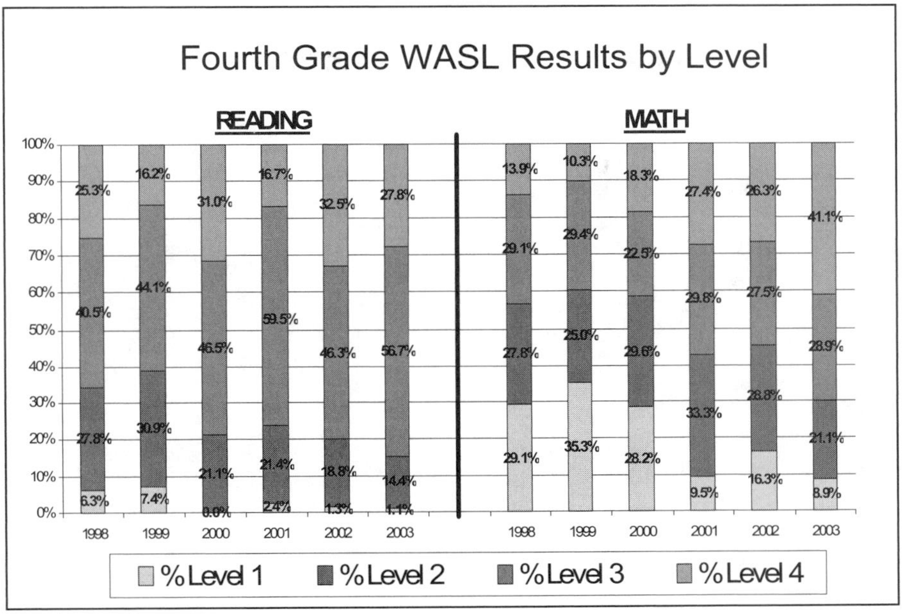
Fourth Grade WASL Results by Level
READING
MATH
100%
90%
80%
70%
60%
50%
40%
30%
20%
10%
0%
1998
1999
2000
2001
2002
2003
%Level 1
%Level 2
%Level 3
%Level 4

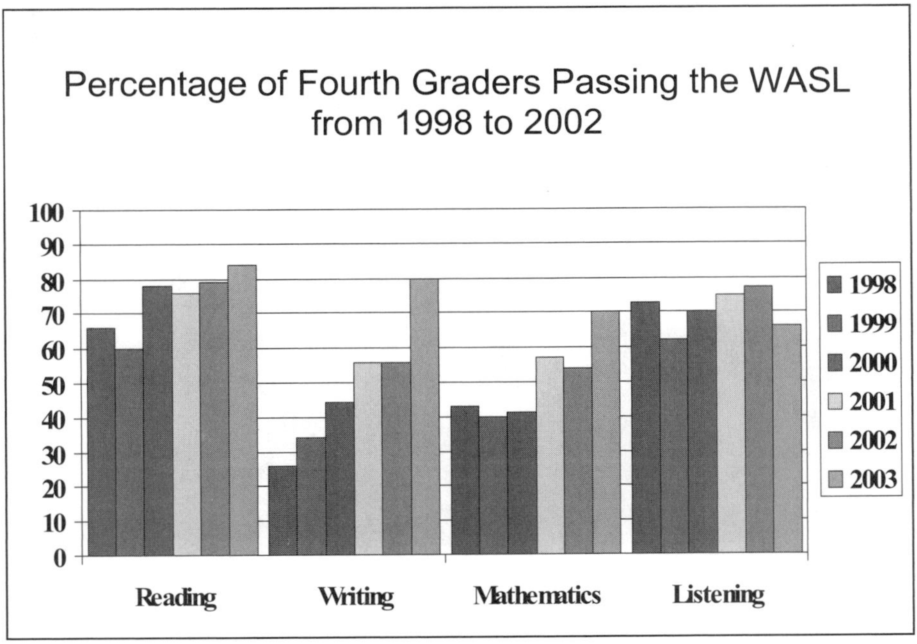
Percentage of Fourth Graders Passing the WASL from 1998 to 2002
100
90
80
70
60
50
40
30
20
10
0
Reading
Writing
Mathematics
Listening
1998
1999
2000
2001
2002
2003

Appendix E

KENNEWICK'S STRATEGIC PLAN, 2003-2004

GOAL 1. Ensure That Our Schools And Classrooms Are Safe And Orderly.

SUBGOAL	PERSON[1]	DUE [2]	INDICATOR
1.1 Develop baseline report and improve the significant indicators of safety and order for buildings, district, and transportation.	Othene Bell Othene Bell	03-04 03-04	Create longitudinal safety reports similar to reading reports by middle school and by high school. Target a 5% reduction in the categories of *fighting, harassment and bullying*, at the middle and high schools from 2003 baselines.
1.2 Identify students with disruptive, violent, or toxic classroom behavior. Stop bullying, initiations, and profanity.	Paul Rosier Principals Greg Fancher Othene Bell M. Lindbloom	03-04	Continue implementation of the state's new "bullying" law. Provide brief report during board building workshops on reducing profanity among students and student athletes. Address modesty issues at middle and high schools with existing or updated dress codes.

GOAL 2.1 Student Learning Goals: Preschoolers Will Enter Kindergarten Ready To Learn.

SUBGOAL	PERSON	DUE	INDICATOR
2.1.1 The district develops pre-literacy, basic math and social skills targets, tools and training for parents.	Paul Rosier Nancy Kerr	6/03 - 8/03	Revise the 3 quarterly training units for parents for each age group from pre-birth to K with age-appropriate activities and materials.
2.1.2 90% of entering kindergarten students will score 30 or higher on the district kindergarten assessment pretest. Isolate the phonological aspects to verify Yale research.	**N. Kerr/** G. Fancher A. Sparks Lindbloom Tri-Tech	11/03 03-04 6/03-6/04	a. Validate kindergarten targets. b. Continue Kindergarten READY! Program district-wide with targets of 1000/200 attendance. c. Revise curriculum as needed. Develop media modules and community awareness. Begin home visits and video versions.
2.1.3 Second language students will enter kindergarten bilingual.	Paul Rosier READY!	03-04	Explore supporting this with Hispanic and Russian communities in READY! Program. Explore options for Spanish radio programming.

[1] Responsible party/parties include those supervising the listed individual/s.
[2] A short written achievement report on the indicator is due from the responsible person on the timeline date.
[3] See page 313 for list of acronyms.

GOAL 2.2 Student Learning Goals: 90 % Of All Third Graders Will Read At Or Above Grade Level.

SUBGOAL	PERSON	DUE	INDICATOR
2.2.1 District wide, 89% of <u>all</u> third grade students will read at grade level or above by the end of the 2004 school year.	M. Lindbloom	7/03	Provide growth by student in grades 1-5 in Instructional Time and Focus format.
	Greg Fancher	8/03	For elementary schools scoring below 60%: White paper analysis of data explaining lack of growth, changes in 2003-04 and projected spring achievement outcome.
	Affected Principals	8/03	For elementary schools scoring below 80%: Include in board packet a one-page list of 2003-04 initiatives and projected growth.
	Paul Rosier M. Lindbloom Greg Fancher		Continue monthly meetings with elementary principals of schools scoring below 80%.
2.2.2 Adequate yearly progress and WASL reporting.	B. Henderson	8/04	Begin reporting students at or above WASL reading and math standards in the 90% goal format.
2.2.3 Increase the performance of children who live in poverty and/or who are impacted by mobility.	Greg Fancher	03-04	Continue to implement the district's early assessments for move-ins.
2.2.4 Continue to implement the Team Read Volunteer program to assist individual students with reading in designated schools.	Greg Fancher Nancy Kerr	03-04	Determine the yearly program indicators in September 2003. Report against the program indicators in December 2003 and June 2004.
2.2.5 Increase the performance of limited English speaking children.	Greg Fancher Maria Hendrickson	6/04	Board report on goal to increase by 10% in 2002-03 and 2004 the number of limited English speaking students performing at district standards.
		03-04	Continue implementation of the peer coaching strategy with bilingual and ESL teachers K-3.

Goal 2.3 Student Learning Goals: 80% of 6th, 7th, and 8th Grade Students Will Achieve WASL Equivalent Standards.

SUBGOAL	PERSON	DUE	INDICATOR
2.3.1 Normal Annual Growth: All students will be expected to make annual progress in reading and math classes as determined by NWEA quartile growth charts.	Lindbloom Othene Bell MS Principals	7/04	Continue yearly growth report for the board of the number and percentage of students in the top two quartiles making annual growth in reading and math by student, by school.
	MS Principals	10/03	Assure Adequate Yearly Progress.
2.3.2 Catch-up Growth: Students below grade level are expected to make greater of adequate yearly progress or annual growth plus sufficient catch-up growth to be at grade level (WASL standard) before leaving middle school. Targeted accelerated growth shall include diagnostic testing, curriculum aligned to deficiency, increasing direct instructional minutes proportional to needed growth and retesting. For students below standard in core subjects, electives, P.E. and other subject time may be reduced except in exceptional cases which include valid parent concerns.	Othene Bell Principals	2/04	Instructional Time & Focus Reports prepared as of 10/03 and 2/04 for reading & math instructional time for each student in gr. 6-8 below NWEA RIT 51st percentile. All students functioning below 51st percentile in reading & math provided additional instructional time. Reading given the highest priority.
	Marlis Lindbloom M.S. Principals	10/03	Targeted Accelerated Growth reports prepared for board indicating number of students receiving additional time (course schedule) and use of additional time (diagnostic testing, curriculum aligned to deficiency, retesting) to provide sufficient catch-up growth during middle school.
	Board	2/04	The district prepares uniform data graphs for school/board workshops for annual growth reports.
	Paul Rosier Lindbloom Othene Bell	03-04	Begin monthly meetings with middle school principals of schools scoring below 80%.
2.3.3 Increase the performance of children who live in poverty and/or who are impacted by mobility.	Othene Bell Vicki Rynd Dottie Stevens	03-04	Pilot unified district-wide new student induction process using Park and Kennewick High students starting 12/03, including student placement and parent contact.

Goal 2.4 Student Learning Goals: 85% Of Sophomores Will Achieve The Certificate Of Academic Proficiency By 2008.

SUBGOAL	PERSON	DUE	INDICATOR
2.4.1 Normal Annual Growth. All students will be expected to make at least normal annual growth in core classes. Existing high school assessment instruments will be used to measure this growth.	HS Principals Othene Bell	03-04	Assure adequate yearly progress.
		7/03 7/04	Report on number and % of students in top two quartiles making annual growth in reading and math.
	Othene Bell D. Stevens	2/04	Develop policy and expand availability of on-line curriculum and assessment to develop challenge tests.
2.4.2 Catch-up Growth. Students below grade level in WASL subjects will be expected to make the greater of adequate yearly progress of annual growth plus sufficient "catch-up growth" to be at grade level (WASL standard) during their freshman and sophomore year. Targeted accelerated growth (TAG) shall include diagnostic testing, curriculum aligned to deficiency, increasing instructional time proportional to the needed growth, and retesting.	Othene Bell Ron Cone	2/04	Continue to study potential impact of providing only elective credit for D's in math and language arts classes by providing RIT analysis of growth of those getting D's.
	Othene Bell HS Principals	8/02 2/04	Instructional Time and Focus Reports will be prepared as of Oct 1/03 and Feb 1/ 04 for reading and math instructional time for each student in grades 9-10 below a NWEA RIT 51st percentile.
	Lindbloom	10/02 2/04	Targeted accelerated growth reports prepared for board indicating by student whether course schedule (time) or curriculum (diagnostic testing, curriculum aligned to deficiency, retesting) will provide sufficient catch-up growth by end of sophomore year.
	Principals Othene Bell	03-04	The district prepares uniform data graphs for school/board workshops of annual growth reports.
2.4.3 Graduation. Increase the percentage of students who enroll as 9th graders and actually graduate to 95% without compromising high standards.	Othene Bell MS/HS	Quar-terly	Data: Stabilize and continue the "In-Out" report. Separate out the involuntary dropouts.
	Othene Bell McClary	12/03	Provide board options for new valedictorian policy with weighed achievement scores i.e., GPA, honor/IB classes, WASL and SAT.

2.4.4 The next generation. Integrate parenting skills into the curriculum of the high schools including how to raise a reader.	Nancy Kerr Othene Bell	12/03	Implement strategies to assure students grades 5-12 understand importance of reading to a child as component of parenting skills.
	McClary Nancy Kerr	12/03	Explore revising family and consumer science curriculum to include parenting strategies supporting developmental reading.

GOAL 3. Develop and Efficiently Operate Academic Infrastructure Necessary to Support Student Learning.

SUBGOAL	PERSON	DUE	INDICATOR
3.1 District develops and administers grade level assessments for core subjects[3] at beg. & end of school year, where appropriate. Assessment instruments coordinated with national and international learning standards and directly test the state Essential Academic Learning Standards.	Henderson	5/04	Continue 9th grade exit writing assessment. Use '03 data to establish baseline for measuring progress.
	Lindbloom Henderson	8/03	Implement year-end testing for U.S. history and first year world language. Map out schedule for adding other MS and HS core subject assessments.
	Greg Fancher Ardis Sparks	03-04	Implement 2nd generation incoming kindergarten test, which includes appropriate pre-math and basic social skill indicators.
3.2 Standards. The district will develop grade level standards for each subject that it tests.	Paul Rosier	03-04	Move district standards to the 51st percentile summer of 2004 pending result of OSPI recalibration of WASL standards.
3.3. Data Systems. Create and maintain a single integrated database of all significant assessments and indices of academic performances by students, building, and district.	Ron Cone Wilma Miller Rich Buel Ron Cone Paul Rosier Board	03-04 11/03 1/04	a. Implement Power School software in September to combine the student assessment results database and the student demographics database. Communicate to parents. b. Complete student progress reports by student, class, school, district, and quintile (01-02 model). Provide on-line access, growth curve analysis, and charting of scores with appropriate levels of security for principals, teachers, and parents.
3.4 Student data reports. Create and annually produce stable multiple year reports of student academic	Paul Rosier Ron Cone Lindbloom	8/03	Finish initial RIT growth by level format for reading and math for grades 3-8. Extend the RIT growth by level format for all RIT scores.

[3] The assessments will test curricula, which prepare students for post secondary education and/or work. Course offering and course content K-12 shall be justified in terms of relevance to post-secondary education, work, transmission of culture, and personal development and will be coordinated with state, national, and international academic learning standards.

achievement by student, school, and district.	Bev Henderson Othene Bell Lindbloom MS Principals	Fall 2003	Report results of state assessment instruments at grades 4, 7, 10. Meet with all 8th grade students and parents functioning below the standard to pass the 10th Grade WASL to graduate. Explain each student's status and what's needed to meet WASL standards. Indicators include 4th and 7th grade WASL results, FLT results, and teacher recommendation.
3.5 Program data reports. Create and annually produce stable multiple year reports of key indicators of all significant academic, co-curricular, and operational programs.	Othene Bell Ron Cone	2/04	Develop initial reports for SAT scores, IB program performance, AP honors classes, competitive music performance, and other subject areas as defined by the board.
3.6 Data-driven decisions. All district staff will acquire appropriate training and expertise in the use of data to make appropriate decisions.	Lindbloom Directors Principals	6/04	Report amount of training by building and perceived unmet training needs within each building. Schedule appropriate levels of data training.
3.7 Instructional expertise. Develop instructional strategies and programs to assist students to meet the performance standards at 4th, 7th, & 10th grades, including alternative programs.	Lindbloom O. Bell G. Fancher Sparks	03-04	Continue the peer coaching process at middle and high schools.
3.8 Gates Commitments**.** Monitor and fulfill our Gates commitments.	Paul Rosier	1/04	Report on progress of buildings in implementing multi-year plans. Include efforts to obtain attributes of highly effective classrooms.
3.9 Systematically strengthen core curriculum K-12: ➢ Refine K-12 District Curriculum Frameworks using "mapping" strategies in math, science, language arts, social studies, PE, health, world language, and the arts aligned to state essential academic learnings as measured by WASL.	Lindbloom Lindbloom Principals	03-04 03-04	Continue curriculum-mapping process with focus on core content areas K-12. Develop initial plan document at each school that: ▪ Shows alignment of the core content areas to the state essential academic learning requirements; ▪ Helps identify gaps and redundancies in the curriculum sequence from one grade to the next; ▪ Establishes a plan for annual review and modifications.

3.10. Develop student-friendly secondary schools that personalize school climate and create learning environments that engage students.	MS/HS Principals Rich Buel	03-04	a. Identify and report strategies that create small, personalized units and provide appropriate staff training. b. Provide teachers with perceptual data of connections with students (i.e. focus group responses on video)

GOAL 4. Establish A District-Wide Customer Focus

SUBGOAL	PERSON	DUE	INDICATOR
4.1 Annually conduct written survey of stakeholders in each co-curricular and student support program, including attitude and participation.	Othene Bell	03-04	Continue administering instrument at HS at completion of each sports season. Review and revise to add initial overall comment opportunity at beginning. Collate data and report to board by sport by school. Examine increased cross country participation at middle and high school for current non-participants.
4.2 An Individual Student Growth Plan (ISGP) is developed or reviewed annually with the student, teacher, and parent or guardian.	Othene Bell	03-04	Emphasis on consistent implementation at the middle school. By high school, the ISGP identifies potential career paths, corresponding courses of study, and the amount and sources of funding for post-secondary education. ISGP reviewed annually by students and parents.
4.3 Teach and test the costs and savings necessary to fund post-secondary education and the earning power differentials resulting from additional post-secondary education and training starting in the 5th grade.	Lindbloom McClary McClary	 03-04	Integrate into the AODA Survey. Include in district-wide testing. At the middle school and high school levels, introduce the concepts of skill paths and their implications for lifelong learning including the need for and cost of post high school education. Continue poster campaign of facts about careers, lifelong earnings, cost of post-high school education.
4.4 Increase parents' involvement in selection of appropriate classroom teachers for their children.	G. Fancher Othene Bell	03-04	Continue to provide flexibility to meet parent and student needs within the framework of creating the best possible learning environments for students.
4.5 Increase authentic parental participation in district problem solving, site councils, parent-teacher conferences, classrooms at all levels.	Principals	03-04	Each school will develop a parent involvement plan. Include procedures to get parents information prior to involvement in specific activities. (See bldg. Customer Focus Plans). Component of I Board Workshops.

GOAL 5. Ensure That The District Is Efficiently Operated And Fiscally Sound

SUBGOAL	PERSON	DUE	INDICATOR
5.1 Report cost and funding source of negotiated contract changes projected over next 10 years.	Bob Eckert	03-04 12/03	Annually gather data on each contact and develop a projection of costs. Calculate the cost of delivery of education K-12 by quintile.
5.2 Design and implement an energy conservation plan.	Ken Smith	03-04	Continue to implement the conservation plan with an emphasis on the "human factor."
5.3 Maintain a fund-balance-contingency reserve of 5% of the total general fund budget.	Bob Eckert	03-04	Maintain at least a 5% fund-balance.
5.4 Encourage school and district entrepreneurial enterprises.	Paul Rosier	03-04	Implement ideas and encourage risk taking.

GOAL 6. Ensure that Decision-Making Governance and Collective Bargaining Processes Within District Will Always Focus on the Best Interests of Students.

SUBGOAL	PERSON	DUE	INDICATOR
6.1 Decision making within the district will involve, as much as possible, all stake-holders and will occur at the level closest to those affected by the decision.	Paul Rosier	03-04	Continue the District Shared Decision-Making Task Force. Continue to seek collaborative solutions to improving learning for all students. Implement the shared decision-making concepts.

GOAL 7. Ensure that Kennewick School District Employees Have The Highest Quality Staff Growth And Development Opportunities To Build A World Class Staff.

SUBGOAL	PERSON	DUE	INDICATOR
7.1 Create strong, effective teams.	Greg Fancher Othene Bell Principals	11/03 6/04	Determine attributes of effective teams and reliable metric to quantify them. Include Harris Survey indicators. Identify buildings most in need of stronger teams and establish 04-05 goals.

7.2 Implement Peer Assistance and Review to assist teachers who are new to the district and who are experiencing difficulties.	Bev Johnson Jan Fraley A. Sparks	03-04	Provide peer assistance to all first year teachers to KSD. Move toward inclusion of all teachers. Continue to integrate PAR training into peer coaching process. Carefully evaluate effectiveness of PAR program.
7.3 Develop a plan and strategies to prepare a cadre of candidates to replace principals that will retire in the next five years.	Bev Johnson G. Fancher Othene Bell	2/04	Board report on plan to identify and encourage candidates to prepare for credentials necessary to qualify for principal position as well as providing training opportunities that will encourage potential principal candidates.
7.4 Design a comprehensive staff development program.	Marlis Lindbloom B. Henderson Principals	8/03	Implement district comprehensive staff development plan that focuses on student engagement, purpose, rigor, and performance assessment with classroom. Increase support for staff of students not achieving expected annual growth.
7.5 Enhance instructional leadership of principals and other admin. Goal of 2 hr/day or 10 hr/week engaged in instructional activities.	Paul Rosier Principals	Ongoi ng	Implement monthly staff development meeting with principals and support administrators focusing on effective teaching and video training.
7.6 Implement the partnership with WSU to create a five-year induction plan for new teachers.	Paul Rosier Bev Johnson Consulting Peer Educators	03-04	a. Implement year 3 of partnership plan. Revise first year actions as needed. b. Provide series of survey data of historical and future costs to KSD students and staff of lack of local 4-year university program.
7.7 Seek relationships with colleges/ universities to meet unique needs of Kennewick School District.	School Board Paul Rosier Rich Buel	03-04	Actively support and campaign for the consolidation of CBC and WSU Tri-Cities into a four year plus graduate school for Tri-Cities.

ONGOING SUBGOALS AND ACTIONS

The following sub goals and actions are operational. They are no longer future goals and actions. They will be continued. The intent is that the current level of performance will be maintained.

Goal 1.

- ✓ Continue to support and utilize the FOCUS Partnership, SAFETOWN and the Student Protection Team.
- ✓ Continue the No Tolerance Policy toward weapons and violence using a common-sense approach.

Goal 2.

- ✓ Continue with each school reporting annually to the School Board at workshops on the progress toward the third grade goal and the goals of the Strategic Plan.
- ✓ Continue to implement the K-3 information system of tests, results, and reporting and parent involvement.
- ✓ Continue to support The Reading Foundation.

Goal 3.

- ✓ Continue the Functional Level Tests in reading, math, and science.
- ✓ Continue the implement the District algebra test to determine placement of middle school students in high school and as a challenge test for credit
- ✓ Continue to implement the elementary and middle school accountability programs.
- ✓ Continue the annual school reports to parents and the public.
- ✓ Continue annual district progress report to community.
- ✓ Continue to assure that vision and auditory handicaps are identified.

Goal 4.

- ✓ Continue to conduct the Harris Survey of primary clients every two years.
- ✓ Continue to administrate and report the AODA Survey.
- ✓ Continue the student assistance support programs.
- ✓ Continue to include parents and community people on district curriculum advisory committees.
- ✓ Continue the semi-annual meetings with the area clergy through the FOCUS Partnership.

Goal 5.

- ✓ Continue financial review committee (Fiscal Task Force).

Goal 6.

- ✓ Continue to work toward collaborative decisions among the PSE and KEA, and district administrative units that reflect the best interests of children.
- ✓ Continue to create an atmosphere of mutual respect permitting a vigorous exchange on the merits of ideas.
- ✓ Continue to work toward win-win bargaining with all labor groups including monthly and weekly meetings as needed.

Goal 7

- ✓ Encourage innovation and flexibility throughout the district operations.
- ✓ Continue to recruit the best-qualified candidates for positions within the district.
- ✓

GLOSSARY OF ACRONYMS:

AODA	**A**lcohol and **O**ther **D**rug **A**buse
IB	**I**nternational **B**accalaureate
ISGP	**I**ndividual **S**tudent **G**rowth **P**lan
NWEA	**N**orth**w**est **E**valuation **A**ssociation
PAR	**P**eer **A**ssistance and **R**eview
PSR	**P**ersonal and **S**ocial **R**esponsibility
RIT	**R**asch Un**it**
SAT	**S**tudent **A**ssistance **T**eam
TAG	**T**argeted **A**ccelerated **G**rowth
IB	**I**nternational **B**accalaureate

APPENDIX F

SUGGESTED TECHNICAL AMENDMENTS TO THE ELEMENTARY AND SECONDARY EDUCATION ACT (ESEA), 2001

1. Incorporate a growth criteria into the process of determining adequate yearly progress (AYP) for all students including those above state standards.

2. English language learners need more time to become proficient in English to demonstrate proficiency in assessments in English. Students should live in the United States for three or four years before they are included in AYP calculations.

3. Establish criteria for special education students within their Individual Education Program (IEP). If students meet their IEP, they should meet AYP.

4. Reduce the punitive aspects and add positive incentives. At a minimum, create a better balance.

5. The various state performance standards vary from the 10th to the 85th percentile. Create a range of standards and performances that all states must meet. Consider eliminating the sanctions for states that meet selected standards at or above the 45th percentile.

6. NCLB currently restricts the state assessment to grade level content, effectively providing very poor measurement for students significantly below and above state standard. Accurate measurement of growth and achievement of all students should be required after inital data indicate that students are above or below standard.

7. The data dissagregation requirement makes it virtually impossible for schools with diverse, mobile populations to achieve adequate yearly progress. Retaining the reporting requirement but creating fewer out-of-compliance categories assures more even-handed results between dissimilar schools.

APPENDIX G

MAKING GROWTH CHARTS IN EXCEL

A prerequisite for this kind of report is having data systems that can measure annual growth in core subjects.

The "Above and Below the Line" school level graphs from Chapters 16 and 17 are constructed in four simple steps.

First, sort the students from top to bottom at the beginning of the year based on their incoming scores.

Next, separate the long list of descending scores at the national quartiles breaks. This step will result in the division of the school's students into four national achievement groups: the top 25%, the bottom 25%, etc. It will not necessarily result in equal fourths in each group. This step is instructive because it shows how a given school stacks up against national distributions. (If the result is to be in quintiles, divide by the national quintiles in this step.)

Third, subtract the previous fall's scores scores from the spring scores to determine student growth. If that growth is measured as a RIT point number, annual growth should be eight points in third grade. Double annual growth will be 16 points. After calculating growth in this step, then sort each column again so that growth appears in descending order.

Lastly, place each quartile (or quintile) side by side for each grade. Then adjust the cells in each column upward or downward so that the report format highlights the growth criteria of the district.

APPENDIX H

RANK ORDER CORRELATION

Microsoft Excel provides a data analysis package that can be purchased for its spreadsheet application. The application allows the operator to run a simple regression analysis between two columns of data. By listing students with their reading or math scores as third graders in one column and their scores as fourth graders (or any other year) in a second column, you can use the program to calculate the correlation between the scores in the two columns.

The correlation can be displayed as a statistic or as a scatter gram. For example, if student reading scores at the end of third grade are very similar to their scores at the end of fourth grade, then the correlation should be in the range of .8 to .9. Over a longer period of time from third grade to sixth grade, the correlation is more typically in the range of .65. Correlations can be negative as well. Negative correlations run from 0 to -1 with strong negative correlations closest to -1.0. Scatter grams allow the user to visually see patterns in the data.

Given this tool, it is simple to rank order the scores of incoming kindergarten students and then compare these scores with their reading achievement scores at the beginning of third grade. When Dr. Joe Montgomery ran this kind of comparison, it showed a .58 correlation ($r = .5861$, $N=563$, $p=0.00$).

In non-statistical terms, this indicates that in Kennewick, there is a very high probability that students who are behind in third grade were also behind on entering kindergarten three years earlier.

Correlation does not necessarily equal causation, however. For example, there is a very high correlation between math achievement and shoe size. That is, the larger the shoe size, the higher the student will probably score on math tests. However, everyone will agree that larger shoe size does not cause increased math achievement or vice versa.

APPENDIX I

STATE CONTENT STANDARDS

Council of Chief State School Officers, *State Content Standards: A 50-State Resource* (Washington, DC: Council of Chief State School Officers, 2003). Used by permission.

State	English/Language Arts	Mathematics	Science	Social Studies/History	Foreign Language	Arts
Alabama	English (1999)	Mathematics (1997)	Science (2001)	Social Studies (1998)		Arts (1998)
Alaska	English/Language Arts (1995)	Mathematics (1995)	Science (1995)	History (1995)	World languages (1995)	Arts (1995)
Arizona	Language Arts (1996)	Mathematics (1996)	Science (1997)	Social Studies (2000)	Foreign and Native Languages (1997)	The Arts (1997)
Arkansas	English Language Acquisition (2002); Language Arts (1998)	Mathematics (1998)	Science (1999)	Arkansas History (2002), Social Studies (2000)	Foreign Language (1999)	Fine Arts (2001)
California	English/Language Arts (1997); Reading/Language Arts (1999)	Mathematics (1997), (2000)	Science (1998, (2003)	History-Social Science (1998), (2001)	Foreign Language (2001)	Visual and Performing Arts (1996), (2001)
Colorado	Reading-Writing (1995)	Mathematics (1995)	Science (1995)	History (1995)	Foreign Language (1997)	Visual Arts (1997)
Connecticut	Language Arts (1998)	Mathematics (1998), (1999)	Science (1998)	Social Studies (1998)	World Languages (1998), (1999)	The Arts (1998), (2002)
Delaware	English (1995)	Mathematics (1995)	Science (1995)	Social Studies (2001)		
Florida	Language Arts; Reading (2001)	Mathematics (2001)	Science (2002)	Social Studies	Foreign Language	Visual Arts
Georgia	Language Arts	Mathematics	Science	Social Studies	Languages and International Education	Fine Arts
Hawaii	Language Arts (1999)	Mathematics (1999)	Science (1999)	Social Studies (1999)	World Languages (1999)	Fine Arts (1999)
Idaho	Language Arts (2003)	Mathematics (2003)	Science (2003)	Social Studies (2003)		
Illinois	English/Language Arts (1997), (2002)	Mathematics (2002), (1997)	Science (2002), (1997)	Social Studies (2002)	Foreign Languages (2002), (1997)	Fine Arts (1997), (2002)
Indiana	English/Language Arts (2000)	Mathematics (2000)	Science (2000)	Social Studies (2001)		
Iowa	None	None	None	None	None	None

STATE CONTENT STANDARDS
(Continued)

State	English/Language Arts	Mathematics	Science	Social Studies/History	Foreign Language	Arts
Kansas	Communication Arts (reading and writing) (1998); Reading (2000)	Mathematics (1999), (2000)	Science (2001)	Social Studies (1999)	Foreign Language (1998)	Communication Arts (Reading Writing) (1998)
Kentucky	Reading (1999); Writing (1999); English/Language Arts (1998)	Mathematics (1998), (1999)	Science (1999), (1998)	Social Studies (1999), (1998)		Arts and Humanities (1999), (1998)
Louisiana	English/Language Arts (2002)	Mathematics (1997)	Science (1997)	Social Studies (1997)	Foreign Language (1997)	The Arts (1997)
Maine	English/Language Arts (1997)	Mathematics (1997)	Science and Technology (1997)	Social Studies (1997)		Visual and Performing Arts (1997)
Maryland	English/Language Arts (2001)	Mathematics (2001)	Science (2001)	Social Studies (2001)		
Massachusetts	English/Language Arts (2001)	Mathematics (2000)	Science and Technology/ Engineering (2001)	History and Social Studies (2002)	Foreign Languages (1999)	Arts (1999)
Michigan	English/Language Arts (1996)	Mathematics (1996)	Science (2000), (1996)	Social Studies (1996)	Word Languages (1998)	Arts (1998)
Minnesota	Language Arts (2003)	Mathematics (2003), (1998)		Social Studies (1999)		Arts (2003)
Mississippi	Writing (2000); Reading (2000); Language Arts (1997)	Mathematics (2002), (2000)	Science (2001)	Social Studies (2000)	Foreign Language (2000)	Performing Arts-Dance, Music, Theater, Visual Arts (2003)
Missouri		Mathematics (1997)	Science (1998)	Social Studies (1999)		Communication Arts (1998); Fine Arts (2000)
Montana	Reading (2000); Writing (1999)	Mathematics (1998)	Science (1999)	Social Studies (2000)	Word Languages (1999)	Arts (2000); Communication Arts
Nebraska	Reading/Writing (2001)	Mathematics (1998)	Science (1998)	Social Studies (2002)		

State	English/Language Arts	Mathematics	Science	Social Studies/History	Foreign Language	Arts
Nevada	English/Language Arts (2001)	Mathematics (2001)	Science (1998)	Social Studies (2000)	Foreign Language (1999)	Arts (2000)
New Hampshire	English/Language Arts (1999)	Mathematics	Science	Social Studies (1996)		The Arts (2001)
New Jersey	Language Arts Literacy (1998), (2002)	Mathematics (2002), (1996)	Science (2002), (1998)	Social Studies (1996), (1999)	Word Languages (1996), (1999)	Visual and Performing Arts (1996), (1999)
New Mexico	Language Arts (2000)	Mathematics (2002)	Science (1999), (1996)	Social Studies (2001)		Arts (1997), (1998)
New York	English/Language Arts (1996); Language other than English (1996)	Mathematics, Science, Technology (1996)	Mathematics, Science, Technology (1996)	Social Studies (1996)		Arts (1996)
North Carolina	English/Language Arts (1999)	Mathematics (2000)	Science (2001)	Social Studies (1997)		Arts Education (2001)
North Dakota	English/Language Arts (2003)	Mathematics (2003)	Science (2002)	Social Studies (2000)	Foreign Languages (2001)	Arts (2000)
Ohio	English/Language Arts (2001)	Mathematics (2001)	Science (2002)	Social Studies (2002)		
Oklahoma	Language Arts (2002)	Mathematics (2002)	Science (2002)	Social Studies (2002)		The Arts (2002)
Oregon	English Lang. Learner (2001); English/Lang Arts (2002)	Mathematics (2002)	Science (2001)			Arts (2001)
Pennsylvania	Reading, Writing, Speaking, and Listening (1999)	Mathematics (1999)	Family & Con. Science (2003), Science & Tech. (2002)	History (2003)		Arts and Humanities (2003)
Rhode Island	English/Language Arts (1996)	Mathematics	Science (1995)	Social Studies (2001)		Arts
South Carolina	English (2002)	Mathematics (2000)	Science (2000)	Social Studies (2000)	Foreign Language (1999)	Visual and Performing Arts (2003)

STATE CONTENT STANDARDS
(Continued)

State	English/Language Arts	Mathematics	Science	Social Studies/History	Foreign Language	Arts
South Dakota	Communications/Language Arts (1998)	Math (1998)	Science (1999)			
Tennessee	English/Language Arts (2001)	Mathematics (2001)	Science (2001)	Social Studies (2002)		
Texas	English/Language Arts and Reading (1997); Languages Other than English (1998)	Mathematics (1997)	Science (1997)	Social Studies (2000)		Fine Arts (1997)
Utah	Language Arts: K-6 (2003); Language Arts: 7-12 (1999)	Mathematics: K-6 (1993); Mathematics: 7-12 (2002)	Science: K-6 (2002); Science: 7-12 (1995)	Social Studies: K-6 (2000); Social Studies: 7-12 (2002)	Word Languages: K-12 (1997)	Fine Arts: K-6 (1997); Fine Arts: 7-12 (2001)
Vermont		Mathematics (2000)	Science (2000)	History (2000)		Arts (2000)
Virginia	English (2002)	Mathematics (2001)	Science (2003)	History/Social Sciences (2001)	Foreign Language (2000)	Fine Arts (2000)
Washington	Reading (1998); Writing (1998)	Mathematics (2001)	Science (1998)	History (2002)		Arts (2001)
West Virginia	Reading and Language Arts	Mathematics	Science	Social Studies	Foreign Language	Fine Arts
Wisconsin	English/Language Arts (1998)	Mathematics (1998)	Science (1998)	Social Studies (1998)		
Wyoming	Language Arts (1998)	Mathematics (1998)	Science	Social Studies (1999)	Foreign Language (2000)	Fine and Performing Arts (2001)

APPENDIX J

NATIONAL HIGH SCHOOL GRADUATION RATE BY STATE AND RACE, 2001

Appendix Table 1: High School Graduation Rate by State and Race

	Total	American Indian	Asian	Hispanic	Black	White
Northeast Region	**73%**	**56%**	**76%**	**45%**	**52%**	**79%**
Connecticut	70%	I	I	47%	56%	77%
Maine	74%	I	I	I	I	75%
Massachusetts	73%	I	76%	49%	65%	78%
New Hampshire	72%	M	M	M	M	M
New Jersey	84%	M	M	M	M	M
New York	65%	63%	75%	42%	47%	77%
Pennsylvania	78%	I	85%	49%	58%	83%
Rhode Island	71%	I	66%	56%	63%	75%
Vermont	79%	M	M	M	M	M
Midwest Region	**77%**	**54%**	**82%**	**54%**	**53%**	**82%**
Illinois	74%	64%	94%	53%	53%	84%
Indiana	74%	I	84%	59%	53%	78%
Iowa	85%	I	89%	I	58%	87%
Kansas	76%	M	M	M	M	M
Michigan	73%	56%	82%	53%	56%	78%
Minnesota	80%	46%	67%	I	I	86%
Missouri	74%	I	91%	I	58%	77%
Nebraska	84%	40%	83%	I	55%	89%
North Dakota	89%	50%	I	I	I	93%
Ohio	78%	I	92%	61%	52%	82%
South Dakota	85%	I	I	I	I	88%
Wisconsin	81%	54%	I	55%	44%	87%
South Region	**65%**	**70%**	**83%**	**55%**	**57%**	**72%**
Alabama	66%	I	79%	I	59%	70%
Arkansas	75%	I	94%	I	69%	78%
Delaware	70%	I	I	44%	58%	74%
District Of Columbia	63%	I	I	I	I	I
Florida	56%	I	80%	48%	47%	61%
Georgia	56%	I	72%	I	46%	63%
Kentucky	71%	M	M	M	M	M
Louisiana	70%	54%	89%	74%	62%	76%
Maryland	74%	I	88%	62%	66%	78%
Mississippi	64%	I	65%	I	61%	68%
North Carolina	63%	M	M	M	M	M
Oklahoma	77%	72%	I	I	66%	80%
South Carolina	57%	M	M	M	M	M
Tennessee	60%	M	M	M	M	M
Texas	67%	61%	83%	57%	62%	77%
Virginia	74%	I	84%	I	64%	77%
West Virginia	84%	I	I	I	70%	85%
West Region	**69%**	**56%**	**81%**	**55%**	**57%**	**75%**
Alaska	64%	50%	I	60%	64%	68%
Arizona	69%	M	M	M	M	M
California	67%	64%	84%	56%	58%	77%
Colorado	68%	46%	75%	47%	56%	74%
Hawaii	70%	I	73%	64%	51%	64%
Idaho	81%	M	M	M	M	M
Montana	81%	53%	I	I	I	85%
Nevada	61%	55%	I	I	50%	69%
New Mexico	67%	62%	85%	62%	73%	79%
Oregon	66%	47%	76%	43%	50%	69%
Utah	87%	62%	74%	I	I	90%
Washington	66%	48%	77%	48%	53%	69%
Wyoming	77%	40%	I	65%	I	79%
National	**70%**	**54%**	**79%**	**52%**	**51%**	**72%**

M = Missing racial group data
I – Insufficient data to calculate graduation rate

Source: Jay P. Greene and Greg Forster, "Public High School Graduation and College Readiness Rates in the United States," *Table 1: High School Graduation Rate by State and Race*. Funding for this study was provided by the Bill & Melinda Gates Foundation. Retrieved on May 9, 2004 from http://www.manhattan-institute.org/html/ewp03.htm. Used by permission of the Manhattan Institute for Policy Research.

INDEX